KV-638-228

The RSPCA Book of British Mammals

Edited by
Leofric Boyle

Illustrated by
Priscilla Barrett

COLLINS
St James's Place, London

William Collins Sons & Co Ltd
London · Glasgow · Sydney · Auckland
Toronto · Johannesburg

First published 1981

ISBN 0 00 219118 0
Filmset by Jolly & Barber Ltd, Rugby
Colour reproduction by Adroit Photo-Litho Ltd, Birmingham
Made and printed in Great Britain by
William Collins Sons and Co Ltd, Glasgow

Contents

CONTENTS

Colour Plates

Acknowledgements

The editor would like to thank the following for their assistance in the preparation of this book: Mrs Anne Beale and Mrs Marianne Ormrod, both of the RSPCA staff, for their secretarial help; Mr Colin Booty, of the RSPCA staff; Mrs Valerie Boyle, for proof reading, and Mrs Susannah Jack for advice on quotations. He is also grateful to Mrs Diana Spearman for the suggestions given in her book *The Animal Anthology* and to the editor and authors of *The Handbook of British Mammals*, which has been invaluable to him.

The following have kindly given permission for the inclusion of copyright material: The poet and the publishers, the Hogarth Press for part of 'The Desertion of the Women and Seals' from *Winterfold* by George Mackay Brown; the poet and the publishers, Faber and Faber Ltd, for lines from 'An Otter' from *Lupercal* by Ted Hughes; David Higham Associates and the Trustees of the estate of T.H. White for passages from *The Book of Beasts* by T.H. White (published by Jonathan Cape); the author and the publishers, Methuen Children's Books, for a passage from *The Wind in the Willows* by Kenneth Grahame; Laurence Pollinger Ltd and the estate of D.H. Lawrence for a quotation from 'Bat' by D.H. Lawrence; and Mrs Ann Wolfe for a quotation from 'The Grey Squirrel' from *Kensington Gardens* by Humbert Wolfe.

Foreword

Richard D. Ryder

Long before Darwin's theories shook the Victorians' complacent assumption that man was a being apart from the animals, many peoples had felt a basic sense of kinship with the rest of creation. In cultures around the world respect for wild animals had taken forms ranging from admiration to deification.

However, Judaeo-Christian doctrines encouraged a sense of mankind's separateness and superiority. Man was claimed to have 'dominion' and the other species were said to have been placed upon Earth for his subjugation and convenience. The nineteenth century saw the climax of this attitude among the educated classes of Europe and North America, whose own highly mannered and artificial lifestyles tended genuinely to blind them to the fact that man was himself an animal. If Darwin's theories had been promulgated in the previous century they might have caused less indignation; certainly they would not have outraged Jeremy Bentham or Dr Johnson whose common attitude towards the other animals was one of down-to-earth fellowship.

Yet, the basic moral implication of Darwinism – that physical kinship should logically entail moral kinship – is only now beginning to be recognized. High Victorian culture, despite all its merits, encouraged attitudes of separatism: the behavioural differences between men and women were exaggerated as was the distinction between one class and another. In a society where men honestly believed themselves innately superior to women, intellectually and physically, it is hardly surprising that the other species were regarded as mere 'brute beasts' or 'lower animals'. Nineteenth-century compassion and charity did little to undermine the ineffable feelings of superiority attached to what our own century calls sexism, classism, racism and speciesism. It is only now that these barriers between life and life are being broken down and the fact that we share life and sentience with the other species is being realized as important.

To those who retort that 'the survival of the fittest' is another major message of Darwin, it is as well to point out that 'fittest' is not synonymous with 'strongest'. The ruthless oppression of the other sentients by man, with its attendant ecological and psychological effects, is likely to do mankind little good in the long-term. The question to be answered is whether man is 'fit' enough to change his attitude towards this planet and the other inhabitants with whom he shares its limited resources; and indeed we have in the Animal Rights movement part of this major debate about man's relationship with his environment. Nor is it correct to argue (as some zoologists have been known to do) that certain of man's impulses to kill and dominate are quite 'natural' and that therefore they are right. Rape and murder could be justified in similar terms.

It is sometimes said that there is a fundamental difference of opinion between the lobbies for conservation and for animal protection but, in practice, the two schools are moving closer to each other. They are beginning to work together to protect the interests of whales, seals, otters and other animals. In particular the RSPCA more than ever before, has been co-operating with the major conservation groups. In the past conservation has emphasised the survival of *species* rather than the well-being of the *individual* animal; but so often, the two aims lead to the same action. What is more, there is a swing towards consideration of animal welfare within the conservation movement itself. The revival of interest in the proposition that animals have moral rights and the claim that such rights should more fully be safeguarded in legal terms, has restored intellectual respectability to these concepts after half a century of neglect. Mass attention has been focused on the predicament of individual animals. The RSPCA has been closely associated with this revival and we have seen the aims of animal protection given political acceptance at national and European levels.

The current trend towards defining the rights of the *object* (or victim) rather than emphasizing the responsibilities and duties of the *subject* (or exploiter) stretches across the species-gap. It can be seen in the great international political drive for human rights, so that the two concerns for the rights of both human beings and animals are united in their sense of compassion for the underdog, whether human or non-human. They are indeed facets of the same concern for the suffering of others.

It is sometimes argued that man is the only moral animal as if this, were it true, would justify our immorality towards the others. But I believe that the spark of morality is to be found in other species; elementary altruism, for example, is displayed by many animals in the defence of their young and, in a few species, in the defence of the wounded. Such behaviour can even extend across the tenuous dividing line between the species. Even if this were not so, it is still true that man should observe a moral code in his treatment of animals, however 'amoral' such animals may be; just as he does in his treatment of immoral or amoral individuals of his own species – whether they be delinquents, infants or the mentally handicapped. One does not say of a child 'I can exploit this child just as I like, because he has no mature sense of morality' – and there are no rational grounds for saying likewise of non-humans.

In the case of wildlife, the basic principles of justice have been turned on their head. It is rare, for instance, to find an alleged 'pest' species considered innocent until proved guilty. Farmers have always sought to find scapegoats for crop and livestock failures.

In a society where witchcraft can no longer seriously be blamed, man has increasingly accused wildlife in its stead. Animals are usually presumed guilty upon ecologically superficial evidence: a predator competing with man for a common prey will often automatically be persecuted without a thorough scientific analysis of local population dynamics. Otters, for example, have been killed because they are known to eat trout, but without knowing the possibly beneficial effects that otters may have upon the trout population, by catching competing species such as eel or by removing individual trout infected with disease. Every wild mammal is a pest in somebody's eyes, yet the price of tolerance would be quite small in comparison with the tremendous interest and excitement which the presence of wild animals can bring.

Furthermore, man's control of a rival predator usually takes the form of killing, in the absence of any evidence that killing is the most effective means of control. The actual methods of control usually lack any scientific subtlety and frequently involve crude techniques of trapping and poisoning that would be frowned upon in wars waged between man and man. Although the snare, the leg-hold trap and poisons such as strychnine are fairly obviously cruel methods, the animal is rarely given the benefit of any possible doubt; instead with outrageous impertinence, the trapper and the poisoner demand of the welfarist scientific *proof* that such methods cause suffering, before they will even contemplate abandoning them. Such topsy turvy 'justice' must be ruled quite out of court.

The RSPCA believes that the principle of minimal interference with wildlife should be applied generally. Thus, humane methods of control which are alternative to killing should always be the first choice and should be evaluated properly when in operation. If killing is deemed eventually to be necessary (and the RSPCA itself is opposed, in principle, to the taking or killing of any wild animal) then only methods proven to be humane should be used. Economic reasons alone do not, in the Society's view, justify the infliction of any suffering – which effectively rules out most contemporary means of killing wild animals for their skins, furs or plumage, as collectors' items, or because they are alleged to be pests. Similarly, to make any creature suffer in the name of sport must be totally condemned and the RSPCA is specifically opposed to any hunting of animals with hounds.

A new and widening form of abuse is suffering inflicted upon wildlife in pursuing research. Scientific study in the field can cause considerable distress through the unwise use of nets, traps, tranquillizers and other methods of capture; techniques for marking and the attachment of apparatus to wild animals may also cause suffering. Far worse is the tendency to use live wild animals for experiments in the laboratory and the numbers of native and foreign animals used for this purpose is on the increase – ranging from the badgers experimentally infected with tuberculosis by the Ministry of Agriculture, Fisheries and Food, and rabbits afflicted with myxomatosis, to the many monkeys captured in the wild and imported for research. The RSPCA is opposed to all experiments which cause suffering to animals, unless performed as part of the treatment of the same individual animal.

As one manifestation of its expanding role, the RSPCA in recent years has set up a full-time Wildlife Department and an expert Wild Animals Advisory Committee. From these this book has sprung, chiefly as the brainchild of Leofric Boyle, one of the Committee's senior members and this book's untiring Editor; to him the Council of the RSPCA owes deep gratitude. Much cruelty continues to be based upon custom and ignorance, and the Society shares with the Editor the hope that this book will modify man's treatment of wild animals by conjoining scientific knowledge with humanitarian philosophy.

Editor's Introduction

Leofric Boyle

In 1960 the Royal Society for the Prevention of Cruelty to Animals set up a Wild Animals Committee and gave it a threefold task. This was: to bring scientific knowledge to bear upon man's treatment of wild animals, to consider how man's treatment of wild animals could be modified by the light of human ideals, and to help to resolve misunderstandings in the field of wildlife, between humanitarians and conservationists.

The Committee started work after a difficult period in the Society's history. People were deeply questioning man's treatment of wild animals in the field of sport, and some were fiercely attacking the Society's policy of moderation on that question. Indeed the RSPCA had in the past been almost exclusively concerned with domestic animals and with animals which, whether indigenous or foreign, had been brought into captivity and so could be regarded as pets.

The Society's first practical expression of the extension of its role had been in 1952 when the flagrant cruelty of the wildlife trade had become so obvious and so intolerable that the Society had established its animal hostel at London Airport, in order to succour animals in transit, whether wild or domestic.

It was not only the flagrant cruelty of the wildlife trade which was intolerable, but also the sheer bulk of the traffic, with its disastrous effect upon wild animal populations everywhere. These two aspects demanded joint action between humanitarians and conservationists and their collaboration in this field has been an encouraging feature of the modern world.

The Wild Animals Committee, which was itself mainly scientific, set about its task by inviting scientists who were expert in the natural history of individual British mammals to witness before it. At first there was no plan to publish the information which the Committee would compile, but it soon became apparent that a book, at least one about mammals, should be attempted. Collins Publishers viewed the proposition favourably and the present volume is the result.

Most of the articles in this book have been written by those specialist zoologists who gave evidence before the Wild Animals Committee but, in order to include every British mammal, some other authorities have kindly contributed studies. But what mammals are truly British and which are truly wild? The *Handbook of British Mammals* includes the Cetacea, whales and dolphins (an Order not covered by this present book), some species now extinct in Britain, and other species whose claim to being both British and wild seems doubtful. We have decided to deal with only those species – whether or not introduced by man – which are now well established in Britain and are living in freedom without man's aid.

Our book begins with a general study of the Class Mammalia, and mammals are then presented in their zoological orders. The discussion of each Order is followed by individual studies of each species. The illustrations have been prepared in close consultation with the authors to ensure that they are not only accurate and attractive but that they also amplify and illuminate the text.

We hope that this book will both stimulate interest in British wild animals and encourage co-operation in their conservation, but we also hope to alleviate cruelty and to this end must first ask ourselves what we really mean by that word. The familiar definition 'causing unnecessary suffering' will not do, for it merely raises in its turn the question: What does 'unnecessary' mean? Must we not accept that any act which is done for pleasure and which causes suffering is cruel, if the perpetrator knows, or would know if he gave thought to the matter, that suffering was likely to follow his action? This means I believe, that no animal except man can be cruel; but surely it also refutes any claim by man that he is merely treating animals as they treat one another. We have said 'for pleasure' but must we not go further than that? If a man, even under economic stress, lays a painful poison or sets an agonizing trap – without considering whether he could not use a less painful poison or trap, or indeed whether the damage caused by his quarry could not be tolerated – is he not also being cruel? These questions are very relevant to human treatment of wildlife, so we offer a chapter about them and also a chapter about the nature of pain itself.

It is hardly necessary to add that no contributor has been asked to bring his or her article within the boundaries of RSPCA policy, and it may be that differences from that policy can occasionally be detected. Readers will, I think, find that such differences between the scientific and the humanitarian views are surprisingly few.

Class Mammalia: The Mammals

David W. Macdonald

For centuries our poets have lauded, even romanticized, the nightingale and the lark. The literary world has been less charitable to mammals which, with the exception of the 'lordly' lion, are often cast in a derogatory role; men are not complimented by being likened to rats, dogs, weasels or wolves; women do not consider endearing the labels 'catty', 'mousy' or 'shrew'. Possibly the basis for this prejudice is that few of us ever catch more than a glimpse of wild mammals. Yet with patience one can overcome the mammalian insistence on privacy and so begin to understand their natural history and to appreciate their diversity which, when combined with their evolutionary kinship to ourselves, makes them among the most exciting and challenging of all animal classes.

The mammals vary widely in appearance ranging from enormous whales, once classed as fish, to bats, winged creatures previously classified as birds. Structure reflects function and indeed the behaviour of mammals is as varied as their shapes. However, there are two obvious features that are shared by all the species – four thousand and more – which belong to the Class Mammalia, and which also distinguish its members from the other ten million animal species. Firstly, all mammals, both male and female, have hair. Secondly, the female mammal always has mammary or milk glands. Most mammals also give birth to living young; but there is a small group (the Monotremes of Australia) which lay eggs.

It might seem strange to argue that mammals are of outstanding interest when they have only two special features, both of which sound rather unspectacular. However both are important landmarks in the evolutionary history of the animal kingdom and presage many other features that differentiate the mammals from other vertebrates and which culminate in the high development of the mammalian brain and consequent complexity of mammalian behaviour.

Hair The possession of hair reflects a critical physiological difference between mammals and their reptilian ancestors: mammals can regulate their internal body temperature independent of the outside environment (a process called endothermy) while reptiles' body temperatures vary with the temperature around them (ectothermy). The everyday description of ectothermic animals is 'cold-blooded', but this is a misnomer. For instance, the major heat source for a lizard is outside (ecto) the body, so that under a desert sun a lizard's blood heats up, perhaps becoming even warmer than that of 'warm-blooded' animals. But in cold conditions when a reptile, or an invertebrate of any sort, would be reduced to a state of torpor as the temperature of its body fell, a mammal can continue with its everyday activities. It can do this because its internal temperature is held constant under the control of a built-in thermostat – in fact part of the brain called the hypothalmus. Not only does this allow the mammal to live under varied conditions, but it also ensures internal biochemical stability. Anybody who has suffered delirium as his temperature rose even a few degrees above normal, can testify to the disastrous effects of this thermostatic system failing. Without this delicate balance, the chemical stability needed for the complex reactions required in long term memory and other aspects of mammalian intelligence, might be impossible. Of course other vertebrates, and indeed invertebrates too, can learn and remember, but apparently not to the same level of sophistication as can mammals.

The possession of hair was the ancestral mammals' method of heat insulation and is unique to them, but this is not the only way to obtain a stable internal temperature. Birds also are endothermic although their insulation is feather, not fur, so both birds and mammals have accomplished the same evolutionary trick to liberate them from the physical restraints of their environment. But, as so often happens, there is an exception in each group: the temperatures of both the roosting bat and of the sleeping humming bird fall to that of their environment. When the bat's temperature falls to 30°C it is incapable of flight and it must perform physical jerks to generate heat for take-off.

However fur and feathers are not the only, nor necessarily always the best method of heat insulation. Whales, for example, have shed all their hair, except for a few whiskers – the insulating property of hair becoming redundant to whales when they evolved a thick layer of blubber to streamline their bodies in water, and 'found' that blubber would serve also as a heat insulator. The naked molerat, which spends most of its life snugly underground, does not need heat insulation and has lost most of its hair. It is also blind and has no external ears. It is an animated mechanical digger.

Hair is dead tissue and must be replaced when worn away or shed, often in seasonal moults, which also provide an opportunity to change to a coat more appropriate for changing seasons. At the moult an animal may change both the thickness of its coat and its appearance, for instance its colour. The coat of the mountain hare is not only thicker in winter but also turns white instead of brown, helping the animal to blend with its surroundings. The role of hair as an insulator is more subtle than simply to cater for predictable weather changes. Moment to moment variation in temperature can be matched by effective changes in coat 'thickness', by raising each hair individually and increasing the volume of air trapped in the coat. Humans experience this effect as 'goose-pimples'. The same delicate control of hair position can be used for other purposes too, for instance communication: an aggressive wolf erects hair on its shoulders and back when it 'raises its hackles'. Even the structure of hair can be shaped to fulfill different functions, for example, in the protective quills of porcupines or of the lesser known spiny mice of the Middle East. The armoured plates of armadillos and pangolins, the straining plates through which a baleen whale sifts its planktonic food, the whiskers around the muzzles or lower legs of many mammals which provide them with sensory information: all these are modified forms of hair.

Mammary glands The mammary glands, second typical and unique feature of mammals, are the glands which produce milk and should not be confused with the mammillae or teats. The teats are merely the means of delivering the milk. Monotremes, for instance, do not have mammillae, but they do have the underlying mammary glands which secrete the milk on to the skin. Therefore they qualify as mammals. The mammary glands are a development of a less obvious but no less special feature of mammalian skin – the sebaceous glands. These glands are associated with each hair and secrete an oily substance which keeps the hairs supple and helps to make them waterproof. The sebaceous glands have been modified in many other ways, for instance into the scent glands involved in odour communication.

Reproduction Even amongst mammals there is a diversity of variation in the techniques of reproduction. For example, in humans and some other mammals the female spontaneously ovulates (sheds ripe eggs into the oviduct for fertilization) at the appropriate stage of her oestrous cycle. However, in some species, notably in several of our carnivores, ovulation is not spontaneous, but induced by the very act of mating. Various species of mammal, among them the grey seal and the domestic cat, are induced ovulators.

For some species it is important not only to organize their life cycle so that cubs are born at the 'right' time – for instance when food is abundant – but equally it is important that the mating period falls at a convenient season for the adults. For example, badgers have a gestation period of about eight weeks so that if cubs are to be born early in the year (the optimum time for finding plentiful food at the end of weaning to build up fat for the following winter), the parents would have to mate at a time when they are normally torpid. To overcome the conflicting requirements of conception, pregnancy and birth season, some mammals evolved an intriguing adaptation of their reproductive physiology: delayed implantation. In most species the newly fertilized egg continues along the oviduct until it reaches the uterus in the wall of which it becomes implanted and thereafter begins to develop. In delayed implantation, the egg reaches the uterus as a so-called blastocyst, but it then becomes inactive, ceasing to grow or to undergo cell division. The egg remains in this state of suspended animation until the optimal season for gestation arrives, whereupon it implants in the uterus wall and continues its development. This disassociation between mating and gestation (and hence birth season) is found especially in species which face a seasonally variable food supply. Among the British fauna, badgers, common and grey seals, pine martens, stoats, mink, common shrews and roe deer all show delayed implantation (the latter being the only artiodactyl known to do so). A quite different dodge, called delayed fertilization, has been evolved by the noctule bat, where the female may store sperm for as long as seven months before fertilization takes place.

Skeleton Another feature of all present-day mammals, not obvious to the casual observer, is that their lower jaws are composed of only one bone, the dentary. More than 225 million years ago, in the Permian geological period, the lower jaw of our reptile-like ancestors consisted of several small bones which have now been incorporated into the complicated amplifying apparatus in the mammalian middle ear. The gradual evolution of the lower jaw and middle ear can be followed in the fossil record and a point can thus be defined at which 'mammal-like reptiles' became 'mammals'. This point is arbitrary since evolutionary change is actually along a continuum and it is merely convenient for the taxonomist to be able to separate mammals on the basis of jaw structure. An 'evolutionary continuum' implies a change, from an animal which can be intuitively recognized as reptilian to one intuitively known to be a mammal, that was imperceptibly slow, with the intermediates blending one to another, differing only in the sort of details a specialized anatomist could detect. Of course it is easy to be mislead into thinking that evolution has progressed in major jumps, because relevant fossils are so hard to find that many links are missing. One Upper Triassic fossil illustrates the real difficulty for those who are intent on delineating neat classes. The skeleton of this fossil, which is called *Diathrognathus* is almost completely mammal-like. It had a secondary palate like present-day mammals. It did not have certain reptilian bones in its skull, for instance, the prefrontal bone or the post-orbital bar. However it still had several bones comprising its lower jaw. Admittedly all these except the dentary were tiny and inconspicuously situated at the rear of the jaw; admittedly also, the dentary articulated directly with the squamosal bone of the skull (as in mammals) but nevertheless these little jaw bones were still there, and one of them, the articular bone, still articulated in the old-fashioned reptilian way to the quadrate bone of the skull. Such is the difficulty in trying to draw an exact line between mammals and their predecessors – a dilemma which is still illustrated to a certain extent by the intermediate anatomy of the monotremes – and indeed it is unimportant to do so. It is also hard to know whether the complicated behaviour that we recognize as typifying present-day mammals, appeared before or after the jaw bones accomplished their journey to the middle ear.

The adaptation of mammals to running, jumping, flying, gliding, swimming and burrowing is testimony to the versatility of their basic building block – the skeleton. This diversity has been achieved not by adding or subtracting bones to create new designs, but by changing the proportions of existing elements of skeletons. The badger with its stocky neck and the giraffe both have seven cervical vertebrae, although giraffes have had to modify their blood vessels to get blood up to their heads. Even whales, with no obvious neck at all, have seven cervical vertebrae, although these are all fused into a single unit. Only the three-toed sloth departs from this scheme, with nine neck vertebrae. Thus the same basic piece of engineering supports both a huge bull moose of 800kg, and a tiny Savi's pygmy shrew, less than 4cm long.

The success of the mammalian musculo-skeletal system is apparent after a glance at some record holders among the animals: the fastest runner is the cheetah, bats fly with more agility than birds, dolphins and porpoises swim faster than can fish or any other aquatic animals.

The evolutionary scale It is a common fallacy that merit can be attached to the evolutionary achievements of different animal classes, rising in an ascending scale towards ourselves. But, for instance, amphibians' hearts, which do not separate arterial from venous blood, are not thus inferior to mammals' hearts; they simply do a different job. Amphibia not only transport oxygenated blood in arteries from their lungs, as do mammals, but can also absorb oxygen into the blood through their skins, so separation of arterial and venous blood would be inappropriate.

Mammals like other animals have evolved a diversity of ways of acquiring their food and so another feature of their class is that, within one month of birth, they normally have different kinds of teeth for different functions. Mammals are thereby able to include amongst their ranks representatives of every dietary taste. Look at the variety just amongst the carnivores. The weasels are strict meat eaters, raccoons take fish, giant pandas are vegetarians. Some mongooses are insectivorous while other viverrids, such as the civets, are more inclined to fruit eating. The dogs are often omnivorous – eating meat, insects and fruit in the course of one night's foraging. To eat these different foods requires different equipment and amongst mammals can be found teeth for shearing, cutting, tearing, chewing and grinding.

Herbivores face different problems from those of carnivores; vegetation may be easy to 'catch' but it is hard to digest, because every plant cell has a wall of tough cellulose, which is resistant to digestive enzymes. This problem has been overcome by various means. First, the spiked cusps of cutting premolars have become 'molarized' into grinding ridges. Second, many ungulates maintain a colony of bacteria in their guts. These bacteria are able to digest cellulose and thus to free nutrients. Both lagomorphs and rodents have a pocket in their intestine, the caecum, which houses this microfauna.

The preparation of vegetable matter for digestion is clearly a difficult and lengthy process. It is also potentially dangerous since the most appetizing foliage may grow in cover that conceals predators, and grazing may necessitate relaxing surveillance for approaching danger. One group of ungulates, the artiodactyls (deer, camels and cattle) have minimized these risks by ruminating – 'chewing the cud'. Their stomachs are divided into sections: the rumen (paunch), the reticulum, omasum and abomasum. Food is eaten with haste and swallowed into the rumen. The animal can then retreat, its 'shopping basket' full, and regurgitate the vegetation to chew it at leisure in some safe place. Some primates and rodents solve the same problem by stuffing food into cheek pouches. A carnivore may have to eat its meal quickly, for fear that a competitor may come and loot it.

The Geological Past A book about the mammals of today's Britain, or of anywhere else, is no more than a glimpse stolen through the keyhole of history; for the world's fauna, and even the shape and distribution of land and sea, have changed through time. Over hundreds of millions of years continents have drifted, mountain ranges sprung up and seas risen and fallen. Each change has affected the local animals of the time and with altering climates and the joining and splitting of continents, many species have come and gone. Britain's mammalian fauna was particularly affected by the Ice Ages of the Pleistocene period, which began some three million years ago.

At the beginning of the Pleistocene, Britain was the home of mammoths 4·5m at the shoulder, rhinoceroses with two-metre horns and huge cave bears – animals which were known right across Europe. Indeed, a puzzling feature of the Pleistocene mammals was their trend to gigantism: amongst the cats, for instance, enormous cave lions inhabited northern Europe, Asia had a giant tiger and North America a huge panther. During the Pleistocene large ice sheets came and went at least four times, with consequent changes in climate and in sea level which in turn united and divided continents. When the sea was low a land bridge named Beringia spanned the Bering Straits and across this chilly bridge faunal migrations occurred, from Europe and Asia to North America. The biggest ice sheet, the Laurentide, covered five million square miles of North America. During that time glaciers, originating in the mountains of Scandinavia, spread over the south of Britain, across the North Sea to Holland and onwards roughly to the position of Berlin, before swinging north to the Urals.

As the ice moved back and forth, so animals migrated. The interglacial periods were warmer than today's climate, and the British fauna (joined intermittently to the European through the then dry 'English Channel') was spectacular: hippopotamuses wallowed in our marshes – becoming extinct about 80,000 years ago – and macaque monkeys were abundant. 'Tropical' plants such as gum trees and swamp cypresses flourished, although their numbers began to dwindle about 100,000 years ago. Seven thousand years ago a warm postglacial period reached its peak and began to cool. Now, presumably, we are heading towards the next Ice Age.

Although the appearance and disappearance of hundreds of species of mammals in evolutionary history puts a perspective on the process of extinction, it does not diminish the seriousness with which we should view the plight of the many species threatened today. This is particularly true since many of them are threatened because of the activities of our own species. The fact that only a few species of mammal are endangered in Britain should not be a source of pride, but rather a grim reminder of the list of recent exterminations; to a large extent the damage has already been done.

The Insectivores

ORDER INSECTIVORA

Kenneth Mellanby

The name of this order – the Insectivores – implies that these animals eat insects, and so they do; but they eat many other things too, mostly of animal origin, so that the order is accurately described as carnivorous. As the following text on the individual species will show, all British insectivores do eat insects, but among them moles also eat earthworms, which generally make up most of their diet, shrews will consume almost any animal small enough for them to kill, and hedgehogs enjoy carrion and slugs and even vegetable foods. One hedgehog kept as a pet appeared to enjoy eating tomatoes and strawberries and drinking a proprietary brand of blackcurrant juice. Non-British insectivores are even more catholic in their tastes – the desman in Spain feeds on fish and crustacea, and the European water shrew, which has a venomous bite, attacks fish and frogs.

The members of this order are of particular interest to the zoologist because they are both primitive and highly specialized. Their primitive features, possibly showing resemblances to some common ancestral mammalian stock, include plantigrade feet, five clawed digits on each foot, continuous tooth-rows with relatively few pointed cusps, abdominal testes, a small smooth brain without convolutions, and a long snout. Some (including our mole) are almost totally blind, all have small eyes and poor sight. On the other hand many possess extremely specialized features. The hedgehog, which lives above ground, has bristles which protect it from many predators; the mole's front feet make it a notable excavator. Among them the shrew has the least obvious anatomical adaptations to its mode of life.

Altogether some 374 different species of insectivores have been described and an equal number may, as yet, have eluded the taxonomist. They are distributed widely throughout the world, but are absent from Australia and most of South America. Madagascar appears to have the richest collection.

The majority of the known insectivores are shrews (of which there are 265 species). There are eight distinct families of Insectivores – only three being represented in Britain. These are the Erinaceidae (hedgehogs), the Soricidae (shrews) and the Talpidae (moles).

The mole is widespread in mainland Great Britain, though absent from Ireland, the Outer Hebrides and Orkney and Shetland. Ireland does not harbour the common shrew or the water shrew, but supports the pygmy shrew. Shrews may seldom be seen, but they are present in very great numbers in many areas of wood and grassland. In cold weather they may even be found entering houses.

At present none of our native insectivores seems to be in any danger from modern farming techniques or from man's other activities. Indeed hedgehogs often are found squashed by motor traffic, and though less easily observed, many shrews and moles suffer the same fate. However, these deaths seem insufficient to affect population densities, and over most of Britain these animals remain reasonably common. But, as our population increases and if farming becomes more intensive, destroying their present available habitat, we may need to take additional measures to safeguard these as well as most other wild animals.

The Hedgehog

Nigel Reeve

. . . then like hedgehogs, which
Lie tumbling in my barefoot way, and mount
Their pricks at my footfall;
WILLIAM SHAKESPEARE (1564–1616) The Tempest

In Britain the European hedgehog, *Erinaceus europaeus*, is a well known and common nocturnal mammal. Adults are about 23cm in length and weigh up to 1kg. Males tend to be slightly heavier than females, but individuals vary very much in size and weight. The hedgehog's most conspicuous feature is its spines but otherwise its body structure is not very specialized. Each foot has five toes and each toe bears a strong claw. The tail is short and inconspicuous. The whiskered snout is long and pointed and has a moist black tip. The eyes are medium in size and the animal can see fairly well, even in rather dim light. The ears are largish but protrude only slightly from the coarse light brown fur which covers the face and underside. The hedgehog's spines are modified hairs with a complex internal arrangement of hollows which make them very light in weight, but at the same time strong. They are creamy white with a broad brown band near the tip, about 2·5cm long and end in a sharp point. Each spine bends and narrows somewhat where it emerges from the skin so that if pressed it will bend rather than be driven back into the skin. Under the skin the spine ends in a rounded knob which serves both as an anchor for the spine and as an attachment for the muscles which erect it. The spines normally lie flat to the body and point backwards, but if the animal is alarmed they are raised and point in all directions.

The hedgehog can roll up into a ball by tucking its head and legs in towards its belly and then, by using a very highly developed skin musculature, it can draw its spine-covered skin down to enclose every part of its body. The animal is able to maintain this position for long periods seemingly without fatigue, keeping itself entirely contained within its prickly armour. This very effective defence ensures that the hedgehog has little trouble from most predators. It probably has fewer natural enemies than have any other mammals of similar size. (Colour illustration facing p.51.)

The sexes are similar in appearance until the underside is examined, and this requires a practised hand if the animal has to be unrolled. Both sexes have five pairs of nipples which range from the base of the foreleg to the groin. The male (boar) has a conspicuous penis placed well forward on the belly where one might have expected to find a navel, whereas the female (sow) has a vaginal opening very close to the anus. The sexes are always easily distinguishable by these characteristics even when very young.

Food The hedgehog has 36 strong teeth capable of dealing with a very varied diet. Studies of stomach contents show that beetles and caterpillars are among the main components of the hedgehog's diet, but the hedgehog will eat a multitude of ground-dwelling invertebrates, such as earthworms, slugs, spiders and earwigs. Carrion may also feature largely in its diet.

When a hedgehog is foraging it moves along at a slow but steady pace, turning this way and that and often turning back on itself. It sniffs constantly, indicating that smell is its main method of finding prey, although sound may play a part in detecting prey moving in leaf litter. Vision is fairly unimportant in the search for food.

In folklore hedgehogs have often been reported to carry away fruit, especially apples, first rolling on them to impale them on their spines. But hedgehogs seldom eat fruit and are not known to store food; however, it would be unwise to discount out of hand stories with such wide currency. Hedgehogs are also accused of taking milk from cows. When a cow with a full udder lies down, some leakage commonly occurs and hedgehogs may easily have been seen licking up the overflow. They certainly enjoy milk, as anyone who has put a saucer-full out for hedgehogs in their garden will have observed. The hedgehog has another intriguing habit. When stimulated by a pungent smell or taste it will produce large quantities of frothy saliva and smother itself with it. The purpose of this is still unknown.

Habitat Hedgehogs true to their name, are often found in hedgerows – but also in copses, farmland and woodland. They seem to prefer the edges of woods to the relatively open interior, possibly because the greater diversity of habitat on the edges provides a large and varied selection of prey. This preference for a fringe habitat is perhaps why the hedgehog can be so successful in suburban areas, where gardens with flower borders, hedges and lawns, parks and golf courses, all provide excellent habitat.

A hedgehog must have winter quarters available – any quiet place where it can make a nest of leaves and hibernate without disturbance will serve.

Hibernation With the onset of winter the invertebrates which make up most of the hedgehog's diet become scarce and hard to find. To survive this difficult period and conserve its energy, the hedgehog must hibernate. Hibernation is quite different from normal sleep. In Britain the only other animals which have the ability to hibernate truly are the bats and dormice. The hedgehog's metabolism slows right down, the heart beat slows to one tenth of its normal rate; the breathing slows down to about ten breaths per minute and the body temperature falls to the temperature of the environment. The hedgehog must prepare for hibernation while food is still plentiful by building up large fat reserves. It has two types of fat tissue: white fat, stored in the mesenteries of the abdominal cavity and under the skin, and brown fat which forms discrete lobes, mainly around the shoulders, and which provides a quickly available source of energy. This energy will be needed to raise the body temperature when the hedgehog wakes from hibernation.

With the warmer days of spring the hedgehog resumes normal activity and feeding. It must now regain condition, for it may have lost one third of its body weight during the winter. If the weather is still rather cold the hedgehog may continue to use a day nest very similar to its winter one. If the weather is very warm hedgehogs often do not bother with a nest but during the day will simply lie up in undergrowth or grass. A hedgehog may have several nest sites within its home range; some may be used several times, others only once. The hedgehog can return to a specific nest after a gap of many days of wandering, so it must have navigational ability and a good memory.

Little is known about the hedgehog's home range, but my own work shows that hedgehogs travel several kilometres in one night and may be familiar with an area of some tens of hectares. Hedgehogs are commonly thought to be slow moving and unathletic but this is far from true, for they are able to run at considerable speed, with a burst of up to ten miles per hour and can keep up a man's walking pace for some hours. They can also scale chain link fences and ivy clad walls with surprising ease. Although hedgehogs seem to be solitary, many may use the same area at the same time; but they seldom meet and it is possible that they try to avoid each other. When there is an encounter a fight may occasionally ensue. The hedgehogs lower their heads, raise their spines and, making threatening snorts, butt each other's flanks.

Breeding Hedgehogs come into breeding condition about April. Courtship is a lengthy ritual. The male circles the female while she snorts vigorously and, turning always to face him, butts aggressively at his flanks. This ritual may go on for hours before the male can successfully mount the female, and it is often inconclusive – the pair losing interest and separating. Pregnancy lasts 30–35 days and, when the babies are due, the mother builds a specially large breeding nest. The litter usually numbers four or five. The newly born hedgehogs have about 90 white spines – later brown spines will grow amongst them. If disturbed in these early stages the female may eat her young, but later she may respond to disturbance either by desertion or by carrying her babies in her mouth to another nest. The mother forages by night returning to the nest to suckle her litter. The young hedgehogs' eyes open in a fortnight and their teeth erupt at three weeks. At one month the young accompany their mother on her outings. At six to eight weeks they are weaned and become independent, although they may still weigh only 200g or less. Sexual maturity is reached in about one year. Some litters are born as late as October, either of females who breed for a second time in the year or those who have not managed to breed earlier. The young of these late litters have little chance of surviving the winter unless the weather is very mild, for they do not have time to build up sufficient fat for successful hibernation – for the food supply dwindles just when they need it most, at weaning, and there is no food available in the winter. Mothers of late litters may also be at risk for they too have to build up reserves after rearing their young.

It is said that probably less than half of all young hedgehogs do in fact get through their first winter but, if they do survive, they have a good chance of living another two years or so. Hedgehogs appear to have a possible life span of up to ten years, but seven is a more usual maximum and not many reach even that comparatively old age.

Parasites Hedgehogs are susceptible to infestation by several ecto-parasites – a flea. *Archaeopsylla erinacei,* which is specific to hedgehogs and does not survive for long on humans or domestic pets; ticks, notably *Ixodea hexagonus,* and also some mites. About 20 per cent of British hedgehogs are infested with a strain of ringworm which can cause baldness, especially on the face, and crumbling skin, especially on the ears.

Predators The spines of the hedgehog render it immune to all but a determined predator; even so foxes are often able to kill hedgehogs, probably by biting the hedgehog on the head before it rolls up completely. Similarly, badgers occasionally kill and eat them, perhaps by scrabbling their way through the spines. Tawny owls use their talons on small hedgehogs and pine martens and polecats may also include an occasional hedgehog in their diet, while large birds, especially crows, can get past the spines with their beaks and they take some hedgehogs in the early morning.

Relations with man Hedgehogs have in the past been persecuted by gamekeepers and at one time they had a price on their heads. Today they are still commonly seen on gibbets, despite studies which have shown that damage by hedgehogs to ground-nesting game birds is insignificant, compared with that caused by harvesting. Hedgehogs feed on agricultural pests and they should be thought of as allies not as vermin.

Generally, hedgehogs thrive in contact with man, especially in the suburbs. Often they are regarded as a free-ranging pet, visiting gardens, eating garden pests, and sometimes being fed by benevolent householders. Captive hedgehogs can make good pets if they are given exercise, a good diet and careful attention; but a hedgehog left free to come and go as it pleases is far more likely to be content. A dab of non-toxic paint on its spines will aid in recognition.

Poisons and pesticides kill some hedgehogs, as do bonfires of rubbish in which they often hide before the pile of twigs and leaves is lit. Hedge and scrub clearance kills some. Others may drown in garden ponds or in drains – although hedgehogs swim well. Road casualties are probably the most significant factor in unnatural death. Nevertheless, despite being one of the commonest mammals to be found killed on the roads, there is no sign of the hedgehog becoming scarce, and its population appears to be in no danger.

Classification and Distribution Hedgehogs belong to the Insectivore family Erinaceidae, which splits into two subfamilies, the hairy and the spiny hedgehogs. The latter consists of three genera, all closely related, which occur throughout the Old World. Some of these are found in arid or desert regions, whereas our own hedgehog inhabits more temperate lands. In Britain it is found in every county and on most offshore islands. It inhabits lowlands from Scandinavia to the Mediterranean, and has even been introduced into New Zealand, where it is now very common. In Eastern Europe it is replaced by a closely related species, the Brown-breasted hedgehog, *E. roumanicus*.

The Mole

Kenneth Mellanby

On every common dozens may be met,
Dangling on bent twigs bleaching in the sun
Whose melancholy fates meet no regret
Though dreamless of the snare they could not shun
JOHN CLARE (1793–1864) The Mole Catcher

The European mole, *Talpa europaea*, is a smaller animal than most people think – the adult male is only about 14·3cm long and weighs about 110g. The female is rather smaller. Prominent among its characteristics are short, silky, black fur, a pig-like snout, enormous spade-like forepaws and a short, narrow club-shaped tail, carried upright to keep contact with the roof of the animal's tunnel as the mole moves along it.

The eyes of the mole are tiny and at the most, probably can distinguish only light from darkness. It has no external ears, though it can certainly hear, for moles have been taught to come for food when called. Its sense of smell is poor for it can detect food only when within a range of about 5cm. Its taste does not seem to be well developed. So, nearly blind and with weak taste and smell, how can the mole be such a widespread and successful animal?

The mole's questing snout, its torpedo body, its shovel-like front feet and its rudder tail adapt it so beautifully to its way of life, that it does not need – or perhaps no longer needs – efficient senses other than the 'cutaneous' senses, which include touch and the appreciation of heat, cold, pain and vibration. The pink, bristled snout is covered with thousands of tiny raised papillae, richly supplied with nerve endings. The tip can be dilated with blood and acts as a very acute organ of touch and perhaps may also be able to detect smells. Although the exact importance of the snout is not yet understood, it must play an important part in the way the mole perceives its surroundings.

The mole's front feet form broad, rigid shovels which are moved by powerful muscles attached to strong arm, breast and shoulder bones. A live mole, if placed upon any but the hardest surface, buries iteself in a few seconds. It almost 'swims' through the earth, bringing the front feet together, pushing them apart and extending an enquiring snout delicately into the cavity. Then comes another stroke forcing the animal further into the ground – repeated again and again until it quickly disappears from view.

If the soil is very soft the mole swims in, pushing the soil which it displaces, up into a ridge above its body. When the ground becomes more firm the mole turns on one side at a time, and bracing itself against the tunnel with both hind feet and one forefoot, drives itself forward with the other foot. Now the earth is too hard to lift into a convenient ridge but somehow the mole must get rid of it. It tackles the problem by pushing up the earth with its foot, making a vertical shaft and raising a mole hill. If the mole is not making a new dig but is merely clearing out an old run, it uses the existing vertical shaft.

A young mole starting an independent life in summer, has usually to make its own burrow system. During this period young males spend much time above ground, scrambling about among grass and roots. Thus the mole hill, although essential, is in a sense an accidental matter – its purpose to get rid of the soil. But occasionally that favourite of the old naturalists, a mole fortress is built. An individual mole, male or female, instead of just pushing up a mole hill, will apparently decide to go one better and build a 'mountain'. In this a female may make her nest and have her young – instead of doing so in the usual small chamber excavated in a burrow. Why this happens is unknown.

Breeding Moles are solitary creatures each keeping to its own system of burrows – male and female meeting only casually, except in the mating season during February and March. After a gestation period of four weeks four tiny young are born. These grow rapidly and, after a lactation period of at least a month, are nearly as long as their mother. Then they gradually gain independence so that, by September, all moles are living an independent life.

Food The mole's tunnel system is not only its home, but its food shop, its store cupboard and its dining room.

Its main diet is worms, though any available insects are acceptable. In a deciduous wood on a clay soil there will be one to two tons of worms per acre, with about two moles per acre, and the moles will have a very easy life. There will be no need for them to dig furiously for worms – which moles do not do anyway – or to come to the surface to hunt, which they sometimes do; for their meals will fall into their tunnels – and this is the standard method of the mole's feeding. What worms the mole does not immediately require it stores in a sort of earthen depository at the side of the run. The worm is mutilated but not killed and will remain there until it regenerates its lost segments, or is eaten.

Moles will eat almost any flesh or carrion – the chasing, catching and eating of a live, wild frog has been recorded – but there is only one well authenticated instance of a taste for a vegetarian diet. J. Oppermann, who studied the diet of moles near Berlin, found forms of truffle (Ascomycetes) in 30 per cent of moles from pine forests.

Territoriality Moles seem to hate each other and to be the most aggressive of creatures. Fights occur between males, between females and between the sexes. Males take no part in rearing the young and there is peace only between mother and young and between the sexes during mating.

Moles have well-defined home ranges in which they remain for considerable periods. A mole may extend its range in one direction and contract it in another, so that eventually it occupies a new territory. In the spring males often move in search of a mate, afterwards perhaps settling down again in their original run system. Streams are no barrier, for moles swim readily. A great deal still remains to be known about the territoriality of the mole for there are gaps in the seemingly simple picture.

Habitat Moles live in many habitats. In deciduous woodland life is easy but in a sandy soil, such as Breckland in East Anglia in which worms and insects are comparatively few, the mole has a difficult life. The Breck appears to be seething with moles – burrows and mole hills are everywhere – but this is a deception. There is actually a paucity of food and to get enough to eat the mole has to make and occupy a network of burrows and must push up many mole hills. The mole has to face a similar situation in chalk grasslands; the food is scarce so there are many burrows and mole hills, but few moles. In both cases the prominence of mole hills in the landscape indicates a low rather than a high level of mole population.

Coniferous woods are usually short of moles – there is seldom enough soil fauna to support a large population. Flooded fenland must be deserted, though moles quickly return after a flood. Pastures and arable lands are well occupied but the large 'prairie' fields of East Anglia and elsewhere are only occupied around the edges; for ploughing destroys the burrows and drives the animals into hedges and ditches.

Natural enemies Moles have many natural enemies. The young are especially subject to predation in early summer, when they have been driven out by their mother and are looking for their first territories. Tawny owls catch them by night, buzzards, ravens and other predators by day. Herons not only catch moles on the surface, but probably, after detecting movement in runs only just below the surface, stab them there with their long beaks. Weasels will go into moles' runs and kill them underground. Various parasites infest moles, including the large so-called mole-flea, *Hystrichopsylla talpae*.

Man and the mole The mole was always considered a pest and destroyed whenever possible. John Woulidge writing in his *System Agricultura* published in 1697 calls them 'a most pernicious enemy to husbandry, destroying the roots of crops, grass, herbs and flowers, and also by casting up hills to the great hindrance of cow pastures.' In 1904 the *Agricultural Gazette* blamed mild winters for the increase of moles and their depredations by which the finer grasses and clovers suffered severely and damage to mangel and turnip drills was enormous. In 1963 the Ministry of Agriculture was more temperate. Their pamphlet No. 318 simply described the runs and mole hills as being, on occasion, harmful to agriculture – the runs by disturbing roots to such an extent that the crops wilt or even die and the mole hills by occupying considerable areas of land (often then infested with ants) and by churning up stones in the soil and thereby damaging agricultural instruments.

That covers the damage that moles can do. On the credit side it may be claimed for the mole that it consumes wireworms and other pests; but against that it eats worms and beneficial insects and it is not possible to strike a balance in this respect. Similarly moles drain the land but they seldom work in waterlogged soils where their efforts might indeed be useful. A bizarre beneficial effect occurs in the fens, for many willow trees now growing there were accidentally planted by mole catchers; they are discarded 'springs' from primitive, home-made traps, which have taken root.

In most cases on arable land the mole is not a serious nuisance. In grass which is to be cut for hay mole hills may cause difficulties but on the whole it is doubtful whether moles cause enough trouble to be worth the bother of controlling.

Mole control When fashionable ladies wore moleskin coats and rural gentlemen moleskin caps and waistcoats, the mole catchers' occupation could be profitable, for in 1900 a good skin known as a 'Best Winter Clear' would fetch 3/6d ($17\frac{1}{2}$p) – more than a full day's wages for many farm workers. Until recently plumbers still used moleskins for wiping joints in pipes; but now the traditional mole catcher is no longer. Moles are still caught, usually using either the Scissor or the Duffus trap. Both are set in the run and both are reasonably humane.

Today, most moles killed by man die from eating poisoned worms which are placed in their runs. Strychnine is the poison most used and it is the most efficient. Strychnine is a deadly poison which may only be used for moles, and it cannot be bought without a permit from the Ministry of Agriculture, Fisheries and Food. Death from strychnine is neither very quick nor painless: in fact it is agonizing.

Many forms of mole repellant have been tried – moth balls, pump oil, carbide, even the planting of Caper Spurge sometimes called 'Mole Spurge'. In 1636 Gervase Markham suggested leeks, garlic and onions, and brimstone burned in a walnut shell. But no repellants can be called satisfactory. If a private individual feels that he must try to oust a mole from his garden (though another will probably replace it) a scissors trap is recommended.

Classification and Distribution The European mole *Talpa europaea*, is a member of the family Talpidae of the Order Insectivora. The mole is common throughout the British Isles and it, or closely related species with similar habits, live in suitable places throughout Europe and Asia. In North America there are similar but quite distinct species. Other less closely related moles, but also Insectivores, live in various parts of the world. There are also burrowing mole-like creatures which are not Insectivores and are examples of convergent evolution.

British Shrews

Gillian K. Godfrey

Common shrew

It is a ravening beast, feigning itself gentle and tame, but being touched it biteth deep, and poisoneth deadly. It beareth a cruel mind, desiring to hurt anything, neither is there any creature it loveth. They annoy vines, and are seldom taken except in cold; they frequent ox-dung. If they fall into a cart-road, they die and cannot get forth again. They go very slowly, they are fraudulent and take their prey by deceipt.

EDWARD TOPSELL History of Four-Footed Beasts (1607)

Shrews are placed in the Family Soricidae of the Order Insectivora. There are two subfamilies. One, the Soricinae, includes animals having teeth tipped with red pigment, and in this are placed the three species found on the British mainland. Shrews in the genus *Sorex* (which include our common shrew and pygmy shrew) are distributed over the land masses of the northern hemisphere, while shrews in the genus *Neomys* (our water shrew and the Mediterranean water shrew) are confined to the Old World. White-toothed shrews (genus *Crocidura*) are found on the Isles of Scilly and the Channel Islands but not on the British mainland. On Jersey both common and white-toothed shrews are found. The white-toothed shrews are a large and relatively uniform group with a wide distribution throughout the southern Palaearctic, Ethiopian and Oriental regions.

Topsell's description is typical of the misconceptions about shrews. More seems to have been written about their alleged evil characteristics than about those of any other British mammal. Shrews do have sharp teeth and most species need to eat with great frequency – though in small quantities at a time – but most of Topsell's facts are wrong.

The Common Shrew

The common shrew, *Sorex araneus*, is the commonest of the three species of shrew found in the British Isles. It is widely distributed throughout the British mainland and on many of the islands, although not found in the Outer Hebrides, Orkney or Ireland.

The common shrew is a small mouse-like animal with relatively small ears, minute eyes and a pointed snout. It measures 60 mm–75 mm from nose to base of tail and weighs about 8–12g. Coloration varies from sandy to chocolate-brown above, and a greyish-white below.

Habitat The common shrew may be found in almost any habitat where there is low cover, including moorland and mountain-top, but it tends to be most abundant in thick grassland, hedgerow and bracken scrub. Few people see the shrew because it spends most of its time beneath the litter or below ground where it often uses tunnels built by mice and voles. Its own tunnels, which are smaller, are distinguished by their oval, instead of round cross-section. Although seldom seen, common shrews are often heard in the hedgerows where their high-pitched squeaks are usually mistaken for those of birds.

Behaviour Anyone catching sight of a live shrew will be impressed by its bustling gait and the swift, almost feverish activity which accompanies its search for food. Periodically it will be seen to stop in its tracks for a few minutes' nap, before continuing the search once more. After about two hours spent in this way, the shrew returns to its nest for a sleep and this pattern of activity continues night and day, because the shrew needs to rest at frequent intervals.

The common shrew can climb and swim well, although it probably only enters the water if forced to do so. However, its sight and smell are poor and it relies mainly on touch to find its food.

Food The shrew is an opportunist – feeding with the guiding principle 'first encountered, first eaten'; its diet tends to be influenced more by seasonal changes in the availability of prey than by taste preference. Earthworms and adult beetles are the main constituents of its diet, but most small soil and litter animals are eaten, except for millipedes and slugs which it apparently finds distasteful.

The animal's daily consumption of food is enormous, roughly equal to its own body-weight. The shrew's need for such a large quantity of food explains why early naturalists' many attempts to keep shrews in captivity were unsuccessful. One aspect of the shrew's feeding is unusual: it eats its own faeces. This habit, known as refection or coprophagy (see also Lagomorphs p.63), has been found to occur mainly during the day, when the rectum contains a milky fluid instead of the normal dark-coloured faeces. Refection probably aids the ingestion of essential nutrients to compensate for the fairly rapid passage of food through the gut.

Breeding A small proportion of shrews breed in the year of their birth but most do not breed until their second year. After a pregnancy which lasts 25 days, a litter of from five to seven young are born. They are blind and hairless to begin with, but grow rapidly and after three days have doubled in weight. Their eyes open after two weeks and at three weeks the young are weaned. A female will produce from two to five litters during the breeding season.

Territoriality The common shrew is by nature a solitary individual. In captivity it is aggressive towards other individuals, regardless of their sex, and this behaviour is suppressed only during the brief period that the female is in oestrus and mating takes place. At other times shrews in a particular area stay within their own territories or home grounds. Paired scent-glands, situated midway between the front and hind limbs, produce a secretion which is used for marking territories.

Enemies Shrews have no defence against the owls and domestic cats which are their principal predators. Their strong odour is obviously no deterrent against owls, in which the senses of taste and smell are poorly developed, and although their odour may prevent shrews from being eaten by cats, this is of little help since they are constantly killed by them.

During the autumn shrews are occasionally found dying or dead beside the road, with no trace of injury, and early naturalists referred to the number of shrews found at this season as the 'autumnal epidemic'. It has since been established that shrews rarely live through two winters, and that in autumn the animals are dying, not from an epidemic but from old age, the maximum life-span of the shrew being about 18 months. The immediate cause of death is probably a combination of cold, shortage of food and physiological changes in some of the internal organs. It is interesting to find that while juvenile shrews undergo an autumn moult during which their summer coat is replaced with thicker winter fur, the adults do not. They remain in their summer coats and, by Christmas, almost all of them are dead.

Relations with man The common shrew, and its smaller relative the pygmy shrew, are among the few British mammals known to be of no harm or nuisance to man.

The Pygmy Shrew

The pygmy shrew, *Sorex minutus*, is the smallest British mammal. It is from 35–60mm long (excluding the tail) and weighs 3–6g. It cannot be distinguished from the common shrew by size alone since juvenile common shrews are sometimes smaller than adult pygmies. However, the pygmy's tail normally exceeds two thirds of its body length and is proportionately thicker than that of the common shrew. The pygmy has a lighter-coloured pelage and its back is less clearly demarcated from the belly.

Habitat and Distribution The pygmy shrew has a wider distribution than the common shrew, being found in Orkney, the Outer Hebrides

The pygmy shrew, Britain's smallest mammal, is distinguished from the common shrew by its proportionally longer and thicker tail.

and Ireland as well as the rest of Britain. Nevertheless its numbers are usually lower and remain low even in habitats from which the common shrew is absent. It is particularly scarce in open woodland. The pygmy shrew is found throughout northern Europe and eastwards into Asia.

Behaviour Many features of this shrew's behaviour resemble those of its larger relative but there are certain important differences; for instance the pygmy does not build its own burrow at all, but relies on the tunnels and runways constructed by other small mammals. In captivity the pygmy has been shown to feed and rest more frequently than the common shrew; nearly half of its feeding periods last less than 12 minutes, and its rest periods are often just as short, rarely lasting an hour. The pygmy is also more active by day than the common shrew.

Food The pygmy shrew has a diet similar to the common but the prey tends to be smaller.

Breeding The pygmy's breeding habits are similar to those of the common with a pregnancy of 25 days; two or three litters containing four to seven young are produced yearly.

Territoriality, Enemies and Relations with man These resemble those of the common shrew.

The Water Shrew

The water shrew, *Neomys fodiens*, can immediately be distinguished from all other British shrews by its large size and striking coloration. It is from 70–95mm long and may weigh over 19g. The coat is glossy black above and greyish-white below with a sharp line of demarcation along the flanks. There is a prominent fringe of stiff hairs on the hind feet and a keel of stiff hairs on the tail.

Habitat Although it has obvious adaptations for a semi-aquatic life, the water shrew is not restricted to the vicinity of ponds and streams. It occurs throughout the British mainland and on several of the Scottish islands. But it is less abundant than either the common or the pygmy shrew and few people will ever have seen one.

Behaviour The water shrew is an able swimmer both on the surface of the water and beneath it. When floating its body stays high out of

A glossy black coat distinguishes the water shrew from the other British shrews.

the water like a duck's, due to the presence of air-bubbles trapped in its coat and to the water-repellant properties of the fur itself. Unlike other British shrews, the water shrew is a poor climber. It is solitary by nature and, in captivity, aggressive to other individuals of its kind.

Food The water shrew catches its prey, which includes both aquatic and terrestial organisms, in the water and on land. Small invertebrates form the bulk of its diet but small frogs and fish are occasionally also eaten.

Breeding After a gestation period of about 24 days the water shrew produces two or three litters of three to eight young every year.

Natural enemies Foxes, owls and carnivorous fish are the chief enemies of the water shrew.

Relations with man There is no evidence that the activities of the water shrew in Britain are harmful to man. Their numbers are in general too low to have much effect upon trout populations, and in water-cress beds, where numbers are highest, the shrews are feeding mainly on freshwater crustaceans. Since these crustaceans can only live in unpolluted water, the presence of shrews is regarded as an indication that the beds are in good condition. Sadly, the current practice of mowing the grass between and around the beds is having a disastrous effect upon the numbers of these shrews.

White-Toothed Shrews

There are two species of white-toothed shrews; the larger being about the size of the common shrew while the smaller is intermediate in size between the common and the pygmy. The differences between the two species are slight and the account which follows applies equally to both of them.

The white-toothed shrew is a greyish-brown animal with a pointed nose, a slightly flattened body and a tail fringed with long, scattered hairs. Its ears are relatively large, giving it a 'foxy' appearance. As its name suggests, the white-toothed shrew has no red pigment on the tips of its teeth.

The common (below) and lesser (above) white-toothed shrews.

Habitat Provided there is sufficient cover, the white-toothed shrew is likely to be found almost anywhere on the islands. It is commonest on the dunes and on bracken-covered slopes but also lives in hedgebanks, in stone walls separating bulbfields and among boulders on the seashore. For distribution see p. 39.

Food Like its mainland relatives, the white-toothed shrew is not particular about what it eats, and as long as the prey is not too large, it will attack and consume most of the small invertebrates that it encounters. In the Isles of Scilly small, semi-aquatic crustaceans similar to woodlice form an important part of the shrew's diet.

The white-toothed shrew normally feeds every 30–50 minutes and consumes its own weight of food in 24 hours. However, it does not need to feed as often as this and if accidentally deprived of food, it will not die nearly as rapidly as common and pygmy shrews under similar conditions.

Breeding There is a long breeding season which lasts from February to October during which a female may produce a succession of litters of up to six young each.

In continental Europe, where it is widespread and common, the white-toothed shrew has long been known to naturalists for the 'caravanning' behaviour shown by mother and young. This occurs only during the second week after the birth of the young and it is usually caused by a disturbance of the nest. The young have by now grown too large to be carried in the mother's mouth but they are not yet capable of finding their own way home. So the leading youngster grasps the fur on the mother's flanks, while the others hold on to those in front until a chain is formed. Occasionally two young shrews grasp the mother and the offspring are led back to the nest in V-formation.

For almost a century this habit has been thought to be confined to white-toothed shrews, but a note published in the Journal of Zoology (Vol. *183*, 1977) contains a vivid description of caravanning in a litter of mainland shrews (*Sorex* sp.) – probably common shrews.

Territoriality The white-toothed shrew appears to be far more tolerant towards individuals of the same sex than other British shrews. The male and female nearly always share the same nest, even when the female is pregnant, and this is the main reason why white-toothed shrews are so easily kept in captivity.

Natural enemies The same as red-toothed shrews.

Relations with man Of all known shrews the white-toothed are probably the most closely associated with man. On the Continent, the larger (common) white-toothed shrew often lives in outbuildings, hence the vernacular name 'house-shrew', whereas in the tropics, another member of the genus is often found in houses where it lives as a commensal with man. White-toothed shrews are not known to be harmful to man.

The Bats

ORDER CHIROPTERA

R. E. Stebbings

Bats, like reptiles, are objects of much irrational, superstitious fear. This is mainly due to their secretive habits, which prevent frequent contact with man. This fear is held by many peoples in cool temperate regions, but generally not in the tropics, where bats tend to be much more conspicuous.

Bats probably evolved in the tropics, and most of the 950 species alive today occur there. The order *Chiroptera* (meaning hand-wing) is divided into two sub-orders, *Mega-* and *Microchiroptera*. The *Megachiroptera* are the Old World 'flying foxes' which occur from Africa (and just into Turkey) east to Polynesia. These bats feed on vegetable diets including fruit, pollen and nectar. They range in size from about 10–1,200g, and have wing-spans up to 2m. *Microchiroptera* are found throughout the world, except for some remote islands and arctic regions. They feed on most types of food from fruit to flesh, including fish, as well as blood, but most are insectivorous. They range from the smallest mammals at 1·5g, to 300g. All bats in Britain and Europe are insectivorous but although most food taken is insects, some species also take other invertebrates such as spiders.

In terms of the number of species, bats represent one-third of Britain's indigenous mammal fauna, yet as a whole little is known of their distribution, their numbers and their habitat requirements. We can assume that distribution and densities will have changed as climate and habitats changed, but historically we know nothing of these changes. As man felled trees forest dependent species probably declined, so that both Bechstein's and barbastelle bats are now very rare in Britain. Conversely, in the past century small bats, such as pipistrelles, may have reached their highest numbers since the last Ice Age due to their adoption of buildings for roosting. These roosts are far warmer than their former roost-sites, in places such as tree holes, and this has probably led to improved breeding success and survival, because less energy would be spent keeping warm and more would be available for producing offspring.

The unfortunate dilemma in which we now find ourselves is that we urgently need a lot of research into the critical habitat and roost requirements of bats, but at the same time, research can easily result in reducing breeding success and survival. Recent research has shown that the female of the endangered greater horseshoe bat may be up to seven years old before the birth of her first baby, and that even when mature, females will not always produce young every year. It is easy to see that recovery from a population crash would be very slow.

Bats are very vulnerable to catastrophes because in summer, entire regional populations usually gather in a single roost to give birth and rear their young. If a householder has such a colony and decides to be rid of it by fumigation or other destructive method, the effect can be widespread. It is thought that the killing of colonies is also occurring accidentally on a large scale due to remedial treatment of timber in buildings, such as spraying roofs against woodworm. The chemicals used contain highly persistent pesticides which are excellent for killing insect pests, but they are equally lethal to bats.

Bats that hibernate, and that includes most species in temperate areas, are more sensitive to organochlorine pesticides, DDT for instance, than are other mammals or birds. The reason seems to lie in the special metabolism and physiology that these bats have. Unlike most warm-blooded animals (Homoiotherms), bats do not attempt to thermoregulate their body temperature. However, they are not poikilotherms (as most reptiles are, changing their body temperature with the environment) but instead are termed 'heterotherms'; that is, they tolerate a wide range of body temperature. The bats' body temperature is selected and adjusted largely by choosing the appropriate roost seasonally, and in response to physiological needs. In hibernation, British bats select roosts varying from 0°C to 12°C, and each species has its own preference. Long-eared bats like to be close to freezing, while greater horseshoes like temperatures between 6°C and 12°C. Within a species the selected temperatures will vary through the winter, from warm in the autumn to cold in spring. In hibernation the bats' body temperature approximates the ambient (the temperature of its surroundings) and its heartbeat may be only a few per minute. When flying, body temperatures can reach 42° (normal body temperature is 37°) and heartbeats can rise as high as 1,000 per minute. At roost, even in summer, bats usually allow their body temperatures to fall to the ambient. Because bats spend much of the time with low body temperatures, the ability to metabolise pesticides is reduced, although accumulation still occurs through ingestion with food, and through skin contact with treated timber. With birds and most mammals that have more or less constant temperatures, pesticides are metabolised and excreted more rapidly, which may avoid the build-up of lethal quantities.

What of the future? Bats are declining throughout the world. Distributions that were once continuous are now becoming fragmented. Habitat change, pesticides and loss of roosts are probably the greatest continuing threats to bats. Through research, education and protection of roosts we hope to prevent their extinction.

British Bats

Michael Thompson

Greater (right) and lesser horseshoe bats

Now air is hushed, save where the weak-eyed bat,
With short shrill shriek flits by on leathern wing,
Or where the beetle winds
His small but sullen horn.

WILLIAM COLLINS (1721–1759), Ode to Evening

Most people are able to recognize a bat, twisting and turning as it pursues its prey, at dusk on a summer's evening. As a group of small mammals they are widespread, but now far fewer in numbers than they were before the use of insecticides. In Britain some species are becoming endangered. To biologists and naturalists, bats are important mammals, in fact they are unique. Firstly, they are the only true flying mammals; secondly, they use sound location to move about their environment and to find their prey; thirdly they use hibernation possibly more skilfully than do other mammals, and finally they use 'delayed fertilization' in their breeding biology.

The pipistrelle is the most common and widespread of the British bats. Sometimes seen during the day, it usually emerges after sunset. This one is hunting threadhorn flies.

The hedgehog is active at night when it may be seen hunting for its food, which may include earthworms, spiders, caterpillars and beetles such as this violet ground beetle.

Anatomy To understand how bats have become adapted to their particular environment, it is necessary to know something about their anatomy and physiology. For an instance, take their flight.

The anatomical structure of the wing of a bat allows for more flexibility than that of a bird, especially at the shoulder or pectoral joint, which in the bat is more mobile. On the other hand most bats do not attain such high flight speeds as do birds. Bats' wings, unlike those of birds, consist of a thin stretchable membrane of skin, between the layers of which are small blood vessels, fine muscles and what is known as 'elastic tissue'. The membrane is stretched over a framework of elongated fingers, and becomes taut when the forearm, which makes the main strut, is fully extended. In the unstretched state, the relaxed elastic tissue gives the wing membrane an appearance not unlike seersucker – the wing, at rest, folds neatly into the side of the bat. The wing membranes are usually dark; some are opaque or translucent when held up against the light.

Bats have thumbs which most of them use, along with their hind feet, to crawl easily over rough surfaces and into crevices and cavities but the greater and the lesser horseshoe bats have difficulty in crawling through crevices and require a reasonably open roof space at their roost. Often bats turn a complete somersault in flight before they alight. When roosting, most species hang upside down by their feet, but some, like Daubenton's bat (*Myotis daubentoni*), may roost head uppermost. Roosting horseshoe bats wrap their wings about themselves, giving them a pear-shaped appearance. Bats are sometimes known to swim.

Like other mammals, bats are covered with fur, which is moulted every June. Generally their fur is medium to dark brown or black in colour, especially on the back, but the under-parts tend to be lighter, varying from white, through light browns to grey. There is, however, considerable variation not only between species, but also within each species. The basal hairs may be dark. Young bats tend to be dull grey in colour. In all species there is sexual dimorphism – females are larger than males. The largest bats in Britain are the noctules (*Nyctalus noctula*), with a wing span of about 36cm and an average weight of 32g, and the rare mouse-eared bat (*Myotis myotis*) which has a wing span of over 40cm. The smallest, the pipistrelle (*Pipistrellus pipistrellus*), has a wing span of about 22cm and an average weight of 5g, depending on the time of the year.

The ears of bats vary considerably in their external appearance and together with an extra lobe within the ear called the tragus, are used as identification characters. The long-eared bat (*Plecotus* sp.)

It is not easy to distinguish bat species on the wing but the pipistrelle (facing p. 50) is very small and, as with some of the other more common species, where you see them can often be a guide. The noctule (*top*) and the serotine (*next top*) fly high, Natterer's bat (*middle right*) is usually seen flying around trees and the common long-eared bat (*middle left*) picks insects off trees, while Daubenton's bat (*bottom*) often flies low over water.

has ears as long as its body, whereas the pipistrelle has small ears, a little longer than its fur.

Each species of bat has different teeth, a useful means of critical identification. Like humans, bats have both milk teeth and an adult set. The milk teeth are shed about 20 days after birth.

Echo-location The vocal chords in the bat's larynx produce the sounds used for echo-location but they are modified and focused by the skull and mouth or nose. As with radar beams the variable echos received from an object allow the bat to interpret the distance it is away, its texture and its size. The bat is continually issuing these ultra-sonic waves, and uses them both for locating its prey and for finding its way about. Bats have eyes, but British bats may not use sight to find their prey. By contrast, fruit bats, which live in the tropics, have well developed eyes but their echo-location system is not well developed, or is absent.

It is possible to analyse some of these ultra-sonic sounds by using a 'bat detector', a piece of electronic equipment available commercially, which is designed to change ultra-sonic into audible sound. The sounds come across as a series of chirrups, cheeps and clicks, depending on the species of bat; but the majority of the smaller species issue such similar sounds, that it is often not possible to say precisely what species is on the wing. However, greater horseshoe bats (*Rinolophus ferrumequinum*) produce echo-location sounds through their noses, with a closed mouth, at a range of 80–85 kilohertz. Pipistrelles produce their sounds through an open mouth at a range of 40–45 kilohertz and make a characteristic chirrup on the detector. But the average amateur, using such a detector, can only tell that a bat is on the wing and whether it is feeding; for the squeak repetition rate increases as the bat 'beams' in on its prey.

Behaviour Most bats emerge from their daytime roosts at dusk, but some, such as the noctule, fly before sundown. Some species remain away from their day roosts throughout the night, whereas others take about one hour's flight at dusk, followed by periods of rest and flight, ending with a pre-dawn feeding period. Noctules tend to fly high, often along with swifts, and their flight pattern is not dissimilar. Other bats, such as Daubenton's, fly low over water, often hovering just above the surface like a swallow. The pipistrelle, Britain's most common bat, often has regular flight paths, usually three to six metres above ground. The two long-eared bats hover near foliage, picking insects off leaves or bark. Although there is great variation in flight pattern and behaviour among bats, they cannot be recognized by flight pattern alone, but must be handled for definite identification.

Habitat The earliest periods from which bat fossils have been unearthed, are the Eocene and the Oligocene. Originally bats must have been either cave or tree dwellers, but they have gradually become adapted to other roosts such as buildings. As a result some, such as the pipistrelle, have even extended their range and numbers. The horseshoe bats have remained basically cave species, only coming into houses where there are large roof spaces. Bechstein's bat (*Myotis bechsteini*) is a true forest species, roosting in trees both in summer and winter. Other forest bats include the barbastelle (*Barbastella barbastellus*), Leisler's bat (*Nyctalus leisleri*) and the noctule, although Leisler's and some of the smaller woodland species have been found in buildings. Noctules regularly use the same tree hole and can often be heard chattering throughout the day, particularly in beech woodland. The function of this chattering, which is found in other species, is probably social communication.

Buildings of the late Victorian period appear to shelter the greatest variety of bats; but bats, particularly the smaller species such as the pipistrelle and the whiskered (*Myotis mystacinus*), may now be found roosting in modern buildings – and it is these roosts which cause such public concern.

On modern housing estates breeding or nursery roosts may be established within a year of completion. The bats usually find access to these nursery roosts between the soffit of the eaves and the outer brick wall at the gable end of the house. The roost is usually situated in the cavity wall, but if there is a gap between the roof felt and the wall, the colony can find its way through to the loft. Other entrances to roost sites in modern houses can be between ill-fitting facing tiles on bay windows or between wooden fascia boards. In some of these situations the size of the colony is determined by the space available. Each roost has one or more exit holes, which can usually be located by the staining on adjacent brick work, or by the accumulation of faecal droppings on the ground below. These droppings consist of chewed insect remains and are black if beetles or flies have been taken – brown if moths were eaten.

Nursery colonies may also be found in churches, caves and hollow trees.

Hibernation Bats change their roosts with the changing seasons, preferring to face south-east to south-west during the summer months, but north or north-west in the winter. They like the warmth of summer but in winter they need a fairly stable low temperature, for hibernation. Seven of the British species may be found hibernating in caves, each carefully selecting its own hibernation temperature. In all cases the hibernaculum will have high humidity, so that the wings will not dry. Although segregation by sexes usually occurs in the nursery colonies, in hibernacula the sexes are usually present in roughly equal numbers; but some species hibernating in caves may have a predominance of males. Bats such as pipistrelle, are gregarious in hibernation; other bats are solitary.

Hibernation begins at the end of October and bats will remain there until the end of March or the beginning of April – the time varying with the species and according to the climate. All bats will come out of hibernation briefly from time to time, depending on weather conditions, and can often be seen flying about in daylight. The greater horseshoe wakes on average every ten days. It will often move its position within a cave as temperatures change. It may also change caves.

Bats come out of hibernation rather slowly, losing more energy (stored partly as fat) than they can replace, unless there is an immediate supply of food. So, if disturbed too often they may not have enough energy left to see them through the rest of the winter. There is some evidence to suggest that female pipistrelles which are under weight at the time they go into hibernation, will be barren in the spring – their infertility being related to the inability of the female to nurture the sperm through the winter (see Breeding below). It is the lack of winter food that forces bats to hibernate in temperate zones. If they remained active throughout the year, they would need to migrate as swallows do.

Food Bats are specialist feeders – British bats depending upon invertebrates, mostly insects. They seem to fill the niche in the environment that is occupied in daylight hours by swifts, swallows and flycatchers. The noctule catches mostly large insects which it eats on the wing. Most other species feed in a similar way. But the pipistrelle is known to carry large prey to a perch, dismembering and eating it there. Spiders are included in the diet of the whiskered bat. The serotine (*Eptesicus serotinus*) prefers beetles (including cockchafers) and large moths. Greater horseshoe bats are known to forage on the ground for dor beetles. Large bats tend to eat large food – small bats small food.

All British bats have an interfemoral membrane. This membrane, extending from one hind foot to the other, is supported in the mid line by the tail and acts as a basket. Into this basket the bat can either transfer its prey whilst in flight or, in some species, actually use it to catch the prey. Also supporting the interfemoral, from the ankle, is a cartilaginous calcar, which varies in size and shape according to the species and so can be used in bat identification.

The weight of a bat can vary considerably within twenty-four hours depending on how much food is available, and some species can eat over half their weight each night. Whatever the source of food – even if it is a large moth or over a thousand midges, it will in every case be caught by echo-location. When the weather is very cold, wet or windy, bats seldom emerge, because there are usually few insects about. When observing nursery colonies a single bat, usually an adult female, is often seen to emerge many minutes before the others and I have wondered whether it was sampling the external conditions. But usually this scout-bat does not return immediately to the roost.

Territoriality Bats are mostly gregarious and in general not territorial. Several bats can often be seen in the air at one time and there never appears to be any rivalry between them. Nevertheless there is some evidence of territorial rivalry between male grey long-eared bats (*Plecotus austriacus*) in the autumn. In the nursery colony situation also there is some evidence of inter-species aggression, so that, for example, the small pipistrelle bat will drive out any intruder such as a whiskered bat. Some bats migrate – noctules have been known to fly several hundred miles. But distances hardly compare with those achieved by birds.

Breeding Bats mate in the autumn and throughout the winter, but mating has been little observed. They are polygamous; the females seek out the males after they have left the breeding colony. After mating the females carry and nurture the sperm within the uterus, throughout the winter, with ovulation and fertilization occurring in the spring. The sperm can therefore retain its fertilizing capacity for many months. This process is called delayed fertilization.

The gestation period varies from species to species. The noctule has an average period of 70 days compared with the 44 days of the pipistrelle. The length of gestation can be extended considerably in poor weather. In most species single, blind young are born, but occasionally twins are produced. Birth normally occurs between the middle of June and the first week of July, when the females come

Heads of the rarer species of British bats, *from left to right: top*, whiskered bat, Brandt's bat; *middle*, barbastelle, Bechstein's bat; *bottom*, Leisler's bat, grey long-eared bat and mouse-eared bat.

together to form nursery colonies. In some species, such as the pipistrelle, colonies can number up to 2,000 bats. The males take no part in rearing the young and at this time, tend to be solitary. The babies are reared by suckling the mother. The young are flying after about 18 days, but do not become fully independent until they are four to five weeks old.

Within eight to ten weeks, again depending on the species, the nursery colonies disband, so that by September the adult females have usually left. In the majority of bats sexual maturity is reached in two or three years, with some bats breeding in their first year. Before they reach maturity females often return to the nursery colonies.

Marking Bats, like birds, can be marked with numbered rings. Ringing has not only given valuable information about their life span and migratory movements, but also about the structure and size of nursery colonies. Ringing returns have shown that females will return to the same roost every year and that each nursery colony will have several alternative roosts within the same area. Rings have also shown that bats have an average life-span of four to five years but some have been recaptured after 30 years. The Conservation of Wild Creatures and Wild Plants Acts 1975 forbids the marking of any bat in any way, without a licence.

Enemies Bats have few enemies except man. Common long-eared and pipistrelles are sometimes caught by owls. Skulls of the greater horseshoe bat have been found in the pellets of both tawny and barn owls. Sparrowhawks and hobbies have been known to take bats on the wing. Even members of the Mustelidae (the weasel family) have been known to take pipistrelles at their roosts. Starlings will drive noctules from their roost holes, and these bats are killed in small numbers during tree-felling operations. Cats also take bats, but these may be sick bats.

Bats and man The survival of many bat species throughout the world depends on man's attitudes towards them; for man's activities, especially during the last decades, have greatly reduced bat numbers. Traditionally, the bat has been an animal of superstitions, especially in our western civilization, because of its association with dark caves, churches and graveyards. In contrast, many Asians, particularly the Chinese, regard bats as good omens of longevity.

The quotation below is from an unrhymed poem that D. H. Lawrence wrote about bats in his series on animals. In another poem, entitled 'Man and Bat', the poet describes how a man found a bat in his bedroom and his frantic efforts to get rid of it. Both poems perfectly summarize most people's attitudes towards bats.

> Creatures that hang themselves up like an old rag to sleep;
> And disgustingly upside down.
> Hanging upside down like rows of disgusting old rags
> And grinning in their sleep.
> Bats!
> In China the bat is a symbol of happiness.
> Not for me!

All the fears that people have about bats are irrational. One is that bats get entangled in hair, but tests show that bats cannot cling on to hair, but just slip off. This fear is probably derived from the time when domestic houses did not have ceilings so that bats roosting in the rafters would, from time to time, fall down onto the occupants below, and probably became entangled in the hair nets worn by women in the seventeenth and eighteenth centuries.

In recent years, especially on new housing estates, people have become increasingly concerned about their bat nursery colonies. When a nursery colony is discovered in a house, the householder seems either to accept it or to ask the local pest control officer to get rid of it – such action usually resulting in the colony being fumigated. As a method of control this is inhuman and ineffectual for, unless the exit holes are blocked up, new bats will occupy the site. Fumigation not only leaves an unpleasant smell of decaying corpses within the roost, but can also have a devastating effect on the local bat population, because all females of one species will collect together from a very wide area into one nursery roost. Bats are not pests and in Britain are not vectors of disease. Admittedly when bats collect in large numbers, their squeaking and their droppings can be a nuisance, but their droppings are not corrosive and can easily be brushed up and used in the garden as a fertilizer. Bats do no material damage to houses.

The only humane way of removing a bat nursery colony from a house is to watch the site for several consecutive nights, counting the bats out on each occasion and noting the main exit hole. Then on a chosen night, after the bats have emerged – before mid-June, or after late-August when their young will be out flying like their parents – block up all entrance holes, leaving the main hole until the last. The bats will, at the end of their feeding period, go to one of their alternative roosts. On subsequent evenings the main hole should be unblocked for two hours at dusk so that any bats remaining in the roost can get away.

Householders who cannot tolerate their bats, should be encouraged to carry out the above procedure at the end of August or in winter when the whole nursery colony will have dispersed. In old churches bats may be a considerable nuisance – even interrupting services – and bat-proofing is very difficult. Nevertheless bats are members of the parish and need to be tolerated.

Bats are declining for a number of reasons. The most serious are the great reduction in insect numbers and the modification of habitats. The replacement of old farm buildings by buildings made of concrete and asbestos, effectively eliminates roosting sites, while the re-roofing and pointing-up of old buildings removes others which may have been in use. Felling old trees and grubbing up hedgerows affects bats and insects alike. Anti-fungal and anti-beetle treatment of lofts, with highly poisonous chemicals, kills many bats, quite apart from fumigation directed against the bats themselves. Insecticides may also cause a reduction in the breeding success of bats.

Bats are so highly sensitive to disturbance that even naturalists studying them may cause deaths. The increased popularity of cave exploration has caused the disappearance of some cave-roosting species from their traditional sites.

Measures can be taken to reduce the killing of bats. Fixing iron grills at the mouth of important caves to keep people out will help. Less poisonous chemicals can be used to treat roof timbers and treatment can be delayed until May, which anyhow is the best month for woodworm control. Bat roosting boxes, resembling bird boxes, but with a 15mm-wide slit entrance in the bottom, have been known to attract several species – especially where there are few natural roosting sites, such as in conifer plantations. Long-eared bats have been found hibernating in bat boxes. Boxes should not be treated with wood preservative.

Advice about bat conservation can best be obtained from the local County Trust for Nature Conservation or the regional offices of the Nature Conservancy Council.

Two species of bat are totally protected by law in the Conservation of Wild Creatures and Wild Plants Act 1975. They are the greater horseshoe and the mouse-eared bats. It is an offence to handle, remove or kill these species without a special licence from the Nature Conservancy Council. Bats are not hunted, but they can be treated very cruelly.

Identification and Distribution (See table) Identification of bats can be difficult, and is best carried out with the aid of a good identification handbook or by going to the local museum for advice. There are 15 species of bats resident in the British Isles. They represent two families, the Rhinolophidae and the Vespertilionidae. The Rhinolophidae or Nose-leaved bats have two species in Britain – the greater horseshoe, *Rhinolophus ferrumequinum*, and the lesser horseshoe, *R. hipposideros*. The remaining 13 species belong to the Vespertilionidae family.

Some of these bats are extremely rare, such as the mouse-eared, with probably less than ten present. Others are becoming increasingly rare such as the greater horseshoe, with some 1,800 in Britain. Other species, because of their similarity to known species, have only recently been scientifically recognized. One such is Brandt's bat (*Myotis brandti*), which was first found in Yorkshire in 1971. The

Table of British Bats

English names	*Scientific names*	*Size*	*Habitat*	*Distribution*	*Status*
Greater horseshoe	*Rhinolophus ferrumequinum*	large	General	SW England, S. Wales	Endangered*
Lesser horseshoe	*Rhinolophus hipposideros*	small	General	SW Britain, W. Ireland	Rare
Whiskered	*Myotis mystacinus*	small	General	England, SW Scotland, Ireland	Rare
Brandt's	*Myotis brandti*	small	Woodland	England and Wales	Rare
Natterer's	*Myotis nattereri*	medium	General	England, Wales, S. Scotland, Ireland	Common
Bechstein's	*Myotis bechsteini*	medium	Forest	England (Dorset to Shropshire)	Very rare
Mouse-eared	*Myotis myotis*	v. large	Open woodland	England (Dorset and Sussex)	Endangered*
Daubenton's	*Myotis daubentoni*	medium	Open woodland	Great Britain and Ireland	Common
Serotine	*Eptesicus serotinus*	large	Open woodland	S. & SE England	Locally common
Leisler's	*Nyctalus leisleri*	medium–large	Forest	S. & C. England, Wales, Ireland	Doubtful
Noctule	*Nyctalus noctula*	large	General	England, S. Scotland, Wales	Becoming rare
Pipistrelle	*Pipistrellus pipistrellus*	small	General	England, Scotland & Ireland	Very common
Barbastelle	*Barbastella barbastellus*	medium	Woodland	England, Wales	Very rare
Common long-eared	*Plecotus auritus*	medium	Open woodland	Great Britain and Ireland	Common
Grey long-eared	*Plecotus austriacus*	medium	Open woodland	S. England	Very rare

NOTES: SIZES – THE SIZES ARE JUDGED BY AVERAGE WING SPAN AS FOLLOWS:

Small	225mm–240mm	Large	360mm–385mm
Medium	250mm–310mm	V.Large	400mm + (Mouse-eared)
M–Large	310mm (Leisler's)		

* Protected by the Conservation of Wild Creatures and Wild Plants Act 1975.

grey long-eared bat, scientifically recognized in 1960, is at the northern limit of its range – in Dorset, Hampshire and Sussex. Other bats, such as the pipistrelle, common long-eared (*Plecotus auritus*), Daubenton's, whiskered and natterer's (*Myotis nattereri*) are still quite common, though greatly reduced in numbers. Migratory vagrants to this country include the parti-coloured bat (*Vespertilio murinus*) and Nathusius' bat (*Pipistrellus nathusii*). Records for the latter species came from Dorset and Hertfordshire during the last decade.

The Rabbits and Hares

ORDER LAGOMORPHA

P. G. H. Evans

The Order Lagomorpha was once considered to be a suborder of the Rodentia. Both are gnawing animals with chisel-shaped incisor teeth. However, unlike rodents, lagomorphs have two pairs of incisors in the upper jaw, though the second pair is much smaller than the first. Both orders lack canines and have a wide gap, or diastema, between the incisors and the cheek teeth. In lagomorphs, the cheek teeth are short but on each side there are six in the upper jaw and five in the lower jaw. Along these teeth runs a pattern of transverse ridges which help to grind up the vegetable matter that forms the food of all members of the order. Whereas rodents have only rudimentary milk teeth (and these only during early life) the young lagomorph develops three upper milk molars and two lower ones, together with two upper milk incisors – although one is rudimentary. The incisors are rootless and continue to grow throughout life. Other distinctive characters of lagomorphs include a large caecum, a short stubby tail, and retracting flaps of skin that cover a hairless groove (called a rhinarium) in which lie the nostrils.

Lagomorphs practice refection, an unusual habit they share with the common shrew and some of the rodents. During the day and in the middle of the night, they produce very soft moist faecal pellets coated with mucus. These are swallowed directly without chewing and in this way the rabbit or hare is able to pass practically all its food twice through the intestine before finally being excreted as hard fibrous pellets. It is thought that bacteria in the food within the large intestine produce B-vitamins, and that these are absorbed in the small intestine when the food passes through a second time.

The rodents are amongst the most successful of all mammalian orders, having undergone extensive adaptive radiation. Lagomorphs have rather few species – only 63 species in the world compared with 1,685 of rodents. However, what they lack in numbers of species, they make up by those few species being very widely distributed and highly successful.

There are two families within the Order Lagomorpha – the Ochotonidae which includes the pikas of the mountains of Asia and western North America, and the Leporidae comprising the rabbits and hares. In Britain and Ireland we have representatives only of the Leporidae – a rabbit and two species of hare. All three British species are grazers upon grasses and perennial herbs, although the mountain hare feeds mainly upon heather. All three closely crop the turf and thus encourage the growth of annual weeds. Rabbits cause a great deal more economic damage than hares.

Hares and rabbits are relatively defenceless animals, easily preyed upon by carnivores. Rabbits are smaller than hares and do not have such powerful hind legs, possibly making them more vulnerable to predators. This may be why they have resorted to using burrows. Although mortality is probably high, particularly in young rabbits and hares, this is compensated for by high reproductive rates, with individuals reaching sexual maturity at an early age – in their first year for rabbits but a year later in hares. Many litters may be born in a season and, if food or climatic conditions are unfavourable, the developing embryos are reabsorbed, so conserving energy for producing litters later in the season. Thus these species may be very successful, and in some areas population increases can result in a great deal of economic damage to farm crops and to pastures. This has been particularly so with the rabbit and has brought the species into direct conflict with man. Since myxomatosis, when numbers of rabbits declined greatly, the brown hare seems to have increased (possibly through less competition) and it may in the future also come into conflict with man.

The Rabbit

P. G. H. Evans

Folks ain't got no right to censuah other
folks about dey habits;
im that giv' de squir'ls de bushtails
made the bobtails fu' de rabbits.
PAUL LAURENCE DUNBAR (1872–1906) Accountability

The rabbit (coney, conyng or cwningen) *Oryctolagus cuniculus*, is surely one of our most familiar mammals, widespread throughout Britain and Ireland including even very small islands. It is easily distinguished from the brown and mountain hares. It has a more squat appearance and shorter hind legs in relation to the body and lacks the black tips which hares have on their ears. The white underside of the tail, conspicuous when running, is a further distinguishing mark. The doe is smaller than the buck, with a less rounded head.

The ears of the rabbit, although relatively smaller than those of the brown hare, possibly because of the shorter grass in which the rabbit feeds, are nevertheless important for quickly detecting potential predators. The eyes are large and prominent, probably for the same reason, and placed well to the sides of the head, giving all round vision. Since rabbits usually feed in fairly open situations, often at dawn and dusk, they are vulnerable to many predators, such as foxes, stoats and, when young, weasels. The long whiskers around the rabbit's snout are sensitive to touch and are probably useful underground. We know rather little about the rabbit's senses of taste and smell.

Rabbits have scent glands at four sites on the body – beside the eye, on the chin, beside the anus and around the rectum (the inguinal gland). Each may serve a separate function, although we do not understand the full significance of each. Marking with the chin gland (chin marking) is usually done by the dominant male of a group and may reflect social status although it is sometimes associated with marking by the anal gland, when it probably has a territorial function. Scent from the inguinal gland passes out with the urine and appears to be important in the female, as a sex attractant. The wide range of scents employed by the rabbit reflect its social organization.

The long hind legs and the powerful muscles in the lower back of the rabbit suit it for rapid motion in leaps, with the forelimbs often moving together. All four feet are covered with a thick coat of hair, giving a firm grip on rocks or sandy slopes. The rabbit's coat is made up of three layers of fur. First there is a dense, soft under-fur. Through this grow longer stiffer hairs, giving the coat its grey-brown colour. Finally, through both grow still longer, sparser hairs banded brown and black, sometimes grey. In winter these last form a thick, warm over-coat.

Burrows and breeding To dig its burrow, the rabbit uses its forepaws, shovelling the loosened earth towards its hind legs, which kick it away. The burrows are about 20cm in diameter and, when extensive, form warrens. The nest is usually either in a blind chamber in a burrow, or in a separate, small burrow or 'stop', one or two metres in length. For their burrows rabbits prefer light, sandy soil, such as is found on dry heaths or maritime dunes, but they will burrow in chalk, shale, loam and even in dry, clay soils. Sometimes they will manage without burrows altogether, nesting instead in dense vegetation such as hazel or hawthorn scrub. In recent years warrens in open ground have become less common, partly because of the extermination of rabbit populations occupying such burrows, and partly as a result of ploughing-up such places for pasture.

A brown hare grooming. In late summer the coat moults to be replaced by denser, redder fur, returning to the summer coat in a second moult between February and July.

The red squirrel, here seen in summer coat, is the native British species. It rarely ventures far from trees, through which it moves at great speed making long jumps from branch to branch.

Mating takes place following a hectic chase, and urination by the female. The buck plays no part in rearing the young – his time is taken up chasing other does.

Young rabbits may be born at any time of the year, but usually between January and August, although before myxomatosis, when rabbits were at high densities, the breeding season was shorter and few litters were born after June. Usually three to seven young are born at a time, although there may be up to eleven. The gestation period is 30 days, and litters may follow one another at intervals as short as a month. A doe rabbit may produce over thirty offspring in a year, but only when the rabbit density is low. At a high density, when many embryos are reabsorbed before birth, only ten or eleven offspring will be produced annually.

Rabbits, unlike hares, are born blind and only sparsely furred, in nests composed of grass and moss and lined with the mother's under-fur. At birth they weigh only about 30g. Fed nightly on milk by the doe they grow rapidly so that at three weeks old, when they are weaned, they weigh 150g – about one tenth of the adult weight. The eyes open at one week old but the young remain in the nest until shortly before weaning. At only three and a half months, the young females are themselves able to breed and the males are sexually mature a fortnight later. By midsummer, young born before March may already have a litter of their own, so it is not surprising that we speak of breeding like rabbits.

A notch present in the long bones of the leg of the juvenile, which disappears as it gets older and ossification takes place, enables the age of rabbits to be judged approximately. If the leg bones from rabbit remains are collected in the autumn the number of those from adults can be compared with those from younger animals. Comparison of remains in recent years suggests that one half of the population is being replaced yearly. This is not what would be expected if the population were increasing.

Social behaviour Most of our knowledge of the social behaviour of rabbits is derived from studies on the islands of Skokholm and Skomer, off the Pembrokeshire coast, and in Australia. These show that rabbit populations are divided into groups, with a definite system of hierarchies. Dominant bucks and does hold a group territory with the main warren as its base. Lower ranking animals are excluded and must instead use short burrows or stops. A buck of high social status will mate with a number of does. The older rabbits are most likely to be the dominant ones. Usually yearling rabbits breed away from the main warren and have a shorter breeding season and their offspring usually suffer higher mortality. When feeding in a group, rabbits signal danger to one another by stamping with their hind feet and they may also stand upright for the same purpose. Perhaps the conspicuous white underside of the tail serves this purpose also, but most communication between rabbits seems to be by scent.

The home range of the rabbit is usually quite small, covering only 150m to 200m from the warren, depending upon availability of food and danger from predators. On moonlit nights rabbits feed close to their burrows, but if it is very dark they may range further afield. On small islands where predators are rare, they may feed throughout the day. Young rabbits do not seem to move very far from their places of birth.

Food Rabbits eat a wide variety of plants, and are very fond of crops such as wheat, barley, oats, clover, turnips, cabbages, lettuces and carrots. They will also feed intensively on a mixture of grasses, choosing the cultivated and erect, but leaving the wild and creeping to dominate. Thus they turn valuable pasture into closely grazed turf or rough grazing, with the annual weeds encouraged by the disturbance of the soil. Rabbits will also damage forestry plantations by browsing on the barks of young trees.

On small islands where rabbit populations are confined and densities high, intensive grazing around the warren may lead to large areas of bare ground and erosion. It is the rabbit's diet that brings him into conflict with man.

The rabbit's second-time-round digestion of food, called refection, has been described in the introduction to the Order Lagomorpha (p.63).

Natural enemies The principal rabbit predators are foxes, stoats and weasels. The long cylindrical bodies of stoats and weasels enable them to enter rabbit burrows, so that even the young in their nests are not safe. The polecat and the wild cat also take rabbits, as do badgers and domestic cats. Among birds of prey, golden eagles and buzzards feed largely on rabbits. Near the coast, greater black-backed gulls, carrion crows, hooded crows and ravens take very many rabbits, although the corvids eat them mainly as carrion.

The rabbit has also to contend with many parasites. On the ears and around the eyes live two mites, a sheep tick, a sucking louse and a flea. The flea, *Spilopsyllus cuniculi*, is found only on the rabbit and its life cycle is closely correlated with that of its host. Rabbit and flea reproduce at the same time, but the flea must ingest the reproductive hormones in the female rabbit's blood before it can itself reproduce. This is one of the main parasites that carries the myxoma virus, the cause of myxomatosis. Another parasite which gives rise to much mortality among young rabbits, especially at high population densities, is the protozoan causing coccidiosis. Rabbits are frequently affected by several internal parasites – several species of nematodes, tapeworms and liver flukes, but normally these do not severely affect their health.

Rabbits and man Rabbits originally came from north-west Africa, Spain and Portugal but spread naturally over western Europe and north Africa. They were introduced into Britain by man during the twelfth century, first to offshore islands but later to the mainland where they were bred for their meat and fur. Probably quite soon afterwards they escaped from captivity and established wild colonies but, even as late as the eighteenth century, they were not looked upon as a nuisance. In fact Gilbert White wrote at the time, 'Rabbits make incomparably the finest turf, for they not only bite cleaner than larger quadrupeds, but they allow no bents to rise'.

In the eighteenth century rabbits probably increased as a result of agricultural changes, such as the introduction of crop rotation and the sowing of winter fodder crops, but the rabbit did not become a pest until the nineteenth century. In the early part of the twentieth century trapping was carried out to control rabbits but the attempt failed and their numbers increased to an estimated population of 50–100 million, with densities of 15 or 20 to the acre (50 to the hectare) – 40 to the acre (100 to the hectare) on some offshore islands. For centuries the rabbit had been hunted for its meat, and fur and that may have helped to keep numbers down, but when rabbit meat ceased to be popular the need to control numbers became even more pressing. Except for man and his domestic animals the rabbit has probably done more than any other mammal to change the British landscape. Similar changes for the worse have followed wherever the rabbit has been introduced – notably in Australia and New Zealand – and it was for this reason that the rabbit disease myxomatosis (to which hares are slightly susceptible also) was introduced into Australia.

Myxomatosis In South America there lives the native wild rabbit of Brazil, *Sylvilagus braziliensis* (a near relative of our European rabbit). In 1942 the scientist Aragão discovered that this rabbit was subject to the disease myxomatosis, itself discovered only in 1897.

To the Brazilian rabbit, myxomatosis was only a mild infection, to which many were even immune, but to the European rabbit it was lethal. From this knowledge there followed several attempts to introduce the disease into Australia and these were eventually so successful that between 1950 and 1953 the rabbit population of Australia, itself introduced by man, was almost wiped out – almost, but not quite. Then, in 1952, deliberate introduction into France led to myxomatosis spreading through most of continental Europe and again to a tremendous reduction in the rabbit population. In 1953 sick rabbits were found in south-east England and on 13th October of that year myxomatosis was confirmed at a farm in Kent. Attempts were immediately made to confine the disease in the hope of eradication, but they failed and the disease spread rapidly throughout Britain.

The exact means by which myxomatosis came to Britain was never discovered, nor whether its introduction was deliberate or accidental, but there is no doubt that, having arrived, it was sometimes deliberately spread by the movement of an infected rabbit to an unaffected area. Although such movement was made an offence by an amendment to the 1954 Pest Act, myxomatosis soon became established in the British rabbit population – with enormous mortality among rabbits but with a great increase in agricultural yields. Eventually rabbits began to develop immunity. A very few rabbits always recovered from the disease and became immune or partially immune to further attacks. These animals could pass on their immunity to their offspring.

Myxomatosis may be transmitted by rabbit-biting arthropods, such as the rabbit flea already mentioned, and by certain mosquitoes or it may even be passed from one rabbit to another by very close contact. It is a horrible disease. The infected rabbit develops a fever, its ears, nose and eyelids swell and it produces a discharge. Blind and dying, it is a truly pitiable creature. Undoubtedly it suffers severely but reports of myxomatosised rabbits feeding voraciously and even attempting to mate within hours of death suggest that possibly it is not in acute pain. But by what criteria can one compare degrees of suffering?

Control How should rabbit control be accomplished? That is a difficult question, but that some form of control is necessary if agriculture is to survive seems indisputable. Now that myxomatosis is established in an endemic form in Britain it can scarcely be eradicated, and myxomatosis may even achieve a balance between successful agriculture and a small, permanent rabbit population.

Hares

Ray Hewson

Mountain hare

Each outcry of the hunted hare
A fibre from the brain doth tear.
WILLIAM BLAKE (1757–1827) Songs of Innocence

Two hares are known in Britain: the brown hare, *Lepus capensis*, and the slightly smaller mountain hare, *Lepus timidus*. The first is familiar throughout much of lowland Britain, excluding northwest Scotland, while the mountain hare is a creature predominantly of heather moorland which affords it both food and shelter, although it is also found at low levels in Ireland, where the brown hare is absent as a native species. The two species are not easy to distinguish unless the mountain hare is in its conspicuous winter coat.

The Brown Hare

Its large size, long black-tipped ears and long hind legs distinguish the brown hare from the rabbit. Likewise its bright yellowish-brown pelage and black-topped tail separate it from the mountain hare. The hare's keen senses and long legs show how well it is adapted to escape from predators and also that it is better suited to living in open country than in dense cover. When disturbed by man, hares often crouch low to the ground with flattened ears, and become surprisingly difficult to see even where cover is scanty.

Brown hares do not burrow but find daytime refuge in a form or couch in long grass, or sometimes in woods – even in heather. This form – or forms for several may be used – will almost always be within a kilometre of suitable farmland to which the hare can move at night to feed, returning to its form in the morning. Hares move along well defined tracks, but these do not lead directly to their forms. (Colour illustration facing p.66.)

Home range The brown hare is pre-eminently an animal of cultivated land or improved pastures. On mountainside or moorland its place is taken by the mountain hare.

Brown hares are usually found singly or in pairs. In good feeding areas several home ranges may overlap, with numbers reaching one hare to every three or four hectares. Hares do not defend territories, and may amicably share a feeding area with rabbits.

Brown hares may live as long as twelve years, but only about six per cent survive for more than five years. Many leverets (hare young) do not reach their first autumn. Female hares average 3·7kg in weight and are bigger than males, which weigh about 3·5kg. There are two annual moults – into a denser, redder winter coat in late summer, and back into the summer coat between February and July.

Courtship and breeding The behaviour of hares during courtship is spectacular, with boxing, leaping and chasing, and the 'mad March hare' is a well-known rural spectacle. A female hare may even strike at and pursue a male, but the meaning of this behaviour is quite unknown.

Hares, like rabbits, can re-absorb their embryos during food shortage or other stress, thereby ensuring, in hard times, that the mother will survive to breed again. After a gestation period of about six weeks she will produce up to five leverets (but usually two or three) in a concealed place among vegetation. They are born fully furred, have their eyes open, and are soon active. Leverets weigh about 110g at birth and reach adult weight in about eight months. The breeding season is a long one, with hares pregnant in almost every month of the year, but with a peak in April and May. Litters are bigger and breeding goes on later when the first half of the year is warmer than average. Curiously, the breeding season lasts a similar time in New Zealand, Australia, Scotland, Canada, Russia and Poland, which have very different climates and environments. In Britain, brown hares probably have three or four litters each year. They do not breed in the year of their birth.

Food Because brown hares are thought, on the whole, not to do economic damage, their diet has been little studied. They are very obvious when grazing spring corn in May or in pastures at the first flush of new grass, and unpopular in turnip fields where they pull off slivers of turnip peel and excavate shallow cavities in the bulbs. They can distinguish between varieties of turnips, preferring purple bulbs to green ones, but, over-riding any such preference and in order to see approaching predators, they like to have an open space around them to graze away from cover.

Hares feed mostly at night, except before heavy rain or during periods of snow. Inconspicuous at dusk, they graze with their ears almost flat, moving a step at a time and keeping their bodies close to the ground. Like rabbits, hares typically produce hard droppings by night, but soft faeces by day which are then eaten to pass through the digestive system again (see p.63).

Natural enemies Among British predators, only the fox and the golden eagle can readily take a fully grown hare, and foxes can more easily get rabbits. But the young hare is vulnerable to attack by cats, stoats and buzzards.

Man and the brown hare Formerly esteemed as a sporting animal, enormous numbers of hares were shot in the nineteenth century, but the Ground Game Act of 1880, which allowed occupiers of land to kill hares to prevent damage to crops, somewhat reduced the bag obtainable by sportsmen. Thereafter hares were probably less common, though still valued as a game animal. Following the decrease in rabbits after myxomatosis in the 1950's, there was an apparent increase in the numbers of hares feeding on farm crops, and these were then shot as pests. In recent years hare carcases have become more valuable and the brown hare's status may return to that of a game animal.

Hare coursing is vigorously opposed by the RSPCA and other humane people, but all efforts to have it banned have so far failed.

Distribution and classification Brown hares are absent from north-west Scotland and from Ireland (except for recent introductions which mostly have been unsuccessful), but they have been introduced successfully into some Scottish islands, for example, Orkney (Mainland), Mull and Skye, and also to the Isle of Man and other English islands. Formerly known as *Lepus europaeus*, the brown hare has lately been reclassified as *Lepus capensis*, bringing it into the same species as all the hares found in Africa and the Mediterranean region. All bear a strong resemblance. Its distribution is among the widest of any mammal, reaching across Asia to central China, and, in the north, to southern Sweden and Finland. It has also been introduced into Australia, New Zealand, Chile and parts of North America.

The Mountain Hare

The mountain hare is smaller and greyer than the brown hare and, in winter, conspicuously white, but, although both its ears and its hind legs are a good deal shorter than those of the brown hare, the absence of a black top to its tail is the only certain way of identifying a mountain hare in its summer or autumn pelage.

Mountain hares moult three times a year, compared with the two moults of the brown hare. The moult to the white winter coat begins in October and is about complete by December. It is triggered off by decreasing daylight – the rate varying with temperature and the amount of snow on the ground. In March the transition from white to brown begins and the old coat is rapidly shed. By May the grey-brown new coat is fully grown, except on the hind feet. A third moult, from the summer coat to a very similar grey-brown autumn one, occurs between June and August.

The white winter coat, found also in stoats, lemmings and ptarmigan, has evolved as a form of protective colouring and probably provides better insulation. In Scotland mountain hares are often conspicuously white against a snow-free, dark moorland background but when there are patches of snow, hares tend to stay near them, and sometimes make short snow burrows. In Ireland mountain hares rarely attain a fully white coat.

Habitat Mountain hares live in heather moorland, and they are most abundant on the grouse moors of north-east Scotland. They move through the heather along conspicuous trails which are kept clear by biting off obstructing shoots. In much of western and north-western Scotland burning and grazing has led to the replacement of heather by other types of vegetation and, in consequence, hares are rare or absent.

Mountain hares choose to make their forms in long heather but often they dig short burrows in peaty ground and sit at the entrance, usually in the upper part of their home range. In winter the entrances to the burrows are kept open by tunnelling through the snow. The precise use of these burrows is not known; leverets are seldom born in them, although they use them readily for shelter. Adult hares, if disturbed at a burrow entrance, usually run away from it.

Home range Moving freely about open hillsides, mountain hares give the impression of having big home ranges. They may occupy (though not exclusively) home ranges of 20–28ha. These territories are likely to include long heather for shelter and short heather, or sometimes hill pasture, for feeding. Mountain hares are remarkably sedentary: during population studies marked hares were sometimes caught several times in the same run over a period of some years. Young hares did not leave the areas in which they were first caught when about two months old, and appeared to be as sedentary as adults.

Courtship behaviour and breeding The courtship of mountain hares is slower than that of brown hares and therefore easier to watch. One or more males will follow a female along a hare trail, all moving at a steady lope. When the female stops, the leading male stops and then approaches carefully. Usually the female strikes out at the male with her forefoot and pursues him for a few metres. Then the whole business starts up again. It is rare to see mating.

The breeding season starts in February, the coldest month of the year, often with snow lying. Reabsorption of early litters often occurs. In April, after a gestation period of seven weeks, the first leverets, usually only one or two, are born in a form in the heather. There are normally three litters in a year, each of up to three young, occasionally four. On average a female produces about six leverets annually.

Population changes Over a period of years mountain hares are subject to big changes in numbers. If, when they are at maximum density, a springtime food shortage occurs, many will die and this reduction in numbers will persist for several years. Then, when numbers are low, hares will rear more young and they and the adults will survive better. So, gradually, the population builds up again, with about ten years between one population peak and the next.

Food The main food of the mountain hare is heather, of which 90 per cent of the winter diet and half the summer diet may consist. It is supplemented by cotton grass, heath rush and other moorland plants. When snow covers these, hares eat twigs and needles of gorse and juniper, bark and twigs of rowan and willow and, in prolonged severe weather, may eat bark and twigs of birch.

During the first few years after heather burning, hares prefer shorter to longer and older heather, perhaps because they can keep a better lookout for predators. In spring, when most female hares are pregnant, they select a better diet than do the males.

Natural enemies On heather moorland, mountain hares often form the main prey of foxes. Wild cats and eagles also take them. Stoats, buzzards and hen harriers prey on the leverets.

Man and the mountain hare Mountain hares have not so far achieved the status of a game animal. Hundreds may be shot in a single day by gamekeepers, shepherds and others during hare drives.

Distribution Mountain hares occur over much of northern Europe, and the tundra zone of North America and Greenland, although generally at lower densities than in Scotland. In north-eastern Scotland there may be five hares per hectare (2 per acre), but only one hare to 100 hectares (250 acres) in parts of the north-western Highlands. The mountain hares in lowland Scotland are the result of nineteenth-century introductions and they have also been successfully introduced into some of the Scottish islands and into Yorkshire and Derbyshire. They are found at low levels in Ireland, where the brown hare is present only as an introduced species.

The Rodents

ORDER RODENTIA

J. R. Flowerdew

The rodents, or 'gnawing' mammals, are probably the most abundant mammals in every terrestrial habitat. Their distinguishing feature is the presence of two pairs of sharp, chisel-like, front teeth, the incisors. These consist of a hard front layer of enamel backed by a softer layer of dentine, so that they naturally wear to a wedge-shape and are continually sharpened in use. The roots of these incisors are always open so that they grow continuously, making good the loss through wear. Without constant abrasion these teeth will grow in a complete circle and may even pierce the jaw. There are no 'eye' teeth or canines; in their place is a gap or 'diastema' separating the incisors from the grinding molar teeth. This gap leaves room for flaps of skin to shut off the front of the mouth, with the gnawing incisors, from the back of the mouth where the chewing takes place. Thus hard or unsuitable food need not be taken into the back of the mouth, even though the incisors have bitten it off. The order is very similar to the Lagomorphs, rabbits and hares, but lacks their extra pair of incisors.

Rodents are mainly herbivores although they sometimes eat animal food in large quantities. A wood mouse, for example, will feed almost exclusively on insect larvae when these are falling from trees to pupate in the ground. Food is commonly stored, particularly during the autumn, and some species possess cheek pouches to help them carry the food to a safe place. The pouches are internal, opening into the mouth in hamsters and ground squirrels, but external, opening on the cheek, in some New World gophers and mice.

The Order is not very specialized apart from the teeth and the jaw musculature. Its species are generally very primitive in form with a long, low skull, a small brain and unmodified limbs. Locomotion is usually quadrupedal but some species have greatly enlarged hind limbs and are capable of bipedal hopping, like kangaroos. Hearing is acute and many species can hear high frequency ultrasonic sounds which are inaudible to man. The eyes are usually well developed, particularly in those species which are arboreal or live in open areas. Most species seem to see in black and white only, but colour vision is probably present in a number of squirrel species, including the grey squirrel. Smell is very well developed and olfactory communication plays an important part in the life of rodents. Information transmitted by odours includes the recognition of home ranges and territory, social status, sex, maturity, the identity of groups of individuals and even of subspecies. Odours also play a part in the acceleration or inhibition of puberty, in the inhibition and synchronization of the period of 'heat' or oestrus and in the failure of pregnancy. These effects occur in the laboratory mouse and in a few other species of mouse and vole, but it is not known how important they are nor how commonly they occur in the wild.

The skin of rodents may bear scent glands on almost any part of the body, including the tail, and many ground-living species, such as the field vole, have glands which are well placed on the rump, or on other parts of the body, to rub on the sides of runways. Urine and faeces are also involved in the production of odours for communication.

Most rodents are small, having a head and body length of less than 300mm. The largest rodent, the capybara which is a close relative of the coypu, weighs up to 50kg. The rodent tail is very variable in length and it is often used to help with balance or support; only rarely, as in the harvest mouse, is it prehensile.

There are at least 1,600 species of rodent distributed throughout the world. They include terrestrial, underground and aquatic species with many forms of motion including walking, running, jumping, climbing, gliding, burrowing and swimming. The order is divided into three main groups, the myomorphs, or mouse-like rodents, the sciuriomorphs, or squirrel-like rodents, and the hystricomorphs, or porcupine-like rodents. The sciuriomorphs are the most primitive and include the squirrels, gophers and beavers. The myomorphs include the Old World and New World rats and mice, hamsters, voles, lemmings, gerbils, dormice, jumping mice, bamboo rats, jerboas and mole rats. The hystricomorphs include the Old and New World porcupines and the South American cavies, capybaras, agoutis, chinchillas, coypu and other families. In the myiomorphs reproduction is usually rapid with short pregnancies and with the production of more than one litter in each breeding season. This fast reproductive rate sometimes leads to rodent plagues such as the 'lemming years' in Scandinavia, or the abundance of wood mice in eastern Europe. Cyclical changes in numbers, with peaks occurring every two to four years, are characteristic of many myomorphs, particularly the voles and lemmings and this subject has been a popular topic for research.

Britain has fewer species of rodents than has continental Europe; Ireland has even fewer. This situation arose after the last glaciation, when recolonization of Britain and Ireland by rodents from Europe had to occur before the land masses were separated. The land connection between Britain and Ireland is not a certainty. If it occurred it was probably only a small glacial or land bridge between very deep sea channels which lasted for a short time as the climate ameliorated. In contrast, the English Channel was cut much later, perhaps about 5,000 BC, so that many of the species, typical of a present-day, more northerly, colder climate were able to enter England, but those adapted to the more southerly temperate climate were excluded. It is thus not surprising that few reached Ireland and the rodents present are only the red squirrel, grey squirrel, house mouse, wood mouse, ship rat, common rat and bank vole. Of these all except the red squirrel were probably introduced by man!

The muskrat was introduced into Britain and Ireland in fur farms and became feral from 1927. However, an intensive control campaign led to its extermination in the wild by 1937. In Britain many other introduced species have proved more difficult to exterminate. In the last 100 years or so the grey squirrel, edible dormouse and coypu have been introduced and are still with us. Earlier introductions into Britain possibly include the house mouse and the Orkney vole, and many of the island races of the wood mouse. More definite introductions are the ship rat and the common rat. The only native rodent in Britain to become extinct in historical time is the beaver which disappeared during the twelfth century in Wales and, perhaps at a later date, in Scotland.

Many rodents throughout the world are pests of stored food and agricultural crops, but in Britain only the house mouse, common rat and perhaps the grey squirrel are of major economic consequence. Other mice and voles may be damaging to crops and food stores but their economic impact is small. In tropical regions many different species of rodents present serious problems to food storage, agriculture and health. Many diseases of man and his livestock are carried by rodents, although plague, most closely associated with rats, is actually transmitted by the flea of the rat, which carries infection from one human to another. Among other diseases carried by rodents are Weil's disease (Leptospirosis), typhus and pseudotuberculosis. The rodents and man have affected each other in important ways and much of their past history and their present-day adaptations are the result of man's activities.

British Squirrels

A. C. Dubock and J. C. Reynolds

Grey squirrel

Like a small grey
coffee-pot,
sits the squirrel.
He is not
all he should be,
kills by dozens
trees, and eats
his red-brown
cousins.
The keeper on the
other hand,
who shot him, is
a Christian and
loves his enemies.
Which shows
the squirrel was
not one of those.

HUMBERT WOLFE (1885–1940) The Grey Squirrel

We have two species of squirrel in Britain: the red which is native, and the grey, which was introduced from America. The red squirrel appears to be in decline and it is not at all surprising that the grey squirrel has often been 'blamed' for its demise, for the change in the relative population densities of the two species has been recorded during an age when people have had an interest in speculating on the reason for such things. It is understandable that the British human population should feel less enthusiastic about the imported grey squirrel than its 'native' red squirrel. But let us examine the facts.

There is evidence that since Britain became separated from the rest of Europe following the last Ice Age, a variety of red squirrel has evolved here which is different from that now found in continental Europe. Red squirrel populations in parts of Britain suffered extinction in the last century or so (and, although unrecorded, possibly earlier) and have been reintroduced by man. For instance the red squirrel was considered extinct in southern Scotland and Ireland by the early eighteenth century, and nearly so in the Scottish Highlands during the late eighteenth and early nineteenth centuries. Reintroductions were mainly from England, but some continental stock was also brought in. Conversely, immediately before the turn of the nineteenth century, the red squirrel was considered superabundant over much of Britain, especially Scotland, where it inflicted considerable damage to forestry. In continental Europe drastic oscillations in red squirrel numbers are now considered a part of the normal natural history of the species.

Quite a number of anecdotal records exist of grey squirrels chasing 'reds', biting and even killing them; and occasionally of greys killing the young of red squirrels. Research has shown that such physical interactions are at the most a very rare event. Where the two species occur together, as for example in parts of East Anglia and of Ireland, the relationship appears harmonious.

There is of course the possibility that the two compete directly for food, and it may be that this creates a shortage with which the grey squirrel is better able to cope.

Endemic disease in red squirrel populations may have reduced numbers locally, allowing grey squirrels to establish themselves. It has also been suggested that grey squirrels may harbour a pathogen more harmful to red squirrels than to grey. Severe local outbreaks of disease causing crippling losses to populations are known for both red and grey squirrels. The organisms responsible have yet to be isolated, but typical symptoms, in red squirrels, include purulent eyelids, nostrils and general lethargy followed rapidly by death.

The most inexplicable fact of the red and grey squirrel interaction in Britain is that the red squirrel appears to be unable to become re-established in an area which has been 'taken over' by the grey squirrel. But of course a squirrel's world is very different from ours. Grey squirrels are known to 'scent mark' small patches on trees with urine, and it is possible that a squirrel visiting one of these 'marking points' can gain an impression by scent of the number of animals using it. Visits to a number of these points could indicate the size of the congruent squirrel population. Red squirrels also make marking points, but they are not so common, or perhaps not so obvious to the human eye, as those of grey squirrels. When a young squirrel is searching for a place to settle, the scent on these marking points may affect the attractiveness of a patch of woodland considerably. This is a channel of communication which is only beginning to be comprehended, and as yet we have no idea whether red squirrels are at all influenced by the scent of greys, or vice versa. Grey squirrels tend to occur at higher densities than red squirrels and in any particular habitat this may reduce food supplies available to the red squirrel. Additionally, there is some evidence that grey squirrels spend proportionately more time foraging on the ground than red squirrels do and they may thus eliminate stored resources before the red squirrels, to whom they are essential, can get at them. All these factors – scent, marking points, and food competition may have a bearing on the apparent inability of the red squirrel to re-establish itself in a grey squirrel area.

Grey squirrels were first introduced into Britain in 1876 and it is not surprising that they spread rapidly in their new and favourable habitat. Latterly the rate of decline of the red squirrel population and the rate of increase of the grey squirrel range have both decreased. This suggests an interaction which may be coming to equilibrium. However, between the late 1800's and the present time, many other environmental factors have changed and these may have had more impact on the populations of both squirrels, than either of them has had upon the other. So the role of the grey squirrel in the red squirrel's decline still remains uncertain.

The planting of extensive monocultures of conifer forests in the more remote areas of Britain by the Forestry Commission since the 1920's, and the ever increasing recreational mobility of the human population, together with the low amenity value of conifer forests in comparison with deciduous woodlands, may have influenced the present distribution of the red squirrel. The red squirrel is considerably more timid than the grey, and could probably be justifiably regarded as being less adaptable. Moreover the grey squirrel, as a species, has demonstrated its greater ability to benefit from the habits of modern man. These considerations may explain why the red squirrel is almost exclusively confined to the more remote and least populated parts of the British Isles.

At the time of the introduction of the grey squirrel, the red squirrel was considered a major forest pest. Today grey and red squirrels together seriously damage almost one per cent of British deciduous woodland every year by stripping bark. Not only the bark is removed: the channels which carry the sap up through the trunk are lost and the dividing layer of cells necessary for growth is destroyed. If the tree is completely girdled it dies. A.C.D. and J.C.R.

The Red Squirrel

As a species the red squirrel, *Sciurus vulgaris,* occurs throughout Europe and the USSR, extending as far east as China and Korea. In Britain it is now almost restricted to Scotland, Wales and East Anglia. It is present in Ireland.

The size and build of the red squirrel vary slightly throughout this range, as do the colour and nature of its coat, but regional varieties are no longer regarded as distinct sub-species. The colour varieties fall broadly into two groups, so-called 'dark' and 'red' phases, apparently associated with latitude and habitat, but the darker of these is not found in Britain.

Our own red squirrel has a brownish-red coat over the upper parts, head and tail, a white belly and a white underside to the neck. It is quite a small animal, considerably smaller than the grey squirrel, measuring about 385mm from nose to tail-tip, and weighing about 285g. Males and females are much the same size. The summer coat is a richer red than the winter coat. Young fresh out of the nest are an especially deep colour until their first moult. Moults occur in spring and autumn, and the colouring of the hairs gradually fades after each of them. In Britain and Ireland the hairs of the tail and the ear-tufts are only moulted in autumn, so that by the end of the summer many red squirrels have very pale bleached tails – on the Continent these parts moult twice a year with the rest of the coat, and very pale tails do not occur. In this respect, our red squirrel is exclusively British.

The features that adapt the red squirrel particularly to an arboreal life are shared by all squirrels, and many of them are characteristic of rodents in general. Although the build of the red squirrel is quite delicate, even for a squirrel, the hind limbs are surprisingly long and robust. The hind feet can be turned outwards at the ankle through nearly 180°, allowing the animal to descend trees head downwards. The front feet can also be turned outwards, but not to quite the same extent. Front and back toes are long and slender, with strong hooked claws which provide a phenomenal purchase on smooth expanses of bark. The thumbs of the front feet exist only as small stumps, but the squirrel has an almost human ability to grasp and manipulate small items of food, and the thumb stumps are actually used in feeding. The long-haired tail, which with the ear-tufts contributes so much to the human appeal of the red squirrel, is of major importance as a balancer, besides being a very expressive signalling device.

Of the senses, sight is the most developed, as it needs to be for safe manoeuvres in the tree tops, and it is the usual means by which would-be predators are detected. Hearing is adequate but not exceptional. The sense of smell, whilst useless for detecting predators in a squirrel's mode of life, is highly sensitive for short range work, such as hunting-out buried food. (Colour illustration facing p.67.)

Habitat and habits On the ground the squirrel has a dainty hopping gait, but turns out to have a very poor top speed when pursued, relying on its ability to climb to escape danger. Consequently it is rarely found at any considerable distance from trees, and its true enemies, in Britain, are those that can climb: such as pine-martens, stoats and both wild and feral cats. Nevertheless foxes and several birds of prey may surprise squirrels at ground level. The goshawk in particular, increasingly a British bird, can become adept at catching squirrels.

On suspecting danger, a squirrel will usually adopt an alert posture, sitting upright on its hind legs, tail flat against its back. If on the ground, it may first of all climb a little way up a tree to gain a vantage point – in any case red squirrels, whilst foraging at ground level, often prefer to feed on raised perches such as tree stumps. Having gained a view over the ground vegetation, the squirrel may content itself with a suspicious lashing of its tail from side to side; below the body. The alarm call is a repeated 'chuk-chuk-chuk' which gradually becomes 'tok-tok-tok' as the fear of danger increases, and may develop into an explosive 'wrrroouhh' as the squirrel panics and flees.

The red squirrel is active only during the day; at night it retires to a nest or drey, a hollow structure built of twigs, about the size and shape of a football. This is usually 6m or more from the ground, and built close to the trunk of a tree, in the crook of a branch or a fork. Inside it contains soft bedding of moss, grass or leaves. Without regular use and maintenance the structure soon falls into disrepair – the top collapsing into the central cavity – but squirrels sometimes renovate old dreys rather than build new ones. Cavities in the trunks of mature trees may be occupied as dens by squirrels. Often these dens are enlarged and adapted from old woodpecker nests or rot holes; but squirrels do not excavate holes in undamaged tree trunks.

For the most part red squirrels live singly, although in winter two or more may share a drey, presumably for warmth. They do not hibernate – after all, early winter is when the chief food source of red squirrels, conifer seed, is most available – but they may have periods of inactivity during intensely cold, wet or windy weather, or whilst snow remains on branches.

Red squirrels are not territorial in that they do not defend an area against intruders. Activity is inevitably centred around the living-quarters in use at the time, be it drey or den, and the area covered by the animal during its normal routine is known as its 'home-range'. Since there are no defended territories, the home ranges of different individuals overlap considerably – or to put it another way, a patch of woodland may be used by more than one red squirrel. If two squirrels meet whilst foraging one will usually quietly give ground to the other, their relative social position having been determined by previous encounters. If the relative status of the two is disputed, a series of soft 'chuks' from one animal heralds a chase which takes place around the trunk of a tree or more rarely through the canopy – the pursuing animal attempting to bite the pursued. The fleeing squirrel may introduce a tactical element by dodging behind the trunk, thus breaking the pursuit and even gaining the advantage. Severe bites are rare, but many animals carry scars on ears and tail.

Social behaviour accounts for only a very small proportion of the red squirrel's time, most of which is spent feeding and resting. In summer, activity begins soon after first light, and feeding is very intensive for the first few hours after sunrise. Thereafter animals are about intermittently throughout the day – until towards dusk when there is another concerted period of activity. In winter there is only a single peak of activity, around mid-day.

Food The red squirrel's diet centres around tree seed or mast but it can and will eat an enormous variety of seeds, nuts, berries, fungi, tree buds and other vegetation. In the extensive coniferous forests of Wales, East Anglia, northern England, Scotland and Ireland, where the red squirrel now principally occurs, its chief food is pine seeds. These it extracts from the cones by biting off the scales to expose the seed underneath. Seed-bearing cones are only available on the trees from the end of summer to about May, when the seed is shed and scatters. During the summer red squirrels subsist by eating cones which they have cached at ground level (or more rarely in a hollow tree or drey) and by turning to alternative food such as buds and shoots of pine and other trees, fungi, and a small amount of animal matter.

Breeding Mature female red squirrels are capable of producing two litters of young per year (early spring and summer), but the number of young in each litter and the number of litters is probably heavily influenced by the previous food supply and weather. A female on heat is attractive to males over a considerable area, and these collect to trail around behind her in a 'mating chase'. Eventually only the dominant male amongst her attendants is allowed to mate. After mating the male has no further role and plays no part in rearing young. The young are born and reared in the drey or den. They begin to emerge and explore at about seven or eight weeks old. At eight to ten weeks after birth they should be fully weaned but their mother continues her protective care for a short while after weaning.

Relations with man One hears little of the damage caused to trees by the red squirrel, such tales being totally eclipsed now by the reputation of the grey squirrel. Yet when it was common in the past, control of the red squirrel was often necessary to protect timber crops. Red squirrel damage to deciduous trees, by removing patches of bark especially near the base of trees, is very similar to that caused by grey squirrels. Usually this bark-stripping occurs during late spring and early summer, but the reason for it is unknown (see p. 90). The red squirrel will also attack coniferous trees, often killing the crown by removing rings of bark from the main stem near the top. The extent of this damage can be considerable. In 1977 as many as 80 per cent of one crop of Scots pines in East Anglia were affected in this way. The cumulative effect of this over several years could cause quite large losses to a timber crop. Nevertheless such damage is now very much a local problem, and on the whole it is ignored, even if it is attributed to its proper cause. In practice, fungal and insect pests do far more damage to forestry. Where it is considered necessary red squirrels can be shot, or trapped in spring or cage traps. (Recently however, research workers have experienced considerable difficulty in live-trapping red squirrels). Legislation prevents the use of Warfarin-poisoned bait in counties where red squirrels occur.

On the Continent the red squirrel is hunted for its pelt, as food and for sport. In Britain it is generally too scarce to make such activities possible, even were they desirable J.C.R.

The Grey Squirrel

The grey squirrel, *Sciurus carolinensis,* is possibly the most frequently observed wild mammal of the British fauna, especially in towns. As such it undoubtedly has an unquantifiable amenity value. Although mainly introduced to Britain from the eastern USA in the 30 years or so following 1876, when the first introduction was recorded, its range on mainland Britain now covers more than 40,000 square miles of central and southern England and central Scotland. It is still expanding. The grey squirrel was also introduced into east-central Ireland, where it is still present.

The physical appearance of the grey squirrel and its agility endeared it to the landed gentry of the late nineteenth and twentieth centuries and, ignoring any qualms suggested by the depredations of the native red squirrel, they imported the grey and introduced it into their parklands. It is ironic that the grey squirrel has so often bitten the kindly hand that fed it in those early captive days, for many estates now suffer its ravages in their hardwood plantations. Slowly the mistake was realized and the importation or keeping of squirrels, except under licence from the Ministry of Agriculture, Fisheries and Food, has been prohibited since 1937.

An adult grey squirrel weighs about 450g. Its familiar and expressive tail, powerful hind limbs and strong claws identify it unmistakably. Its muscular body, excellent sight and special eye structure adapt it well for its mainly arboreal existence, although the squirrel is equally at home on the forest floor, or in gardens and urban parks.

The colour of the grey squirrel is not always what might be expected from its common name or from its appearance at a distance. The dorsal surfaces consist of long guard hairs and dense underfur. On close examination the guard hairs are seen to be banded black, white and brown. Although the general impression is grey, the dorsal surfaces of the paws, the flanks and the muzzle are frequently quite chestnut in colour, especially in summer. This has led to the mistaken suggestion that red and grey squirrels may interbreed. The ventral fur is white, and, in winter, small patches behind the ears are white also. Only occasionally do the ears sport prominent tufts of fur, similar to those of the red squirrel. Males and females are indistinguishable at a distance but, upon close observation, a sexually developed adult male can be seen to have prominent scrotal testes which are often quite dark and thereby differentiated from the white ventral fur. A lactating female is obvious by the bare patches of skin around her enlarged mammae, of which there are normally eight.

The grey squirrel has a life span of from four to six years although, in captivity, individuals have reached 20 years.

Enemies Probably man, with his cats, dogs and especially his motor car, is the squirrel's worst enemy. At times of dispersal of the young, especially in September and October, many newly independent squirrels are confused by traffic and succumb on busy roads. Wild predators are few, but include owls and foxes.

Breeding Females usually attain sexual maturity at about one year or eighteen months old, depending upon whether they were born in the spring or summer. In their first year of sexual maturity females usually have only one litter, but older females may have two. Males usually become sexually mature at about one year old. Each year there are normally two periods of litter production and the timing of litters occurs as a result of cycles of sexual development and regression, particularly noticeable in the male reproductive organs. The testes dramatically enlarge to about ten times their previous size and their position changes from scrotal, in the sexually active state, to abdominal in the non-breeding season. These cycles appear to be affected by the length of day – regression following the summer solstice – but food availability and social interactions may also be important. In some years sexual development and therefore production of young is completely inhibited, for one or even both breeding seasons. Mating normally occurs in late December or in March. The male, who is by no means monogamous, mates with a female in oestrous after a 'mating chase' involving one female pursued by several or many males. After mating the female is aggressive to all males, and the father of her brood takes no further part in the proceedings. The gestation period is about 44 days, and weaning occurs at about ten weeks. An average of three or four young are born in each litter, with an approximately equal sex ratio. Young are born blind, furless, without teeth and with closed ears. New born squirrels weigh about 15g.

Young squirrels begin to forage for food on their own at two to three months, although the family group may share a drey and feed together until the mother becomes pregnant again or until the offspring become sexually mature.

The Home Grey squirrels use leafy twigs to construct approximately spherical nests called dreys, 30–60cm in diameter, set in the forks of branches. Suitable twigs are bitten off and painstakingly woven into this structure. During winter, dreys nearer to the centre of the tree tend to be used, for there they are less liable to be dislodged by high winds. Old winter dreys are often repaired and re-lined. It is not uncommon to find layers of old bedding in the bottom of a drey, including the remains of past occupants who died in residence! The entrance to the drey is not normally visible. Holes in trees are also used (often year after year) and, like dreys, lined with soft materials such as leaves, grass and soft, stripped bark. A number of dreys or holes may be used by individual squirrels, and a number of squirrels are quite likely to share dreys or holes.

Food Squirrels are basically diurnal creatures, with major peaks of activity around and just after dawn, and just before dusk. In bad weather grey squirrels, which are particularly susceptible to fatal chilling when wet, may remain in their dreys for three or four days before hunger forces them to venture out to feed. The food shortage of late winter is preceded by the most abundant food supply of the year – the autumn fruit of trees, especially acorns, beechnuts and hazel nuts. Stores of body fat are built up at this time, and excess food is buried. Neither the grey nor the red squirrel hibernates in winter. Before spring buds appear, when food is scarce, individual squirrels will re-discover food buried just below the surface in times of plenty – probably using smell to locate it. Probably only by chance do individual squirrels re-discover food which they themselves had stored. Large hoards of food buried in one place are not characteristic of grey squirrels, but may be made by yellow-necked mice. More typically grey squirrels carefully bury individual items of food and then disguise the disturbed ground – a delightful activity to watch in autumn.

Habitat Grey squirrels live by choice in mature deciduous forest, especially oak, beech and sycamore; but they may also inhabit conifer forests. Although mainly vegetarian – feeding on buds, flowers and fruit – the grey squirrel is an omnivore. As opportunity offers it will eat fungi, insects, bird's eggs and fledglings. Its vegetable foods come chiefly from woodland trees, but any other available source will be made use of, for example, standing corn or fruit in orchards.

Man and the grey squirrel Grey squirrel damage is most important in beech, oak and sycamore woods of 10–40 years growth, where excessive bark-stripping may destroy whole plantations. Nobody completely understands why squirrels do this but the most frequently accepted theory is that it is the work of young subordinate males, frustrated by their lack of mating success. Another idea is that the damage is done by hungry squirrels seeking the nutritious sap of the tree, especially the trace elements. Most bark-stripping occurs in May, June and July. There is also 'bark chipping' with urine marking of territories, especially by males, although as territories appear to overlap, 'home ranges' would seem to be a better name.

In a few districts grey squirrels (as well as red) damage conifers. This is economically important especially where the leading shoot is removed, for the resulting kinked conifers may be less easily harvested and handled than undamaged trees.

Control During the 1950s a bounty scheme to control squirrels was tried, with shooting as the main method. It was unsuccessful, as bounty schemes for pest control almost invariably are. But shooting in the trees and trapping on the ground (with traps that may either kill or catch alive) remain the most usual methods of control. Both are inefficient. Shooting can also be inhumane for squirrels have extremely tough skins and badly injured squirrels can continue to run and jump through the trees after receiving several cartridges of shot.

Since 1973 it has been legal to use the anticoagulant poison warfarin for the control of grey squirrels in areas where red squirrels are not found – provided that a special hopper, designed to limit access by other animals, is used. The use of anticoagulants is usually considered humane, but efficiency in the field may be low due to immigration of squirrels from other places, unless large areas are controlled at the same time.

All the above control methods are most effective if carried out just before and during the period of maximum tree damage – May, June and July.

A method of exploiting a squirrel's behaviour to facilitate shooting it, can equally well be used to observe a squirrel which circles a tree always keeping out of sight. If two people are present but only one moves, the squirrel tends to move to the side of the tree opposite the moving person, allowing the other a good view!

Although not yet in use, long-acting reproductive inhibitors may well have a future in controlling grey squirrel populations. Offered on food baits, for a short time only, in late autumn when other food is scarce and squirrels are already sexually regressed, these inhibitors would reduce the number of young squirrels born in a population during the following year, and the stable social hierarchy of the remainder would limit immigration of other squirrels. If, as suggested above, tree barking really is the work of young, unsatisfied male squirrels, this new method of birth control might prove more effective than the 'removal' methods of shooting, trapping and poisoning.

Some people believe that grey squirrels can be important predators of game bird eggs and nestlings, although this has never been fully substantiated. When they are a nuisance in gardens, the easiest and most effective solution is to regard them as an amenity to be enjoyed, as much if not more than the roses or the bulbs – in which case no control is necessary! If, however, control of squirrels is essential, single-catch live traps, baited with whole maize, is probably the simplest method available to the gardener. Then the RSPCA may be asked to deal with the offending squirrel. But unless the garden is unusually isolated, the removal of a small number of squirrels will only be the prelude to immigration of others. Better the devil you know. . . .!

A.C.D.

British Voles

J. R. Flowerdew

Water vole

Then, as he looked, it winked at him, and so declared itself to be an eye; and a small face began gradually to grow up round it, like a frame round a picture.

A little brown face, with whiskers.

A grave round face, with the same twinkle in its eye that had first attracted his notice.

Small neat ears and thick, silky hair.

It was the Water Rat!

KENNETH GRAHAME (1859–1932) The Wind in the Willows

There are four species of vole representing three genera which may be found in Britain. The voles and the closely-related lemmings have a rounded head and a short tail. These characteristics, together with the relatively shorter limbs and smaller eyes, serve to distinguish the group from the mice and rats. The vole and lemmings often cause economically important damage to crops and forestry in Europe and, in this respect, Britain is fortunate in having only a small, more or less harmless, selection of voles and no lemmings.

The Water Vole

The water vole, or water rat, *Arvicola terrestris*, is the largest of the voles found in Britain and is probably the species most often seen. In common with the other voles its head is rounded, with a blunt nose, and its ears are partly concealed in the long fur. The water vole is often mistaken for the common rat. Despite being called the water rat, it does not deserve this title for in Britain it is usually quite innocuous. It is also easily distinguished from the rats by the 'vole' characteristics and the shorter tail. The head and the body measure about 200mm and the tail is only half to two thirds of this length. The fur is very variable in colour and texture but in the usual form is dark brown. The variants include a darker brown and a black type – the latter being found in northern and north-western Scotland and in some areas of East Anglia. The lightly-haired tail and the hairy feet are very similar to those of the terrestrial voles and probably help the water vole in swimming; but they are not particularly adapted to a semi-aquatic life.

The species is distributed from Europe to Siberia. It resembles *Arvicola sapidus* of Iberia and western France and only in France do the ranges of the two species overlap.

Breeding The breeding season lasts from about April or May until September, but may be shorter if the summer is wet and cold. Pregnancy lasts three weeks and the female may conceive again immediately after giving birth – having up to four litters yearly. The young are born in a nest built either below ground or in good cover at ground level. There is usually a short tunnel leading to the nest and to this there will be more than one entrance, which the vole will block off after entry. Newly born water voles weigh about 5g, are naked and have their eyes closed; they develop quickly and by 14 days old are weaned. In Britain water voles rarely breed in the year of their birth.

Habitat and habits The habitat of the water vole varies from small streams to large rivers and canals, wherever it can burrow into the bank and find suitable vegetation to eat. Water voles restrict themselves to the edges of waterways except for an occasional sally into fields, where, as in Holland for example, they may become pests. They make tunnels in the banks, with exits above and below water level, and often eat bare an area close to their nest sites. Their food consists of reeds, grasses and other vegetation – even on occasion, carrion. In winter root crops and rhizomes will be taken if they are available.

Water voles are more active by day than by night, moving silently in search of food; but once feeding starts their biting and chewing can make them quite noisy. Their sight is poor but their hearing is good. Smell is thought to play an important part in their social life.

Home ranges At six weeks of age water voles take up home ranges which usually form a linear strip along the waterway. On the edge of their ranges they establish latrines where faeces and urine, together with a secretion from glands on the flank (placed on the ground by the hind feet) act as olfactory marking points. These points, often established on prominent spots close to the water's edge, indicate the area to other water voles.

The social system seems to be based upon the family group, which occupies a home range and fights off intruders. There may be a dominance hierarchy within the group.

Numbers are lowest in the spring but early litters soon add to the population which increases up to the end of the breeding season. Later litters survive less well than early ones. In the wild, individuals are unlikely to live for more than three winters.

Natural enemies Predators of water voles include the heron, owls, otter, mink, stoat, weasel, pike, trout and eel, but probably the most important is the common rat which sometimes drives water voles from a stretch of water and eats their young.

Relationship with man In Britain the water vole only rarely causes damage to agricultural crops or to the banks of water courses, but on the continent of Europe it can be a pest in bulb fields and to potato crops.

The Bank Vole

The bank vole, *Clethrionomys glareolus,* is distinguished from other small rodents by its chestnut-brown upper fur. The under-fur is grey or cream-coloured. The hairs are not quite as long as those of the field vole, so that the ears are not completely covered by fur. The tail is long for a vole, being half the length of the head and body which in adults together measures about 100mm. This longer tail, and slightly smaller size, also help to distinguish the bank vole from the field vole. Both species have compact bodies and short legs which ideally suit them for their secret but active life in underground burrows and in open runways worn by their passage between the stems of plants. (Colour illustration facing p.98.)

Habitat and habits The habitat of the bank vole is primarily dictated by the amount of cover available. As long as there is enough cover this species will be found in all types of woodland, scrubland, hedgerow, and even in grassland and areas of marshland and fen.

Bank voles are active by day and by night, leaving their underground nests to search for food and to explore. During their normal activity, they continually release drops of urine, presumably to mark their range and to inform other individuals of their presence. The home range may be as much as three quarters of a hectare (nearly 2 acres), but smaller areas are more usual. Dominant and subordinate individuals may definitely be recognized in social encounters, but little else is known of the bank vole's social behaviour in the wild.

Breeding Breeding usually starts in April and ends in October; but if food is abundant, especially acorns, it may continue into the winter and perhaps even through to the next spring. Pregnancy lasts 17 or 18 days and will be prolonged by a few days if the previous litter is still being nursed. The average litter is about four. Young are born hairless and with their eyes closed, but development is rapid and after two and a half weeks they will be weaned. Females may become pregnant at four and a half weeks old, so that by the end of the breeding season many generations will be present in the population.

Enemies Natural enemies of the bank vole include birds of prey such as kestrel, tawny owl, and barn owl and many of the predatory mammals, particularly weasel and stoat.

Food The bank vole's diet is mainly vegetarian with fruits, seeds and green leaves predominating. They will also take dead leaves, fungi, moss, roots, flowers, grass, insects and worms. Hazel nuts are extracted from their shells through an opening, which leaves few teeth marks on the shell surface – in contrast with the ragged, tooth-chiselled, opening made by the wood mouse and the precise, smooth-edged, but surface-marked hole of the dormouse. Nuts and other foods are often stored in underground chambers.

Populations Bank vole populations commonly reach their lowest density at the start of the breeding season in the spring, and then increase through the summer, to reach a peak in autumn or early winter. This pattern is however affected by the availability of cover and, if cover is lost in the winter, numbers may decline earlier than would otherwise happen. The annual changes in numbers are very variable and may include a decline in mid-summer, or even, if winter breeding occurs, an increase through the winter into the next summer. Failure of the autumn mast crop may cause so many voles to die or disperse during the winter, that it will take two breeding seasons to regain normal winter densities. Variable food supplies may thus cause changes in bank vole numbers which will take more than a year to make good, but there is little evidence from Britain to suggest that bank vole populations show long term cycles over a period of three or more years, as do some populations of the field vole.

Relations with man The bank vole is an occasional pest in forestry plantations as it eats seeds, seedlings and the bark of small trees, but it is generally of little importance to man.

Distribution and classification The bank vole is distributed throughout most of Europe and extends eastward to Lake Baikal. In Britain it is found on the mainland and the Isle of Wight, also on Jersey and the islands of Raasay, Mull, Bute, Anglesey, Ramsey and Skomer. In 1964 it was first found in the southwest of Ireland, where presumably it had been introduced some time before, perhaps deliberately. Island forms of the bank vole are larger than those of the mainland.

Four subspecies are recognized – on Jersey *Clethrionomys glareolus caesarius*, on Skomer *C. g. skomerensis*, on Mull *C. g. alstoni*, on Ramsey *C. g. erica*. The Skomer vole is so docile that if captured it will sit calmly on the palm of the hand.

The Field Vole

The field or short-tailed vole, *Microtus agrestis*, is well named; for its main distinguishing feature is a short tail. The head and body together measure 90mm–115mm, but the tail is only about 40mm long. The fur of the adult is grey-brown in colour except for the belly which is grey-buff. Juveniles have slightly darker fur than adults. This species is often heavier than the bank vole (adults weighing 30g–40g in the summer) and their appearance is generally much more substantial, because of the longer fur which makes up much of the field vole's bulk. They may be confused with juvenile water voles but the relatively smaller feet and longer tail of the latter should distinguish them.

Habitat and habits Typical habitat for the field vole is long, uncultivated grassland but they may be found anywhere where grasses occur within other habitats. They avoid short grazed pasture but find hedgerows, road verges and even some areas of moorland very suitable. Young forestry plantations thick with grass are ideal but slowly become less attractive as the trees grow and the grass declines.

The field vole has a short tail and is more bulky than the bank vole.

Field voles make short underground tunnels and construct nest chambers, but the nest is just as often found at the base of a grass tussock. Much of the vole's activity is confined to the open runways which weave around the bases of grasses and other vegetation. These clear-cut pathways, well worn by use, will reveal the presence of field voles on grassland and it will be confirmed by piles of faeces or of chewed vegetation. Field voles feed on leaves, stems and seeds of grasses, and on many herbs.

The vole's periods of activity span both day and night, and as the individual explores its home range, it marks the area with aggregations of faecal pellets and probably also with urine. The size of the home range is very variable but anything up to 1000 square metres is typical. The social behaviour of the field vole in the wild is poorly understood, but if studies in enclosures are to be believed then a dominant male will associate with females and exclude other males from his home range – thus making it a territory. Yet, it is commonplace to find as many as half a dozen voles under one piece of corrugated iron, so perhaps family relationships overcome individual antagonism, making a group territory.

Breeding usually occurs from April to September with litters of three to seven young being produced after a 21-day pregnancy. The young are born without fur and with their eyes closed; they will be weaned after 14 to 28 days. Breeding will sometimes continue into the winter, but there is no obvious connection with an increased food supply, as there is with the bank vole.

Natural enemies and populations Almost all birds of prey and carnivorous mammals are natural enemies of the field vole. Numbers usually decline from winter to spring, when breeding starts again, although this pattern is by no means constant. If winter breeding occurs or if survival over the winter is unusually good, then numbers may increase from one breeding season to another. This may lead to the classical population cycle in which numbers reach a peak every three to four years – to be followed by a severe decline and a period of scarcity, which may last for a year or longer. Two explanations given for these cycles involve changes in genetics and behaviour, or reactions to stress caused by high densities; but the evidence for either is far from conclusive. If predators are involved at all they are probably most important in keeping vole numbers at a low level, after they have already declined.

Vole 'plagues' may cause damage to forestry plantations but otherwise their effect is economically negligible.

The field vole is distributed throughout the British Isles but is not to be found in Ireland. It is present on some of the Scottish Islands and on the Isle of Man. The range of the species extends to the Arctic coast in the north, the Alps and Pyrenees in the south and to Lake Baikal in the east. Island forms of the closely related European common vole, *Microtus arvalis*, are found on Orkney, and on Guernsey.

The Orkney and Guernsey Vole

The islands of Orkney and Guernsey both support populations of the European common vole which have been given subspecific status as *Microtus arvalis orcadensis* and *Microtus arvalis sarnius* and named after the islands in which they live. Both are usually larger than the field vole, weighing up to 63g on Orkney and up to 45g on Guernsey compared with a maximum of about 40g for the field vole.

A male bank vole (right) encounters a female (left), but she is unreceptive. Bank voles may climb into hedges and bushes. They are active by both day and night.

A yellow-necked mouse suckling her week-old litter in her burrow. This species climbs well and is equally at home in trees and on the ground.

The only sure way to distinguish these subspecies from each other or either from the field vole is by comparing their teeth which show slight characteristic differences. However, since they are confined to their own islands and the field vole does not occur in either territory, the problem only arises with collected specimens. The Orkney vole may be light or dark brown above and grey with orange-buff or creamy buff fur below, there being some variation between the islands. The Guernsey vole is similar in colour to the field vole except that it has pure grey underparts.

The Orkney and Guernsey voles are subspecies of the European common vole and are larger than the field vole.

Little is known about the Guernsey vole except that the litter size is probably low; the average embryo number for eight pregnant females was 3·3, similar to the average litter size of 2·7 given for Orkney voles born in the laboratory. The Orkney vole easily interbreeds with the European common vole.

The life of the Orkney vole is very like that of the field vole. It lives in similar habitats as well as in heather and in growing crops. Its nest sites, feeding and behaviour are also similar. Its runways are said to be very conspicuous. Its predators include hen harriers, short-eared owls and domestic cats. Populations of the Orkney vole may be very dense, but numbers are more stable than those of the field vole. The species does no serious damage on Orkney although it appears in grain stores and stacks of hay and oats.

The European common vole is not found in either Scandinavia or northern Finland, but its range extends throughout Europe south of the Baltic, to the Mediterranean. It is found as far east as Iran and the Altai mountains. The two subspecies of Orkney and Guernsey *may* both be the result of human introductions but there are strong reasons for thinking that this may not be true of the Guernsey vole. A recent study of many variable characteristics of bone structure in the skulls of voles from Orkney, Guernsey and many locations in Europe, indicates that the Orkney populations show more affinities with populations from the south of Europe than from elsewhere. Other evidence leads archaeologists to conclude that the early farmers on Orkney came from the eastern Mediterranean; so it seems possible that these people introduced their vole into Orkney, about 4,000 years ago. The vole populations on the various Orkney islands were once considered to be five distinct subspecies of *Microtus arvalis*, but this view is no longer held as their differences are very slight. Some islands in Orkney may have held populations in the past which have since become extinct and this is known to have happened on Shapinsay.

Skull characteristics of the Guernsey vole show strong affinities with populations from Germany, Greece, Hungary, Yugoslavia and Iberia and are very similar indeed to the German population. This probably means that the Guernsey vole is a true relict rather than an introduced species, having remained from the time that Guernsey was connected to the French mainland.

Wood Mice

J. R. Flowerdew

Wood mouse

> *Mus, the Mouse, a puny animal, comes from a Greek word: although it may have become Latin . . . Others say it is 'mice'* (mures) *because they are generated from the dampness of the soil (ex* humore*). For* 'humus' *is* 'hu-Mus', *you see?*
>
> Twelfth century Latin bestiary, translated by T. H. White

Two representatives of the wood mice (genus *Apodemus*) live in Britain. There are three other species of the same genus distributed in Europe but only our wood mouse and the yellow-necked mouse occur in Britain. In North America a similar-looking genus, *Peromyscus*, fills the same woodland and field niche, but is more closely related to the voles.

The Wood Mouse

The wood mouse, *Apodemus sylvaticus*, is probably the best known of the country cousins of the house mouse and although it may not be seen very often, it is the most widely distributed mouse in the British Isles. The common ability of mice to dart quickly out of sight, balance on very narrow supports with the aid of their tails, and to depend mainly on touch, hearing and smell for sensing their environment, make them ideally suited to their retiring and often nocturnal way of life.

The wood mouse has large, bead-like eyes which are more prominent than those of the house mouse or of the voles. The ears are also larger than those of the house mouse and stand erect at the top of the head. The fur is dark brown above, becoming yellowish brown or buff on the flanks, and pale grey or white on the belly. Juveniles have a darker, greyish-brown coat until about eight weeks of age and this is when the wood mouse may most easily be confused with the house mouse. A buff-coloured spot may be present between the fore legs, sometimes extending down the belly, but it never reaches the dark upper fur as does the yellow 'collar' of the yellow-necked mouse.

Wood mice caught on the mainland of Britain and Ireland measure about 75–110mm from the tip of the nose to the base of the tail, this being only slightly longer than the tail itself. Individuals from island populations are often larger than mainland mice – adults weighing up to 50g compared with the mainland weight of 18–30g.

Habitat and habits An alternative name for the wood mouse is the long-tailed field mouse and, together, these names accurately describe the usual habitats of the species, although they are also found in hedgerows and gardens and even on moorland. In all these places wood mice live in underground burrows containing food stores and nest chambers, but sometimes the nest may be found above ground in a hole in a tree or wall.

What use the wood mouse makes, at night, of its sense of sight is uncertain, but presumably its large eyes make the most of the poor light available to a strictly nocturnal animal. Young mice are able to attract their mother by making squeaks at very high frequencies inaudible to the human ear, and similar ultrasounds are produced in exploratory and social behaviour. The night activity of wood mice reaches two peaks, after dusk and before dawn, but during short summer nights these peaks are amalgamated. The movements of a wood mouse in search of food and in exploration may cover an area of two and a half hectares but often the home range is smaller than this – the actual size depending upon sex, age, breeding condition and habitat. Wood mice generally move greater distances in summer than in winter and this increase coincides with the start of the breeding season.

Social behaviour of wood mice seems to be based upon the family unit. In the breeding season males and females are associated in pairs but there is little evidence of territorial behaviour, for adjacent individuals of the same sex have widely overlapping home ranges. There is, however, an indication (from field observations) that a dominance hierarchy exists between pairs of mice at a feeding place, for one male and female will wait until another pair have finished feeding, before they themselves venture out of the shadows.

Breeding Breeding usually starts in March or April so that the first young are born in April or May. The last pregnancies usually occur in October and November, although an abundant crop of acorns or other mast may provide enough food to allow breeding to continue into the winter. The gestation period is 25 or 26 days, the average litter five or six. The young are born naked and blind but develop quickly and are weaned by about 18 days of age.

Enemies The natural enemies of the wood mouse include fox, weasel, stoat, badger, pine marten, domestic cat, the owls and the kestrel. Predators above ground, such as the tawny owl, find it much more difficult to hear wood mice walking on damp leaves than on dry; so wet weather helps to protect the mice. Badgers and foxes will dig up runways in search of nests and so take the young as well as adults.

Food The diet depends upon the availability of food but there is a definite preference for seeds and insects, though seedlings, buds, fruits and snails are also taken. In hedgerows and bushes old birds' nests are used as both feeding platforms and stores; indeed they are often found full of the remains of past meals such as hips, haws and blackberry seeds.

Populations Wood mice have a well-defined yearly cycle of numbers in both woodland and open arable land. In winter, numbers decline from a peak reached around December, at the end of the breeding season, continuing to fall until May or June when juveniles are recruited into the population. After a good seed crop in the autumn, woodland populations remain at high levels throughout the next summer, but if trees then produce very little fruit or seed a very great drop in the population may follow.

Juvenile survival in the summer is usually poor, probably as a result of antagonism between established adults and the new recruits. But the survival of juveniles improves by the end of the breeding season, as many of the older mice will have died; very few live through two winters. Numbers then quickly rise to the winter peak. The yearly cycle is sometimes complicated by movements from harvested fields into woodland in the autumn and from woodland to fields in the spring.

Man and the wood mouse The wood mouse may become a pest when it enters houses or outbuildings and raids stores of food including stored fruit and vegetables, but this is usually in winter and rarely serious. They have been known to raid bee hives for honey and they commonly dig up rows of peas or beans just after sowing. They are easily controlled by using the conventional break-back mouse trap baited with cheese. Wood mice become agricultural pests when they dig up and eat sugar-beet seed.

Distribution The wood mouse is distributed throughout Great Britain and Ireland and is present on most of the off-shore islands. It reaches north to Iceland and Scandinavia, east to the Himalayas, and south to the north of Africa and to most Mediterranean islands.

The Yellow-necked Mouse

The yellow-necked mouse, *Apodemus flavicollis*, is very similar in appearance to the wood mouse except that it is larger. Adults commonly weigh 27–29g and the tail is often longer than the head and body. The only difference in coloration is the presence of a yellowish-buff 'collar' of fur joining the brown upper fur on both sides of the neck. This 'collar' is also visible in the greyish-brown fur of a juvenile. Yellow-necked mice are more vigorous than wood mice, biting and squeaking (almost a screaming sound) at the slightest opportunity, when held. These large mice are equally at home in the branches of trees, on the ground or in their underground burrows. They jump and climb excellently and may even be found sleeping during the day in disused bird nest-boxes, some feet off the ground. (Colour illustration facing p.99.)

Habitat and habits The typical habitat of the yellow-necked mouse is woodland but they are also found in hedgerows and occasionally in fields. Their general behaviour is similar to that of the wood mouse, except that they have a larger home range.

Breeding and enemies The breeding season is sometimes shorter and the litter size a little smaller – on average five. The yearly cycle

buildings, cornricks, hedgerows and arable land will support populations of house mice. When mice densities are high, females may share nests and the rearing of young. When living out of doors they excavate tunnels and nest chambers, making nests of any available material.

House mice are usually most active at night although they will venture out in the day. Compared with their other senses sight is not very acute. Individuals recognize members of their own group and members of the opposite sex by smell, for olfactory communication plays a very important part in the life of a mouse.

In indoor situations, if there is plenty of food and cover and mouse density is high, movement of individual mice may be restricted to only a few square metres. Under these conditions house mice may become very aggressive and two strangers will fight regardless of sex. Fighting such as this leads to the development of a dominance hierarchy in which subordinate individuals – at the bottom of the 'ladder' – will be harassed by those dominant to them. Subordinates may even avoid activity when the dominant mouse is awake and may be prevented from taking part in any reproductive activity. Dominant males usually defend a territory and, in outdoor situations, subordinates may not remain in the neighbourhood for long, preferring to move away to another area.

Breeding Breeding usually occurs throughout the year, except in temperate climates out of doors, when there is a decline in the number of litters born in winter. Under urban conditions the usual litter size is five or six, but it may be much greater. Pregnancy lasts about three weeks and lactation for 18–20 days. One female may produce up to ten litters in a year and the young may start breeding at the age of six to eight weeks.

Enemies and Populations The most important natural enemies of the house mouse are the barn owl, weasel and stoat. The common rat is also said to be an enemy, because mice tend to become more abundant when common rats have been removed. The domestic cat is useful in preventing movements from a mouse-infested area to one free of mice, but has little effect on general population levels.

Indoor mouse populations may build up to very high densities and remain at a peak infestation level for some time. Out of doors numbers usually increase during the summer, reach a peak in winter and then decline until the next spring. Few mice survive for two winters. Juvenile mortality is heavy, particularly between birth and weaning. On islands such as Skokholm, winter mortality is related to the mean temperature in February, either directly or through a food shortage.

Food House mice eat whatever food they can get but, in food-stores, prefer cereals, proteins and fats to vegetables and fruit. When living in the open they eat, among other foods, cereals, weed seeds, stems, roots and insect larvae.

Man and the house mouse Indisputably the house mouse is a pest but its economic impact is uncertain. It causes direct damage by consumption of food and agravates it by spoiling the remainder. Damage to building materials, electrical equipment and packages is common. A further possible hazard is transmission of disease.

The house mouse may be controlled by the familiar mouse trap, but anti-coagulant or acute poisons are more commonly used. One usual anti-coagulant is warfarin, but in some places mice have become resistant to it and alternatives must be found – otherwise householders may be feeding rather than poisoning mice!

Distribution House mice have been present in Britain since the Iron Age and are now distributed throughout the world. Wherever man is, there will mice be found, even on small islands.

A number of subspecies have been described, each slightly different in colour or size.

The Harvest Mouse

Stephen Harris

One of these nests I procured this autumn, most artificially platted, and composed of the blades of wheat, perfectly round, and about the size of a cricket-ball . . . It was so compact and well filled, that it would roll across the table without being discomposed, though it contained eight little mice . . .

GILBERT WHITE (1720–93)
The Natural History and Antiquities of Selborne

The harvest mouse, *Micromys minutus*, is the smallest British rodent. Adults weigh 5–8g, pregnant females up to 15g. British specimens have an average head and body length of 57mm, with a slightly shorter tail (average 55mm). Unlike the other British mice, the face is blunt and rounded, the ears hairy and projecting only a short distance beyond the fur, and the eyes not prominent but small, round and black. The colour of the harvest mouse is also distinctive. When adult, it has black-tipped guard hairs on the back overlying orange or russet fur on the back and flanks. The belly is usually white and clearly demarcated. Colour variants are rare, but occasionally mice are found with white markings on the dorsal fur.

When the young harvest mice first leave the nest, they are brown or sandy-yellow in colour. The moult to the adult coat normally starts at about 31 days old, beginning at the rear of the body and finishing, at 42 days old, on the dorsal side of the head. With late-born litters this moult may be much delayed, or interrupted when only partially complete.

The harvest mouse spends most of the summer climbing in rank vegetation, and this life-style is reflected in its anatomy. The skeleton is light, and the outer toe of the hind foot is large and opposable, to ensure a firm grip on grass stems. The end of the tail is prehensile. When the mouse is stationary or climbing downwards, it uses its tail as a fifth limb. When climbing upwards the tail is usually held stiffly and helps the animal to keep its balance.

Harvest mice hunt insects by sight and by sound. They respond to small movements, noise and vibrations and when disturbed either freeze or move rapidly through the vegetation, often ending up in a crash-dive to the ground. Several forms of communication have been recorded. Distinctive sounds are made during mating and fighting, and the nestlings utter audible distress calls if handled during the first day or two of life. Nestlings also produce ultrasonic sounds of unknown function.

The urine and faeces are deposited as scent marks on grass stems.

Habitat In the winter the harvest mouse is predominantly ground-dwelling, and lives in the base of grass tussocks or in similar situations. It used to occur commonly in cereal ricks, and can still be found amongst stacks of bales. During the winter, harvest mice occasionally enter houses, and can sometimes be found living in disused birds' nests in hedgerows. In the spring, with the onset of grass growth, harvest mice spend an increasing amount of their time climbing, and continue to do so throughout the summer into the early winter. The harvest mouse is a poor burrower.

During the summer the harvest mouse is found in a wide variety of habitats, from coastal salt marshes to ungrazed mountain grasslands. All these consist predominantly of tall grasses. It is in such places that the harvest mouse builds its characteristic nests, ranging in size from loose constructions about 4cm in diameter, used as a temporary shelter by a single mouse, to the intricately woven breeding nest, 6–10cm in diameter. The height of the nest above ground level varies from a few centimetres in short grasses, to over 150cm in tall reeds. It is built from the shredded free ends of green grass leaves, but the bases of the leaves are left attached to the grass stems so that the nest hangs freely between them. The nest is packed inside with finely chewed grass or thistle down, and there is no obvious entrance when in use. Each nest is used for a maximum of three to four weeks, and many breeding nests may be built but never used at all.

Habits The harvest mouse is active by both day and night, especially at dusk and dawn. During a twelve-hour day only about a quarter of this activity occurs in daylight, but in winter harvest mice are more active during the day. Rainfall and heavy dew reduce their activity. Harvest mice may migrate from their summer quarters, particularly if it is a marshy area, to a drier winter site. Such migration occurs in twilight and during the early hours of darkness.

Breeding and development In Britain mating begins in April, with the first litters born in late April or early May. In a dry autumn breeding may continue until December, but three-quarters of the litters are born in August and September.

In the wild, harvest mice may reach sexual maturity at 45 days old but earlier breeding may occur in captivity. During mating the male noisily pursues the female through the vegetation and they eventually mate, usually at ground level. The gestation period is 17–19 days and it is followed by a post-partum oestrus, so that the female harvest mouse can produce a litter every three weeks. Litters vary from three to eight (mean 5·4) but occasionally litters of up to twelve have been recorded. The young are born blind and naked. By five days old they have developed dorsal fur, and belly fur by seven days old. By nine days old the ears and eyes are open. The young first venture from the nest at 11–12 days. At 15–16 days, when about 85 per cent of their adult size, the young are deserted by the female. They remain near the nest for a day or two, but then disperse. In the wild virtually all litters are born in nests built in standing grasses.

When the young mice first become independent there is a heavy mortality from predators, wet and cold. Life expectancy is low and very few harvest mice exceed six months of age.

Territory Little is known about the territorial behaviour of harvest mice. In grassland, home-ranges of males average 400 square metres, those of females 350 square metres. These ranges overlap, but the female probably defends a small breeding area, and breeding nests tend to be evenly distributed throughout a habitat – for example a minimum distance of about five metres apart in reeds, with an occasional clump of two or three nests, presumably the work of one female. Outside the breeding season harvest mice may collect together in sheltered places such as barns and ricks, but aggression is intense, and fights may result in the loss of part or all of the tail, and sometimes the ears and hind feet.

Mortality Harvest mice are eaten occasionally by a wide variety of animals, ranging in size from toads and blackbirds upwards, yet rarely form a major part of the diet of any of them. They are infrequently found in the pellets of tawny owls, which hunt mainly in woodland, but more frequently in those of barn and short-eared owls, which hunt over open ground. The remains of as many as ten harvest mice have been found in a single barn owl pellet. They are eaten occasionally by foxes and weasels.

Being small, the harvest mouse has a large surface area to volume ratio, and so heat loss is a problem. As a result, they often die of exposure, particularly during frosts and heavy rain. Harvest mice are very occasionally found in discarded bottles.

Food The food of the wild harvest mouse has been poorly studied. In captivity they will eat a wide variety of seeds, hedgerow fruits and insects, and it is assumed that this reflects their natural diet. They are cannibalistic and will also eat the bodies of other small rodents. The daily food intake is up to 30 per cent of their body weight, and the energy requirements of an 8g harvest mouse are the same as those of a 20g wood mouse or vole.

Conservation The harvest mouse is locally distributed, and in some habitats is the commonest small mammal. Although easily over-looked, it is an adaptable animal. It readily colonizes new places, and no special measures are required for its conservation. The current theory that it has undergone a dramatic decline with the advent of the combine harvester is false, for it can still be found in a wide variety of habitats including fields of cereals and other crops.

In parts of Europe and in Eastern Russia, the harvest mouse occasionally becomes a pest, damaging cereals. In Italian rice fields harvest mice excrete the bacterium *Leptospira bataviae*, which causes 'rice field fever' in the crop workers. In Russia it has been recorded as the host of a number of other bacteria and viruses.

Distribution The harvest mouse is the only living member of the genus *Micromys* and is found from south-east Asia (China, Japan and Assam) across to northern Spain and north-western Europe, as far north as the Arctic Circle. In Britain it is found in most parts of England, on the east coast of Scotland near Edinburgh, and in most of the north and south coast counties of Wales. It is most abundant in the south and east. It is not found in Ireland.

The Ship Rat and the Common Rat

K. D. Taylor

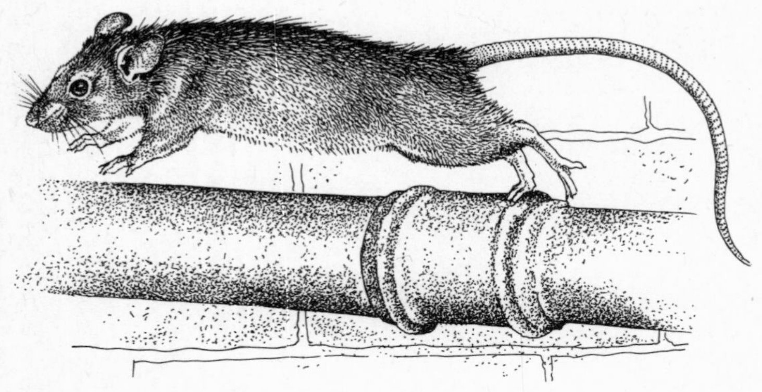

Ship rat

Strange that you let me come so near
And sent no questing senses out
From eye's dull jelly, shell-pink ear,
Fierce-whiskered snout.

But clay has hardened in those claws
And gypsy-like I read too late
In lines scored on those naked paws
A starry fate.

Even that snake, your tail, hangs dead,
And as I leave you stiff and still
A death-like quietness has spread
Across the hill.

ANDREW YOUNG (1807–1889) The Rat

In many people rats evoke only feelings of revulsion, hatred, horror and fear. Some claim that they cannot bear even to contemplate their scaly tails, while, in the warmth and cosiness of public houses, dark stories are recounted of rats 'as big as cats' that when cornered, will jump at a man's throat. Many widely-held beliefs about rats have their roots largely in ignorance and prejudice. Rats share many common features with other mammal species such as cats and dogs, which attract great devotion and respect. So let us take an unbiased look at these interesting and resourceful animals that have spread to and successfully colonized all corners of the world, despite having the hand of almost every human being turned against them. Surely such an achievement deserves a measure of attention and even a modicum of admiration?

There are many hundreds of species of rats in the world today. Most live uncomplicated lives in the forests and savannahs of warm countries. Just a few have learned to feed on agricultural crops, but only two have developed such a close relationship with human activities that they have been carried, in ships and boats, to all parts of the world inhabited by man. These two species are the ship rat and the common rat. They used to be known respectively as the black rat and the brown rat but colour is not a reliable means of distinguishing them, since the so-called black rat, *Rattus rattus*, is usually brown in colour, while occasionally black variants of the so-called brown rat, *Rattus norvegicus*, are found. This situation became so confusing that the old names have been replaced.

Whatever their colour, it is true to say that ship rats and common rats are wholly distinct from each other and never interbreed. Nevertheless, they are superficially very similar, with long almost hairless tails, pointed snouts and coarse fur, generally brown on the back shading to greyish underneath, but a close look at the living animals will quickly reveal differences between them. The common rat has relatively smaller eyes and ears and its tail is shorter and thicker, dark coloured above and pale beneath. The tail of the ship rat is much longer and is coloured uniformly dark; its large ears are also much less furry than those of the common rat.

Common rats do not usually exceed 350g in weight although occasionally they may reach 750g. This can only be described as kitten-sized, since even small adult cats are bigger. Ship rats are generally somewhat smaller than common rats.

Spread and distribution The earliest record of an association between rats and man comes from archaeological excavations in the Far East. Very long ago the wild-living common rats in northern China and the ship rats in Thailand or thereabouts began to find that in and around the emerging settlements of early man the accommodation was comfortable and the pickings easy. Over the course of many centuries, both rats gradually changed their ways until they could live in the growing cities, wholly dependent on the spoils of civilization. Later still, as trade routes were opened up, the ship rat spread into India and the Near East and thence to Europe, perhaps reaching Britain around the eleventh or the twelfth century. For many years it ruled supreme in Europe and was responsible for the spread of the great plague or Black Death that swept across the land in the Middle Ages, killing an estimated 25 million people.

The common rat did not put in an appearance in Europe until the eighteenth century. Exactly how it came to Europe from China, no one really knows, but its spread was dramatic. A bustling trade was in progress at that time and within the course of a few years this rat appeared in Russia, Norway, France and Belgium, probably reaching Britain in the early nineteenth century. The common rat found Europe much to its liking. It had evolved to thrive in the snows of northern China and was well able to cope with our temperate climate and lived happily outdoors. The ship rat on the other hand, being a tropical creature, needed the warmth of human habitation to survive.

The ship rat's need for warmth is probably the main reason for its downfall in twentieth-century Europe. As building methods improved, there were fewer places for rats to hide within houses; but above all, people became aware of the need for hygiene. Rats within buildings therefore became a primary target for extermination. It was mainly the ship rat that suffered – understandably, since the outdoor-living common rat was less of a health hazard. Today, the ship rat is something of a rarity in Britain, occurring at only a few localities in major ports, such as Glasgow, Liverpool and London. The common rat however is still widely distributed in farmland, towns and cities and even along the sea shore.

Behaviour Rats have been persecuted by man for so long that they have become mainly nocturnal and are very shy and difficult to observe. Probably for this reason there is a wealth of legend and folk-lore about their habits. Some of these tales contain more than a grain of truth. For instance, in the West Indies it is widely claimed that a rat can climb up a coconut palm, but cannot climb down. So, the story goes, when the rat wants to come down, it gnaws a hole in a coconut, gets inside and then leans out to bite through the stalk. Just before the nut strikes the ground, the rat jumps out. Many different people will tell this story with conviction. Once, when walking through a coconut grove on the island of Nevis and finding, amongst many holed nuts, one with a dead rat inside, my companion took this as proof of the story, and told me the dead rat was one that had forgotten to jump out.

Now the truth of the matter is that rats – particularly ship rats – are able to climb perfectly well both up and down palm trees, and they bite holes in coconuts in order to feed on the nut itself. The fact that a rat will occasionally come down with a falling nut is quite understandable since any damage to the nut quickly causes the stalk to rot, and the extra weight of a rat returning to feed on a nut already holed, may often cause it to fall. And what is more natural, when you feel yourself falling, than to jump for your life! The rat and coconut story is therefore a nice example of good observation but faulty interpretation.

The rat and egg story, which is widely told and apparently believed in Britain is another matter. The gist of this is that a single rat cannot pick up and carry a hen's egg because of its smooth rounded surface, and so two rats co-operate – one lying on its back holding the egg in its forepaws and the other dragging the first along by its tail. A little understanding of the ways of animals and some rational thought on the matter suggest that this method of moving eggs is entirely impracticable. In the first place no self-respecting rat is going to permit itself to be dragged along by its tail for anything more than a very short distance – to say nothing of having its tail bitten. Secondly, the rat is supposed to be dragged backwards; against the lie of the fur, making for extremely hard going on anything but the smoothest surface.

The fact remains however that rats do remove and store eggs and the question of how they do it is to some extent still open. There is no doubt that they can and do roll eggs to move them, but it is also possible that they can pick them up by grasping them at the pointed end with their incisor teeth.

Other stories have no more than a grain of truth in them, for instance the one about a cornered rat jumping at a man's throat. Certainly a cornered rat will jump, but it jumps to escape, and would never stop to bite, even if by some remote possibility it landed somewhere near a person's throat.

The facts of rat behaviour are in many ways more interesting than the fiction. Rats are social animals. Each colony contains some animals that are dominant over others; the dominants live in the best burrows, have first choice of food and rear more offspring than other animals in the colony. In some cases, the second class citizens may be chased by the dominants to such an extent that they cannot feed while the dominants are active, and are forced to come out to feed in daylight, or to emigrate. Migrant rats have a very thin time of it since, having no safe refuge, they are easy targets for predators. They are also generally attacked and driven off by the rats in any other colony they come across.

Recognition amongst rats is by smell, and within a small colony all rats know each other and know their social positions. Any stranger is recognized immediately and attacked. In large colonies, consisting of several hundred or even thousand individuals – such as occasionally exist on refuse tips – a breakdown in the social order occurs. Rats no longer recognize each other and strangers may slip in unnoticed. Just as in human cities, the lower and higher ranking inmates of rat cities jostle each other in underground passageways and none stops to greet his fellows. Compare this with rat villages where every animal knows its position and greets its neighbour with a sniff of recognition – the lower orders stepping aside to let dominant animals pass.

Habits and habitat Rats have a remarkable capacity to adapt their habits to a wide variety of circumstances. Adaptability is the key to their success. Common rats living beside rivers and along the dykes and ditches of fenland become expert in the water, diving and swimming many yards beneath the surface. Ship rats are less good in the water and rarely enter it voluntarily, but have a much greater climbing ability than common rats. As already mentioned they climb palm trees readily and often build nests in trees, similar to squirrel dreys. In buildings they can climb vertical pipes, and cables and even walls, provided the surface is rough. They frequently cross streets by means of overhead wires. The greater climbing ability of ship rats may lead to their occupation of the upper storeys of buildings in which common rats are established in the ground floor and basement. For this reason the ship rat is sometimes known as 'roof rat'.

Being more of a ground-living animal, the common rat is the principal burrow digger, and prefers to live in a burrow wherever possible. Burrows are generally dug in banks or other raised ground and are complicated branching systems with nest chambers at intervals, and sometimes extend for several yards at a depth of up to 50cm. Some rat burrows last for years and are occupied in turn by several generations of rats.

Rats are very often thought of as dirty animals and it is true that they sometimes live in dirty places such as farmyards and even sewers, but in fact they generally manage to keep themselves remarkably clean. Grooming, as with other small mammals, is a very important activity.

Breeding takes place at all times of year, provided food is plentiful. Generally, between five and ten naked and blind young are born at a time, but up to 16 have been recorded in a common rat's nest. Development is rapid, and within three weeks the young rats are scrambling after their mother for short distances outside the nest burrow, and at the age of three months can themselves breed. It is not surprising that suitable habitats, such as refuse tips, quickly become populated by rats. It has been conservatively estimated that the breeding of a single pair could result in 2,000 rats at the end of one year, if numbers were unchecked. The fact that rat numbers do not usually explode like this is a good example of the effectiveness of the natural processes that regulate animal numbers. Competition for food and the establishment of a social order within rat populations usually combine successfully to limit growth.

Common rats are very much creatures of habit. Individuals tend to use the same pathways repeatedly, making clearly visible runs between their burrows and their feeding places. They learn the position and appearance of all the various objects in the immediate vicinity of their homes, so that any new object – for example, a brick or a rat trap – is immediately recognized and avoided. This behaviour has led to the assumption that rats are intelligent enough to recognize traps as potentially dangerous, whereas in reality their avoidance of a trap is merely a response to an unfamiliar object. They would similarly avoid the brick or an old shoe.

Food Rats will eat almost anything, although they do have preferences. Ship rats are particularly fond of fruit and will often climb trees to get it. The staple food of common rats is grain, but in the fields they will eat nuts, seeds, snails, earthworms and even grass. Rats living by the sea live on crabs, sand hoppers and any edible debris. In towns rats eat any food intended for human or animal consumption and are very good at extracting the edible bits from garbage. When hard-pressed, they will eat soap, candles, bones and even the resinous knots from pine boards.

Predators and disease Young rats are easy game for predators such as owls, foxes, stoats, weasels and cats. Foxes and stoats will also take full grown rats, the latter tackling them in their burrows. Some farm cats will also kill big rats but most prefer them small or half-grown. Even gulls will prey on rats and a pair of lesser black-backed gulls were seen to take a rat that was foolhardy enough to try to cross a busy London street in daylight.

Rats are particularly disliked for their capacity to spread human diseases, and it is probably the deep-seated fear of bubonic plague, passed from generation to generation, that is the cause of so much prejudice against rats. But plague is no longer the scourge it used to be. Rats are now more effectively controlled; the fleas that transmit plague from rat to man can be killed with modern insecticides, and even the disease bacterium itself is highly susceptible to antibiotics. Other less well known and less serious diseases that can be spread by rats are salmonellosis (a form of food poisoning) and leptospirosis (a disease that causes flu-like symptoms and sometimes jaundice). By no means all rats are infected with disease, however; the truth is that rats are not much more dirty or disease-ridden than other mammals, including household pets such as dogs and cats.

Relationship with man The close association of rats with mankind over the centuries has resulted in a wealth of folk-lore and tradition regarding our attitude towards these animals. Even today in developed countries many people have had at least one experience involving rats. In less developed parts of the world rats are often so commonplace that people ignore them. Our Western prejudices against rats are not universally shared. In parts of Africa and the East rats are regarded as welcome items of protein in an otherwise deficient diet – and some of the larger species are indeed good eating. In India there is a temple devoted to the worship of the rat, and several hundred free-living ship rats are fed daily by devotees. The Ancient Egyptians also revered rats because they noticed that the animals had sufficient wisdom to choose the best bread.

There is no doubt however that the influence of rats on mankind has been mainly detrimental. Not only have there been the catastrophic outbreaks of plague in Europe, and more recently in other places such as Madagascar and Indonesia, but there is also the extensive loss that rats cause to agriculture and stored produce. Rat damage to growing crops is particularly severe in tropical countries. Almost all food crops are attacked to some extent but rice, coconuts, sugar and cocoa are particularly hard hit. Often the rats that cause the damage are neither ship rats nor common rats but local species that have learned to like the agricultural environment. In food stores and warehouses, on the other hand, our two familiar species can be found throughout the world, gnawing holes in sacks and cardboard cartons to feed on the contents.

Control Rodent control in Britain used to be the preserve of local rat catchers whose various methods often contained an element of secrecy; but during the Second World War a unit was set up to improve rodent control on a national level. What had largely been an art then became a science. The unit recommended various means of inducing rats to eat lethal doses of acute poisons such as arsenic. Much success was achieved but little consideration was given to the cruelty of poisoning and this is very understandable when it is remembered how much human suffering there was during the war.

A new generation of poisons emerged in the early 1950s: the anticoagulants, of which warfarin is the best known. Anticoagulants cause death by haemorrhage, apparently without the very considerable pain that results from acute poisoning. They are also very successful poisons and have been the mainstay of rodent control for nearly 25 years. Acute poisons are now used infrequently in Britain. When they are, only quick-acting kinds such as zinc phosphide and fluoroacetamide are employed. Poisons that cause highly distressful symptoms (for example, strychnine) must not be used against rodents. This regard for the welfare of such notable pests can be considered something of a breakthrough in the humane treatment of animals. However rodent control, even in Britain, still involves cruelty. Rats probably have about the same level of pain appreciation as, say, dogs and there is no fundamental reason why cruelty to the one species should be accepted while to the other it is abhorred. The argument that rat control is necessary in spite of its cruelty cannot be sustained, since control can often be effected without killing. In fact proofing buildings against rodents, although more expensive, produces more satisfactory and much more lasting results than poisoning. Even in agriculture, proper land management can do much to alleviate rodent problems.

The old adage that prevention is better than cure has application in rodent control. It is better to prevent the problem by proper management than to have to cure it by poisoning. There is no doubt that what can be broadly termed 'bad housekeeping' is at the root of most rodent problems. This being so, the problems are preventable.

Laboratory rats A question that is often asked is, do rats serve any useful purpose? This question takes for granted that, to be in any way considered worthy, an animal must serve mankind. It ignores the fact that all plants and animals – ourselves included – evolved together; none was put there for the use of another. If the question must be answered, then it can be said that laboratory rats, derived from an albino strain of the common rat, have been of service in medical research. Laboratory rats also give increasing numbers of people pleasure as intelligent and responsive pets.

Dormice

Elaine Hurrell

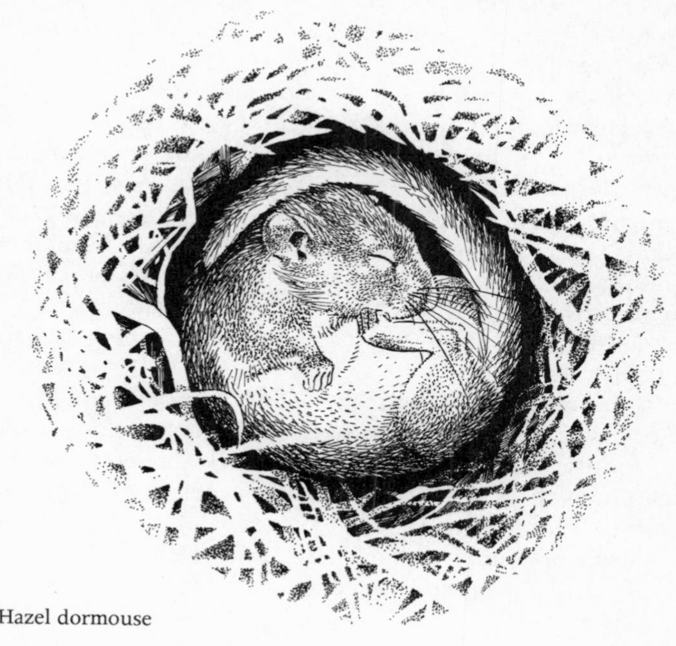

Hazel dormouse

'The dormouse is asleep again' said the Hatter, and poured a little hot tea upon its nose.

LEWIS CARROL (1832–98) Alice's Adventures in Wonderland

In Britain there are two representatives of the dormouse family or Gliridae: the common dormouse, *Muscardinus avellanarius*, often known more appropriately as the hazel dormouse, and the larger grey dormouse, *Glis glis*. The smaller species has been here for thousands of years and is a long-established and welcome member of our native fauna; the larger one, the grey dormouse, is a very recent introduction which it is hoped will not spread further in this country.

The Common Dormouse

The common or hazel dormouse is an attractive small mammal with the head and body measuring about 7–8cm and the tail 5–7cm. It can weigh between 23g and 43g. It has dense fur, soft in texture and of a rich, sandy brown colour. Its black eyes are prominent and its whiskers long and sensitive. Its tail is the same colour as the body and is thickly furred on all sides, with hairs which are sometimes darker at the tip.

It is hardly surprising that the dormouse has a reputation for sleepiness, since not only does its name suggest this but its habit of hibernating for lengthy periods throughout the winter means that it shows little activity for almost half the year! Yet, it is far from accurate to think of it solely as a sluggish, sleepy animal. When it is awake, its ability to move through the canopy of the hazel bushes is truly astonishing. Its feet are adapted to assist its arboreal life: the toes on both its front and back feet turn out laterally making it easy for the dormouse to grasp the twigs or stems on which it climbs.

Habitat Dormice are likely to be found in places where there is plenty of undergrowth, such as woods which have thick secondary layers, copses, thick hedges, and overgrown commons. Frequently in such places there is plenty of prickly vegetation – gorse brakes, bramble patches and hawthorn thickets providing much needed security from predators, particularly during the breeding season. As woodland becomes mature dormice move away in search of more suitable habitats.

The best time to catch glimpses of a live, wild dormouse is in the late evening, before the light has quite gone. They have been seen by wardens watching at nesting sites of rare birds and also by people engaged in quiet evening pursuits, such as badger watching. Try sitting inside the edge of a wood where dormice occur and look outwards so that the twigs and leaves of bushes are silhouetted against the sky. If a dormouse is moving through the canopy, you may see its tiny shape against the pale-coloured sky. Your view is likely to be a brief twilight one since most dormouse activity takes place after dark.

Breeding Dormice have two breeding periods. The first is during May and June, the second during August and September.

The loosely constructed nest of the dormouse is frequently placed on the arched stems of a bramble bush, just below the leaf canopy and about a metre from the ground. The material used to weave it may be grass, honeysuckle strippings, sometimes moss and nearly always leaves.

The gestation period is 22–24 days. The young, of which there are usually three or four, remain in the nest for a month. This is a crucial fact to bear in mind when considering dormouse conservation, for it follows that a breeding female must have an undisturbed period of at least a month if she is to raise her young successfully. Young dormice have duller and greyer fur than adults. They do not breed until the year following their birth.

Territories Little is known about the amount of space required by dormice. Wolfgang Wachtendorf, who studied dormice in the foothills of the Alps, says that normally they will not move much further than 10m from the nesting area to reach food and that 40m is the furthest he has recorded them travelling to a food source. Probably they favour particular parts of a wood rather than being distributed throughout it.

Enemies Analysis of barn owl and tawny owl pellets suggests that neither owl preys on dormice to any great extent. If they did so, the characteristic molar teeth of the dormouse would often appear in the pellets and they are but rarely found. Probably owls find difficulty in catching this small rodent which lives most of its active life off the ground in thickets and bushes. No doubt dormice are most vulnerable when they are hibernating and it is then that ground predators can take their toll.

Food In late summer and autumn, when dormice are putting on fat before hibernation, the edges of mixed deciduous woodland provide a variety of valuable food sources from the fruit of bushes such as bramble, guelder rose, hawthorn, hazel and wild rose. Other vegetable matter is also eaten as can be seen from the honeysuckle leaves which have been bitten off and nibbled, and from which the mid rib vein has frequently been nipped out. At times the spurs of honeysuckle flowers are opened to reach the nectar.

When dormice emerge hungry from hibernation in the spring it must be more difficult for them to find food – there would certainly be honeysuckle leaves but fruit and nuts are not available. They are said to take caterpillars and insects but to what extent is not known. Much more information is needed.

The name 'hazel dormouse' reflects the attraction that areas where hazel bushes are found have for dormice. In autumn the nick-name 'chisel-mouse' also becomes appropriate, for the dormouse is an exceedingly neat and precise carpenter. On a still night in late August or September you may hear the sand-papery and chiselling sounds made by a dormouse's teeth as it files and cuts the hard shell of a nut. At intervals the sound stops and then the dormouse is eating the kernel. The chiselling continues in an intermittent way for about a quarter of an hour and afterwards there is a sharp plop as the empty nut shell drops to the ground! Close examination of the hole made in a discarded nutshell will show a smoothly finished edge – the effect of the dormouse's very precise carpentry. This style of nut-opening is characteristic of the species and their discarded nutshells provide a most useful indication of their presence. The tooth marks made by both bank voles and wood mice around the edge of the hole are quite different. They leave a ribbed effect, rough to feel, like the rim of a 10p coin.

At the end of October and early in November when, the dormouse is fat and ready for the winter, it builds a new nest either under the leaf litter or in a hollow stump of a tree and sinks into hibernation. At intervals of some weeks it wakes up, is active for a few days and then goes into hibernation again. Mild winters are not beneficial to the dormouse, it is likely to be awake too often and so lose too much energy. By April, or certainly by early May, dormice are very active, for hedges and copses are coming into leaf and cover is growing again.

Conservation It seems certain that the hazel dormouse has declined in numbers and many factors are now ranged against it. Not only has urbanization increased but mechanical farming methods have intensified, removing hedgerows and clearing scrub; native deciduous woodlands have been replaced by conifers. Although dormice can live in the deciduous hedges sometimes left to border conifer plantations, the conifer plantations themselves, often in bleak and exposed situations, are unlikely to provide enough food for them. Their ecological niche is transitional, so that dormice cannot do well when woodland becomes mature. They live on a knife's edge and those naturalists' trusts which provide them with strongholds are indeed doing important work. It is good to record that the RSPCA's own nature reserve at Mallydams, Sussex, has been able to play its part in this, for nest boxes in the reserve, put up and checked by John Goodman, have often been occupied by dormice.

Distribution The hazel dormouse occurs in Europe and into Asia Minor but is not found in Spain, the Mediterranean islands, Denmark or northern Scandinavia. In England and Wales, which are on the fringe of its range, it is chiefly found in the southern counties. Even where it occurs it is found sporadically and locally and it is often difficult to know why it should favour one area rather than another which, to human eyes, looks equally suitable.

Relations with man Hazel dormice pose no threat to man's interests. Once they were the pets of Victorian school children but nowadays this should be completely discouraged since, like any nocturnal creature which spends half the year asleep, they are disappointing animals when brought indoors.

The Grey Dormouse

The grey dormouse, *Glis glis*, is an introduced animal in Britain. It was first released in 1902 at Tring Park in Hertfordshire and then spread rapidly into Buckinghamshire and Bedfordshire. It has remained in a comparatively restricted area of some 100 square miles in the Chilterns, although there are sporadic reports of grey dormice turning up outside this area. It is found widely in continental Europe, in general inhabiting more mature woodland than its smaller relative.

The grey dormouse makes a nest of mosses and fibres, usually in holes in trees, walls or rocks.

In size, the grey dormouse is somewhat like a small edition of a grey squirrel – its head and body measuring on average 150mm and its tail around 125mm. The fur is a silvery grey above, shading underneath to a light grey almost white colour which is sometimes tinged with yellow. There is a ring of black hair around each eye. Its tail, which is thickly furred with long hairs and looks bushy, is much the same colour as its back, except on the underside where there is a parting in the hair which is lighter in colour.

Grey dormice are usually nocturnal and therefore not easily watched. Sometimes they may be easier to hear than to see since they have a habit of entering the roofs of houses, bringing in nuts and fruit and rolling them about! Apples are a favourite. They are also said to catch and eat cockchafers. In the autumn they become very fat and no doubt it was because of this ability to put on weight so prodigiously that the Romans 'farmed' them by keeping them in huge, earthenware jars called Gliraria (the Family name is Gliridae) and feeding them on currants and chestnuts. When cooked they were evidently considered a great delicacy. No wonder they were sometimes called edible or fat-tailed dormice!

In the wild there are many creatures likely to prey on grey dormice including rats, cats, stoats and some birds. Like hazel dormice they must be particularly vulnerable during hibernation.

Relations with man Because of the damage which grey dormice can cause to trees the Forestry Commission considers them a pest. Certainly on the continent they are known to damage crops and timber and there is no doubt that people should be discouraged vigorously from thinking of them as potential pets. In any case they are often sulky and standoffish and therefore temperamentally unsuited to captivity.

The Coypu

L. M. Gosling

Of an evening they are all out swimming and playing in the water, conversing together in their strange tones, which sound like the moans and cries of wounded and suffering men: and among them the mother-coypu is seen with her progeny, numbering eight or nine, with as many on her back as she can accommodate, while the others swim after her crying for a ride!

W. H. HUDSON (1841–1922) The Naturalist in La Plata

The coypu, *Myocastor coypus*, a native of South America, is one of the introduced mammals that form an increasing proportion of the British fauna. Coypus have been living in the wetlands of East Anglia for nearly half a century and, having survived the coldest of British winters, are unlikely to be removed, except perhaps by man. In common with many other introduced species coypus have caused problems, particularly for agriculture, and there have been almost continuous attempts to control their numbers.

In the British context at least, adult coypus are easily recognized by their large size; males reach an average of nearly 7kg and are almost a metre long from the nose to tail tip. When females are not pregnant, which is rarely, they are slightly smaller than males and are more slender in the head and neck. The front surfaces of the incisors are coated with a bright orange enamel which contrasts with the short white fur that surrounds the mouth. The coat is usually brown or yellow-brown and this, together with the long tapering and almost bare tail, gives a somewhat rat-like appearance. In fact this similarity is only superficial since coypus belong to a completely separate group of rodents, the hystricomorphs, which includes the porcupines. (Colour illustration facing p.115.)

The forelegs are short and the feet bear long and powerful claws. These are used for grooming, for excavating burrows and roots and for holding and manipulating food. The large webbed hind feet and valve-like nostrils betray the semi-aquatic habits of the coypu and closer inspection reveals a dense grey underfur, rather like a deep velvet, that remains dry even after prolonged immersion. It was this underfur, known commercially as 'nutria', the Spanish word for otter, that was adopted as a fashion fur and which led to the introduction of coypus into Britain.

The ears, eyes and nostrils are arranged in a line along the top of the head. They protrude just above the water when the coypu floats with only its upper surface exposed. When undisturbed coypus swim in a similar position using alternate, powerful thrusts of the hind feet. The tail is not used actively in swimming but, being slightly flattened from side to side near the tip, probably acts as a rudder. When alarmed, coypus dive noisily and can swim submerged for long distances, often surfacing in the concealment of vegetation. Coypus, like seals, can also slow down important body functions during immersion and, when alarmed by a predator, but undetected, the coypu will sometimes swim noiselessly away to lie submerged for five minutes or more, immobile and with legs outstretched. Presumably these behaviours originated in South America as adaptations to escape native predators.

Waterways inhabited by coypus are a communication system between various resources and fixed points in an individual's range. By regular use, runs – 'swims' might be a more appropriate term – and tunnels are formed in the aquatic vegetation. They lead along water courses and have branches to burrows, grooming ledges (small platforms at the water edge where coypus emerge to rest and groom) and, most frequently, to 'climb-outs' where coypus leave the water and enter a network of runs on dry land. These lead in turn to feeding areas and to surface nests which are of two types: the most common in England are small structures – 30cm in diameter and 2–5cm deep – constructed of dead leaves and shredded bark and hidden in waterside vegetation. More rarely, large piles of plant material, up to a metre high, are built in marshy areas and coypus rest on the top of them. Otherwise they retire to large nest chambers in burrows which sometimes contain over 7kg of nest material.

Social behaviour The social system of coypus is based on a female lineage. A colony may start when a colonizing female occupies a range in the best habitat available, with a good food supply and banks high enough for burrowing. When a daughter of such a female grows up she establishes a range that partly overlaps that of her mother and, when a number of generations are present, a clan of related females is established. Typically the central female, the 'clan matriarch', is in the best habitat and one of her female offspring usually moves into the vacated range when she dies.

One large adult male is usually dominant over other males in a clan area. It is subordinate to large females, except when they are in oestrus, but excludes other adult males. Male offspring are eventually chased from a clan area by both the clan females and the dominant male. The clan male appears to have a closer relationship with the clan matriarch than with the other females and this sometimes gives the impression of a pair bond; however coypus are fundamentally polygynous.

Both males and females have well developed scent-marking behaviour using the secretion of an anal gland and urine, but its function is unknown.

Activity Coypus are nocturnal, becoming active shortly before sunset. Feeding and defecation (usually in the water) occur at night and the coypus return to the nest at a variable time before dawn. Coypus are one of the many rodents which reingest their faeces so that all food passes through the gut twice. This practice, known as refection, is carried out in the nest and occurs sporadically during the first part of the resting period. The function of refection is to absorb the essential nutrients that are released by the action of gut bacteria during the first passage of food through the gut (see p.63).

Feeding habits Except that, like the water vole, coypus will eat freshwater mussels, they are almost entirely vegetarian. In East Anglia they have a complex but ordered pattern of feeding and at any one time of year they select relatively few of their diverse annual range of plants. They also select within an individual plant, choosing a part rich in nutrients – for instance the basal growing point of a sedge – and discard the rest.

In the spring coypus eat a wide range of sprouting plants. In the summer they choose more carefully, feeding commonly on the growing base of the burr-reed and on the great pond sedge. Fruits are added to the diet in autumn and these include blackberries and the seed pod of the yellow water lily. Roots and rhizomes are the primary winter food and they are excavated to considerable depths. The rhizomes of the reed mace are a particular favourite and it is interesting that this species is common in true wetland forest communities of South America. Pasture grass is grazed throughout the year although the amount varies with its quality This use of pasture probably accounts for the success of the coypu on the extensive grazing marshes of east Norfolk and Suffolk.

Breeding In East Anglia coypus breed throughout the year. Although not fully grown until 18 months old, female coypus first conceive at three to five months. Up to 14 embryos are implanted at the start of pregnancy, but the death of individual embryos reduces the average litter size at birth to just over five. Quite frequently whole litters are also aborted.

The mammary glands are situated in two rows of four or five along the top of each side of the female. The young are suckled in a normal sitting position. The position of the glands is sometimes regarded as an adaptation to the aquatic habitat, but this is unlikely because most suckling occurs on nests during the day. Lactation lasts for about eight weeks and at this stage, when weaning, juveniles lose condition and some probably die. Undoubtedly many unweaned juveniles also die from starvation and exposure, when their mothers are killed during control operations.

Predators Young coypus are known to have been killed by a variety of predators including marsh harriers, herons, stoats, foxes and dogs. It seems likely that they would also be taken by owls, hawks, weasels, domestic cats and pike. Adult coypus are probably killed only by large dogs and by men. Several instances are known of dogs suffering severe wounds from the incisors of coypus but contrary to popular belief wild coypus never attack people, unless cornered.

Relations with man In South America, men have killed coypus, partly for food, for a very long time and this has eventually caused their elimination over a large part of their native range. W. H. Hudson records that early in the nineteenth century hunting for their pelts led to coypus becoming so rare that they were protected by an edict of the Argentinian dictator Rosas. As a result numbers increased dramatically until 'a mysterious malady fell on them from which they quickly perished, becoming almost extinct'. Nowadays coypus are protected in some parts of South America, but poaching has reduced both numbers and range. In spite of this large numbers of wild coypus are still harvested each year for their underfur.

In the 1920s an eddy in the vagaries of fashion, and no doubt substantial advertisement, raised nutria to the status of a valuable fur. At first suppliers in South America tried to cope with the international demand by supplying the fur only, but breeding stock soon followed and coypu fur farms became established throughout the world.

Many farms attempting to breed coypus for quick profit were under-capitalized and many of the farmers did not appreciate how slowly coypus bred. Disgruntled owners, as their dreams evaporated, released their stock; other coypus escaped from inadequate enclosures. Many of the free animals perished but some survived to establish wild populations, so that feral coypus are now found in North America, Europe, the Middle East (Israel), the Far East (Japan) and in Africa (Kenya).

Coypus are attractive and interesting animals and at first provided a welcome addition to a number of impoverished faunas, but this view changed as they became more numerous. Unfortunately coypus eat a wide range of agricultural crops and sometimes damage the same crop at different stages of its growth. For example, they graze growing wheat in the spring and, in the summer, eat the mature seed heads. They eat brassicas extensively and indeed almost all the root crops found in Britain: in East Anglia perhaps the most important damage is to sugar beet.

More important than crop damage is the threat coypus pose by burrowing. Burrows are about 20cm in diameter with a half submerged entrance. They often penetrate several metres and have a complex network of tunnels, nest chambers and exit holes away from the water. Coypus choose high banks for their burrows and often dig beneath trees or bushes which provide concealment and give some mechanical support.

Most burrows are excavated in the banks of ditches and occasionally cause inconvenience by disrupting drainage systems. Livestock and farm machinery have also been known to fall into burrows where these are close to the surface. More important is the potential weakening of the extensive banks which run alongside many East

Anglian rivers and which protect the lower, pump-drained agricultural marshes on either side. Coypus rarely, perhaps never, burrow into these banks from the river side of the banks – they prefer quieter backwaters – but burrows originating from the land side, from a 'soak dyke' or ditch, are common. By itself this would present no problem but it does when added to the destructive impact on the river side of the bank of the wash of pleasure cruisers, which are playing an increasing role in the ecology of Norfolk broadland.

In large numbers coypus also make a substantial impact on natural and semi-natural plant communities. They are well known for their ability to clear aquatic vegetation in drainage ditches, lakes and ponds, and were certainly responsible for a huge increase in the area of open water in broadland, up to the winter of 1962–63. There they also severely reduced their favourite food plants such as the flowering rush and cowbane. At lower numbers coypus maintain smaller patches of free water and open up dense fen vegetation. In this way they create a more patchy habitat, with correspondingly diverse plant and animal communities.

During the 1930s, 50 coypu fur farms were established in the south and east of England but all were closed down at the start of the Second World War. By this time escaped and released animals had formed feral colonies and by the mid-1950s coypus were very numerous, particularly in the Norfolk wetlands. By then the damage coypus could do was becoming obvious and in 1962 organized control started, and continues, now under the name 'Coypu Control'.

Methods of Control In the 1940s, in a comparatively small campaign under the Norfolk War Agricultural Executive Committee, gin traps had been used to control coypus, but fortunately these cruel traps are now illegal. Besides the suffering caused to the trapped animal, use of the gin trap, or any other control method involving immediate killing or maiming, unavoidably results in the death of other species. For example, in the 1930s, during a campaign against the musk rat, 945 musk rats were killed, but over 6,500 other animals also perished. Since the present organized operations started only cage traps have been used. Captured coypus are killed, usually with a ·22 pistol, but other species such as moorhen, water rail and water vole are usually released unharmed.

The Outlook By 1970, trapping and a succession of cold winters had reduced the coypu population to less than 2,000. But the following five winters were mild and the small trapping force of six men was powerless to prevent numbers from increasing to almost 20,000 by the end of 1975. Then an increase to a force of 20 trappers and the return of colder winters reduced numbers to a level that, up to 1980, fluctuated between about 6,000 and 14,000. Trapping and climate will no doubt continue to be the most important factors that affect the population in the future, but their impact may well be altered as inevitably the coypu becomes adapted to the British way of life.

The Carnivores

ORDER CARNIVORA

David W. Macdonald

The carnivores are Jacks of all trades and masters of most. The Order embraces animals with a phenomenal diversity of size, shape, and behaviour. Gigantic polar bears are thousands of times heavier than the lithe weasel; cheetahs race whereas badgers lumber and sea otters float, and even the massive rending teeth of the spotted hyaena are reduced to rudimentary pegs in its termite-eating relative the aard-wolf. Indeed the straightforward assumption that all members of the Carnivora are carnivorous, that is to say flesheaters, perched at the peak of food chains, is untrue; many carnivores feast on fruit at least as a supplement to flesh, whilst the giant panda, undoubtedly a member of the Carnivora, is a strict vegetarian. Some 240 species of carnivore survive today, including a fair number which are sufficiently threatened to have been gazetted as endangered, and they inhabit every continent. Admittedly, before man's intervention, Carnivora were absent from Australia and the Antarctic. In Australia their niche was filled by equivalents – marsupial flesh-eaters. In Britain today we have nine surviving species of carnivore and in comparatively recent historic times had two others: the last wolf was killed in Scotland around 1740; brown bears were hunted to extinction sometime around the tenth century.

The only feature which unites all the Carnivora is the construction of their teeth: the first molar teeth of the lower jaw and the fourth premolar of the upper jaw are modified for cutting and shearing and are together named the carnissal teeth. In addition the canine teeth are often enlarged and conical, for holding and piercing prey.

The Order Carnivora is divided by taxonomists into two superfamilies, the Canoidea (dog-like) and the Feloidea (cat-like). The Canoidea include four families – Canidae, Ursidae, Procyonidae, and Mustelidae. The Canidae include some 35 species of dogs and foxes, ranging from wolves, jackals, Arctic foxes and fennec foxes to less familiar creatures such as the long-legged, maned wolf and the webtoed, bush dog of South America. The red fox is the only surviving British representative of the Canidae. The Ursidae (bears) and the Procyonidae (racoons and pandas) have no British representatives, but the fourth family the Mustelidae, includes weasels, stoats, polecats, pine martens, mink, otters and badgers, all present in Britain, together with some 60 other species from elsewhere. The super-family Feloidea embraces three families of which two, Viverridae (mongooses, civets, genets) and Hyaenidae (hyaenas and aardwolf) have no British members but the third, Felidae, includes the Scottish wild cat (and of course, domestic cats).

The differing life-styles of members of the Carnivora has lead to the development of diverse and elegant anatomical features. For example, both the Scottish wild cat and the weasel kill similar prey, such as mice, with their enlarged canine teeth. To deliver the killing bite through fur, skin and bone requires that both species should have powerful jaws. Yet the shape of the skulls of these two species are so dissimilar that the mechanical problem of biting is quite different. This is closely related to their different hunting techniques. In the cat, wild or domestic, which seeks its prey above ground, a ridge of bone called the sagittal crest, runs the length of the skull and to it, from the upper flange of the lower jaw, runs a large muscle, the temporalis. When the cat's jaw is wide open, the temporalis is at its greatest mechanical advantage and can pull the jaws together very hard, thus stabbing the prey with the long canine teeth. But the cat must also dismember the prey it has killed and for this another group of powerful jaw muscles, called the masseter muscles, is employed. In contrast to the 'killing' temporalis, the 'chewing' masseter is at its greatest mechanical advantage when the jaws are nearly closed. In this way the cat is designed to have a powerful bite whatever the position of the jaws.

The weasel's problem is rather different, although it too needs a powerful bite in order to despatch mice, caught after pursuit through their underground burrows. In order to pass through such tunnels the weasel must be long and thin – a high-crowned head, so vital in the cat's killing apparatus, would be a hindrance to an animal whose livelihood depends on being able to squeeze through the tiniest cranny. Perhaps for this reason the weasel's skull is long and low, extending far backwards below the angle of the lower jaw. This provides a greatly expanded area to which the temporalis muscle can be attached and has resulted in the posterior part of that muscle 'taking over' the job of chewing from the reduced masseter. Anatomical structure reflects function and this example shows how the pre-requisites of two life-styles are reflected in two different arrangements both designed for doing the same job. Interestingly, one consequence of the strong backwards pull of the powerful muscles on the elongated mustelid skull is that the animals are in danger of disarticulating their own jaws! To overcome this problem the hinge connecting the lower jaw to the skull has much less play in a weasel than in a cat. Indeed, in the badger (also a mustelid) the hinge is so developed that the lower jaw cannot be disarticulated from the skull without breaking it.

Recent studies have begun to show that the social lives of carnivores are as varied as their anatomy and that there is a subtle interplay between the ecology and social life of the species. The use of radio-tracking has revolutionized the study of mammals and has been instrumental in the exploration of carnivore private lives. Why, for example, do foxes and also badgers sometimes live in groups? The old answer to this general question was that some carnivores hunted cooperatively because this made it possible to pull down prey with which a single animal could not cope. This explanation is probably correct for the wolf, the hyaena, the lion and some others; but cannot apply to foxes or badgers, or to the domestic cat, none of which hunt co-operatively.

As the following pages will reveal, the Carnivora are an intriguing Order whose habits are as tantalizingly baffling to biologists as they are infuriating to many countrymen. Almost every species of British carnivore is somebody's enemy – badgers are accused of transmitting bovine tuberculosis and of damage to machinery when the axles of combine harvesters, which have broken into their underground passageways, are bent; foxes may slaughter reared pheasants and have the potential of transmitting rabies, if that disease should reach Britain. Otters may kill fish which the bailiff struggles to protect; and the mink, besides eating fish, may compete with otters which conservationists struggle equally fervently to protect. Some of these issues are real, others imaginary, but whichever the case, carnivores are invariably controversial.

The Red Fox

David W. Macdonald

Take a skin of bacon, and lay it on a gridiron, and when it is well broiled and hot, then dip it and puddle it in this sauce that is within the pot, and make a train therewith, and you shall see that if there be a fox near to any place where the train is drawn, he will follow it. But he which maketh the train must rub the soles of his shoes with cow's dung, lest the fox vent his footing. And thus you may train a fox to a standing, and kill him in an evening with a crossbow.

GEORGE TURBERVILE (c.1544–97). The Noble Art of Venery.

Generations of man have exercised their ingenuity over concoctions and devices with which to wage war against the red fox, *Vulpes vulpes*. Throughout almost all of its expansive range the fox is deemed a pest, a reputation which was already entrenched well before medieval poets symbolized Renard as the cunning schemer of the Animal Kingdom. What traits of fox behaviour have led it into conflict with men? Are the problems real or imaginary, and are our solutions effective? Simple enough questions, but after centuries of conjecture and decades of research, the answers are still largely elusive.

The fox is an opportunist, a feature which Archillocus perceptively recorded two millennia ago when he allocated each species of animal into one of two categories, typified by the fox and the hedgehog – the former versatile and unpredictable, the latter a dependable, if prickly, drudge.

The red fox is found throughout Great Britain and Ireland and in most of the northern hemisphere, from the arctic tundra to Arabian deserts; in the southern hemisphere it is abundant in Australia, where it was originally introduced to be hunted for sport. Throughout this range there are differences in its appearance; northern foxes are bigger and, not surprisingly, have denser winter coats. Desert races are small, with relatively large ears and of a more sandy hue. In spite of this variation, foxes are clearly recognizable as reddish canids, a bit bigger than the average terrier (adult males averaging 6·9kg and females 5·7kg in weight) with predominantly black lower limbs and ears, together with bushy tails sometimes tipped with white.

Habitat and habits Foxes are found throughout mainland Britain, although they are less numerous in hill country, but are absent from all the Scottish isles except Skye. The 'rurban' fringe between town and country may be ideal fox habitat, providing diverse food supplies and abundant shelter, but foxes are also found in town centres, sometimes at high densities. Indeed, in a recent survey of urban foxes I found them throughout Britain, although much more frequently in towns in the South East and, in general, in coastal towns.

Foxes have long been regarded as solitary animals, often believed to travel prodigious distances. This may be true of some foxes in some habitats but many live in social groups and the distances they travel vary greatly. We are only just beginning to get glimpses of the fox's intriguing social life. The red fox is largely nocturnal and this, combined with its elusive nature, has made it difficult to study, although tracks across snow or sand can be read like a diary of the night's activity. Foxes may excavate a large burrow, or earth, consisting of an entrance passage of a few metres length and a rounded sleeping chamber, or they may take over another creature's den, for example, a rabbit warren or a badgers' set. Foxes do not necessarily spend their days in earths throughout the year. Many, especially dog foxes, probably spend most days lying above ground.

Foxes can now be live-trapped and equipped before release with miniature radio transmitters fitted to a neck-collar which will enable their positions to be pinpointed from a distance. These techniques have at least yielded sufficient information to show us how little we know of fox behaviour. In some areas fox populations are composed of two social categories, residents and itinerants. Residents occupy territories which are shared by other members of their group, but from which other foxes are excluded. The itinerants, of which the majority are usually male, do not defend a territory but travel in irregular patterns over large home ranges. In reality, this picture is grossly simplified; resident foxes may occupy territories which differ in size by a factor of as much as 70 (e.g. from 20 hectares up to 1300 hectares) and each territory may hold a single pair or up to six adult foxes, and may have more or less clearly defined borders. Similarly, the average distance travelled by an itinerant fox varies considerably from one habitat to the next. Records exist of foxes ranging over 250km, but the average is between 20 and 50km for males and between 7 and 15km for females. Some itinerants appear to travel in predominantly straight lines while others meander within enormous home ranges. Still other foxes commute between two or more centres of activity, and the distinction between residents and itinerants is sometimes blurred.

In a species which displays such a diversity of lifestyle what are the factors that influence the social behaviour of each fox and of the fox community within each habitat? So far, it seems that the most important single answer is food, with predation pressure an important second. In general, where prey are abundant, territories are smaller. The relationship between food supply and the size of the group is less obvious but may relate to the *pattern* of prey availability, rather than to prey abundance, with patchily distributed prey favouring larger groups.

Fox groups very rarely include more than one adult male. Where several vixens are members of one group the evidence suggests that they are often close relatives. For instance on several occasions I have found that vixens within a group shared the same colour abnormality, such as a splash of white on the lower leg. More convincing, some young vixens equipped with radio-transmitters have never left their mother's territory. Detailed observations in the wild, supplemented by studies of captive foxes, have disclosed something of the society existing within these groups of foxes. The vixens generally have clearly defined relationships, some being dominant to others: some evidence suggests that the eldest (sometimes the mother of the rest) is the most dominant. For most of the year even she crouches submissively at the approach of the dog fox, although during courtship these roles may be reversed.

Breeding In Britain foxes mate during the winter with a peak in January. After a gestation period of 52–3 days the vixen produces a litter of four or five cubs which are normally born in earths, although occasionally in a tussock of grass or an hollow tree. Signs of re-excavated earths in the early spring are a common indication of the approaching whelping season.

The relationship between vixens in a family group of foxes are most interesting during the breeding season. By examining the uteri from large numbers of vixens, biologists from different countries noted that the proportion of barren vixens varied between wide limits from one population to the next. In some places it seems that all vixens are mated but only a fraction may reach full term or successfully rear cubs. Elsewhere many vixens do not get pregnant at all. Neither the mechanisms involved nor the differences between populations are understood, but one observation is that within a group of vixens it is often only the dominant one which has cubs in a given year. In captivity it has been possible to watch the behaviour of barren subordinate vixens. Once the cubs of the dominant vixen begin eating meat some of the subordinate vixens take on the role of 'nannies'. They take food to the cubs and also act as guards while the real mother is away foraging. One may speculate about what it is that these subordinate vixens achieve by such devoted altruism. One possible answer is that they gain practice in maternal skills, making their mistakes at somebody else's expense! Another idea, which seems rather convincing, is that since all the vixens in the group may be related, each has a vested interest in the cubs of the other as they will share a certain proportion of their genes. If these subordinate vixens cannot breed themselves, then the next best thing, in evolutionary terms, may be to help rear a relative's cubs. After all, an aunt is half as closely related to her nephew as a mother is to her child.

Food The details of fox sociology differ from habitat to habitat and to a large extent reflect differences in diet. Foxes are solitary hunters preying on anything from hares to beetles, fish to pheasants or apples to earthworms. Such diverse prey require great flexibility of hunting techniques: rabbits may be overhauled at breakneck speed, or pounced on as they emerge from their warrens; mice are jumped upon with a characteristic leap high off the ground, so that the fox crashes down with its front paws on the mouse before the latter can spring clear. Earthworms are harvested from the surface like animated spaghetti as the fox picks its way slowly across a grazed pasture.

Man and the fox What then of the conflict between man and fox? This falls into two categories, competition and disease: competition between foxes, farmers and game-sportsmen, and disease principally because in Europe the fox is the principal vector of rabies. The conventional way of combating both damage and disease has been to kill as many foxes as possible. Let us see what information exists on the magnitude of this conflict and on the appropriateness of fox control as a solution.

Rabies Rabies is a viral disease which can infect all mammals and which, in humans, is fatal. It often appears in epizootics (animal epidemics). The present strain of rabies in Europe is transmitted mainly by the red fox. In the Americas the epizootiology of rabies is more complex as many hosts are involved, including foxes, two species of skunks, racoons and bats.

Waves of rabies have swept across Europe for centuries and indeed, the disease was familiar to Aristotle and the ancient Greeks. The present century is in fact the first in Britain's recorded history during which we have been largely free of rabies. The most recent European epizootic originated in Poland in the 1930's and has been spreading westwards ever since. Nowadays the risk to human life in areas where rabies is endemic is seldom great. Although the disease is fatal once symptoms, including hydrophobia, have become manifest, there are good vaccines for both pre and post-exposure treatment. Of course the fear of the disease remains, together with a substantial economic burden for immunizing people, pets and farm livestock.

Each European country where rabies is endemic has massive fox control schemes utilizing professional trappers, often working in collaboration with the World Health Organization. Foxes are killed by a variety of methods but principally by gassing their earths or by shooting. In some areas poison and gin traps are also used. Some evidence suggested that if the fox population density could be reduced below a certain threshold, then the disease would gradually die out and Public Health officials in some countries have been trying to effect that reduction in density. Sometimes this has involved terrible carnage. In Alberta in 1952 as part of an 18-month campaign, 50,000 foxes were killed along with 30,000 coyotes. A back-up campaign accounted for an estimated 70,000 further coyotes. Moreover most economically viable hunting techniques are non-specific and result in the loss of other species also. The badger for instance has almost disappeared from large areas of Germany as a result of extensive gassing of all likely open holes, in an attempt to eradicate foxes.

Anti-rabies schemes The problem with fox reduction schemes against rabies is that in only a few cases is there any evidence that they serve a useful purpose. In spite of intensive fox control, rabies has spread across Europe at a rather uniform speed. Rabies is such a terrible disease that almost any form of short-term onslaught on the fox population would be desirable *if* it resulted in eradicating the disease. What is now coming under serious question is whether the damage to the ecosystem and the huge expense of fox control in Europe is tolerable, in the absence of any sign of the disease disappearing. Present rabies control schemes involve widespread killing which is doubtfully effective, and for both economic and conservation reasons it seems appropriate to look for alternatives. Recently workers like Baer and Debbie at the Centre for Disease Control in Georgia, USA, have achieved encouraging results with oral vaccination of foxes against rabies. The idea, still in its early development, is to immunize foxes in the wild against rabies by distributing baits loaded with oral vaccine. There are still many technical problems to be solved, but such a technique would have many merits, the most important being that it could exploit the foxes' own territorial behaviour to minimize movement of the resident population. Field vaccination might usefully be integrated with other techniques such as killing or sterilization, to reduce for instance the number of dispersing itinerants at critical seasons of the year or phases of the epizootic.

Most of the principles underlying the problems of rabies control are similar to those facing the farmer or game sportsman who kills foxes, in both cases we need to know what effect the control measures have on the surviving population; do they achieve the desired result?

The farmer and the fox Nowadays, intensive farming has tended to make the free-range chicken obsolete and hence has diminished the pest status of the fox to poultry farmers. Many shepherds however still believe it is necessary to pursue a vendetta against foxes. Their methods include poisoning, shooting, snaring, bolting with terriers and hunting with hounds. Debate has raged over the question of whether foxes take healthy lambs, or only dead and sickly ones. It is undeniable that they do feed extensively on sheep carrion and afterbirths and, in sheep farming country, several dead lambs may often be found accumulated around a fox's earth. But it is extremely difficult to prove whether or not these lambs would have survived if the fox had not taken them. Many predators are known to prey by choice upon sickly individuals and foxes may do this also. One detailed study of the causes of lamb mortality was conducted in Australia by Rowley who found that only 14 out of 314 deaths of newly born lambs in his study area were directly attributable to foxes. In a wider study he estimated that foxes were responsible for 15 per cent of lamb mortality. There are no comparable figures for Britain, although an opinion survey recently indicated that most farmers who lost lambs to foxes, actually lost only a small number. However, to the owner of the sheep, each lamb represents a significant sum of money and the few farmers who lose a lot of lambs to rogue foxes, do suffer serious economic loss, even if the problem is small on a national level.

The critical question is whether controlling foxes actually reduces the risk of lamb worrying. Most shepherds agree that serious lamb killers are isolated individuals and that most foxes never kill lambs (in itself rather surprising). If this is so then killing every fox is an inappropriate way of eliminating specific individuals.

Malicious killers? Foxes are often accused of being malicious killers with an insatiable blood lust. Of course, such value judgements are nonsense biologically. Nevertheless, the phenomenon of 'surplus killing' when a fox, or any other carnivore, kills many more prey than it needs, immediately poses an interesting management dilemma. The poultry man (or game-keeper) whose coops are raided by a fox can lose dozens of birds in a few moments. These surplus kills invariably happen in circumstances where the prey cannot run away, for instance in a poultry house or a rearing pen. H. Kruuk has suggested that predators such as the fox are so finely tuned to take advantage of any opportunity to get extra prey, that they cannot 'switch-off' the killing response when a chicken flutters in front of them. Of course, in nature the prey quickly disperses so there is no danger of killing far too many – a couple of surplus items can always be stored for the unknown shortages of the future. Therefore, it is not the fox which is behaving unnaturally but the chicken which cannot run away. Of course, a plausible explanation such as this is small consolation to the man who suffers losses, but it does pose a problem for control.

The most recent study of fox predation on pheasants is Mike Gill's analysis of the fate of almost 500 nests. Half of these nests never reached successful hatching and half of the losses resulted from some sort of predation, of which 30 per cent could be attributed to foxes. Of particular concern to the game manager is that these figures apply to intensively-keepered land, and the evidence was that in about 94 per cent of the nests predated by foxes, the sitting hen bird had also been killed.

Where fox-killing is considered necessary much debate, but little scientific scrutiny, has been devoted to the merits and demerits of various control methods. To an ecologist the most important single criterion by which a method could be judged is its selectivity. To achieve the desired result with the minimum disruption to the ecosystem requires that control should be carefully tailored specifically to eliminate a chosen age class, sex, or proportion of the population of *only* the species in question. At the same time minimizing the cruelty involved in a given method is clearly important, although desperately hard to assess objectively. A Swedish zoologist, Jan Englund, has pioneered the study of cruelty involved in different types of fox control. First he compared the frequency and severity of wounds suffered by foxes trapped in gin traps with those caused by leg snares. He found that leg snares hardly ever resulted in injuries comparable with the hideous wounds inflicted by gins. This information contributed to the banning of gin traps in Sweden. Englund also examined the skull and leg bones of several thousands of foxes for signs of lead and gunshot wounds. He found that the frequency of old wounds rose to a peak in foxes over three years old and that in some areas up to 40 per cent had suffered some shooting accident and up to 16 per cent had signs of serious old injuries. These calculations emphasize, at least for Sweden, the claim that many more foxes are shot at than are shot. Englund speculates that foxes are at much greater risk of wounding now that pelt prices in Sweden have soared to 50–100 times their value in the 1960's. Other methods of fox control have not been subject to the same scrutiny although some, such as snaring, unquestionably involve cruelty, especially if used carelessly. To minimize this the Game Conservancy has issued a 'code of practice' stipulating, for example, that snares must be checked twice daily – but this code has no legal status.

The problems in fox management and their biological implications, not to mention their moral ones, are complex. One dilemma is that the gamekeeper's logic that a dead fox means one less to do damage may only be true in the most trivial sense; it is not the case that killing a fox correspondingly reduces depredation on lambs or pheasants, or necessarily hinders the spreading of rabies. In some cases it can clearly be counter-productive (in creating biological vacua for instance). Much more work is needed to clarify the detail of fox biology and the biological consequences of manipulating fox populations; so that where future management is necessary at all it can be conducted on the basis of an understanding of its likely consequences.

A fox family. The vixen suckles one of her cubs while her daughter from an earlier litter grooms another and the dog fox tolerates the attentions of a playful third.

The pine marten is most frequent in coniferous and mixed woods. It climbs and leaps well. It is sometimes seen by day but is chiefly nocturnal and especially active at dusk.

The Pine Marten

Ian S. MacPhail

Who can outclimb the squirrel,
But the weasel of the trees?
Who can outrun the roe-deer,
And catch the hare with ease?

From an old hunting song

The pine marten, *Martes martes*, is Britain's rarest terrestrial mammal. This handsome little animal is known locally by many other names – common marten, mart, sweet mart, martern, martron, marteron, matron, mantlett, tagham, taogham and tree-cat. One of our most elusive mammals (few readers will have seen one in the wild), it can be very difficult to identify for it is usually seen in a poor light and can easily be confused with a large stoat, a small fox, a feral mink, or even with a red squirrel. Cat-sized and weasel shaped, with a long bushy tail, it measures 450–500mm long and when mature, weighs 1–1·5kg. It has a reddish brown coat not unlike that of a red squirrel – the colour on the back and sides being a rich dark brown, with a thick undercoat of reddish grey. All the year round it has a cream coloured throat patch and sometimes, in the autumn, the centre of this patch is orange or pinkish. Individuals can be recognized by the shape of the throat patch, but this is of little help to the field observer for the animal is constantly on the move. The pine marten has round, pale yellowish ears and carries its tail curved slightly downwards. Its legs are short and powerful, with broad pads and long claws. Its footprints show five distinct toe pads in an arch around the central pad; the claws do not usually show up in footprints. Its foot is large in relation to overall size and this may help it to climb more easily. The female is about two-thirds of the size of the male.

Distribution Until comparatively recent times the pine marten was to be found in 34 English counties, but it is now thought to be almost extinct in England. It has been driven from all cultivated areas, being seen now only in the wilder parts of the Lake District. According to that great authority, H. G. Hurrell (who has kept pine martens in captivity for over 25 years) one was shot near Bristol in 1945 and another was trapped in Essex in 1950.

Pine martens can also be found in Wales (Snowdonia), Scotland (North West Highlands), and Ireland (Connemara and County Clare). The largest populations are believed to be in Ben Eigh National Park in Wester Ross, Scotland, and in the remoter glens of Sutherland; but even there they are very rarely seen, although there is encouraging evidence of their presence.

Pine martens are found throughout northern and central Europe into western Asia.

Habitat The pine marten's habitat is based on woodlands, preferably scrub woodlands with an abundance of fruit-bearing bushes, prey species and good ground cover; but sometimes even bare moorlands or conifer plantations will do.

Behaviour Like most British mammals the pine marten is largely nocturnal and exceedingly shy, so that the best chance of catching a glimpse of one is within an hour or so of sunrise or sunset. It is not as arboreal as the name suggests and forages mostly on the ground, although it will venture right up into the treetops in pursuit of its prey. It is alert, acrobatic, tense and swift-moving. It climbs nimbly and can run fast for short distances. It travels with the speed of a squirrel and is adept in negotiating difficult jumps, often 'flying' from tree to tree. Its movements are graceful whether moving slowly up a tree trunk, or investigating the brushwood underneath. It is often possible to spot the presence of a pine marten by the noise of birds because like an owl or a jay, it is likely to be mobbed when it crouches 'frozen' on a branch or on the ground. One of the bolder birds may approach within a yard, and this will be its swift downfall for there are few animals that can jump and strike so quickly as the pine marten. When running or climbing the tail is held low and straight; when jumping it lashes the tail from side to side to keep balance. It has well developed senses, with keen eyesight, acute hearing and an excellent sense of smell.

The pine marten holds a territory varying in size from 10–100 acres (2·5–25 hectares), depending on the kind of habitat, but one bramble bush, well hung with fruit, will occupy it every night for a week. It patrols its boundaries or some part of them, every night, leaving droppings (scats) in conspicuous places such as on the tops of walls or large stones, in order to warn off intruders. The scats are usually 4–12cm long, cylindrical in shape and often coiled. Usually shiny black or very dark, yellowish or greyish, they can very easily be confused with hedgehog droppings. The well-worn paths of the pine marten's territory are used for generations, and with their clearly-defined latrine points are a boon to naturalists. These tell-tale signs are often the only means by which this shy, nocturnal animal can be detected and then perhaps observed.

Food The pine marten's diet is very varied and is based on whatever food is readily available in a particular haunt. In the wild and remote areas of the Highlands it has been known to feed on young grouse, hares and rabbits. In woodlands its food can consist of small birds, their young and eggs, rats, beetles, and wild fruits. Pine martens are astonishingly catholic in their choice of menu and eat blackberries, ivy berries, hazelnuts, earthworms and carrion. Other food, not so commonly eaten, has been known to include wild honey and bees, slugs, grubs, frogs, lizards, woodlice, wild cherries, crab-apples, rowan berries, wild strawberries and even a stoat and a kestrel. The yearly cycle of a pine marten's activity is partly dictated by the seasonal availability of these foods.

Breeding Pine martens mate in the late summer, but the development of the embryo is delayed until the following January so that the litter of two or three kitts is born in March or April (see p.20). The female selects a site for her breeding den in a small cave, ivy-covered tree, hollow log, among grass under a fallen tree well hidden by scrub, or under a rock. Some females have been known to use the old nest of a crow or magpie. No effort is made to provide a soft bed for the young, which are weaned after six weeks but do not leave the nest until they are about eight weeks old (twice as long as a fox cub takes to leave its den). At that stage the kitts have thin and almost hairless tails and it takes two or three weeks for the hair to grow and for their tails to take on their typically bushy appearance. Like most young mammals they are frisky and will play together endlessly, wrestling and mock fighting, but when handled they can be ferocious little creatures.

A young female pine marten will not mate in her first year, so she will be two years old before her first litter is born. Females do not breed every year and populations are slow to increase – perhaps an important factor in their present scarcity.

So little is known about the family habits of the pine marten that J. C. Millais's description of a captive birth in his *Mammals of Great Britain and Ireland* is of particular interest.

> So far I have been able to ascertain there is no previous instance recorded of the pine marten breeding in captivity; and but little appears to be known concerning its reproduction in a wild state, for in no book that I have met, is mention made of the remarkable difference in the colour of the young when first born, which surely would have been noticed had the fact been known. At about 11 pm on April 7th 1882, I heard the unmistakable whimpering or squealing of young proceeding from one of the bed-boxes in the cage. On the morning of the 10th I ventured to take out one of the young ones. It was about six inches long including the tail, which was about or nearly $1\frac{3}{4}$in. long, and appeared out of all proportion in so young an animal, and was in shape and in proportion to the head and body like that member in an adult stoat. It will, I believe, be a surprise to others, as it certainly was to me, to learn that this species is at first quite white, the coat being, of course, fine and short. On the 14th I again looked at the young and found them to be three in number – two males and one female. They were white, like very young polecat ferrets, coats longer and rougher than before, and bodies heavier and stouter, but not perceptibly longer than on the 10th. Certainly if I had met with these cubs without knowing their parentage I should not have guessed them to be pine martens, but should have been inclined to suppose they were young polecat ferrets, or perhaps, chiefly in consideration of their tails, young stoats. On May 4th the eyes of the young were still closed, on May 20th the young had their eyes open, and on May 25th one of the cubs showed itself outside the nest for the first time. On May 29th, three young

green-finches were given to the mother and she induced her young to eat by uttering a clucking noise. On June 6th one of the young managed to jump on to its nesting box which was a foot high, and on June 25th they were able to climb in and out of their box which was five feet from the ground. The young martens were full-grown by the autumn.

Relations with man The pine marten has always been persecuted by man, as vermin, as a game animal, or for its fur. From earliest times marten fur has been a much prized luxury. In AD 940 the 'Laws of Howel Dda' state that a pelt was worth 24 pence – a sum equal to many pounds today. It is possible that many of the skins that Julius Caesar mentioned as one of Britannica's main exports were marten pelts. Capes lined with marten fur were traditionally worn by kings and nobles, from Viking to Plantagenet times. Up to 400 years ago there was a large export trade to the Low Countries and, as recently as the late 1940's, a good pelt fetched as much money as an agricultural labourer in rural Ireland could earn in a week. Martens were once hunted with dogs for sport. They can still fall prey to a golden eagle but today are more often killed in traps, in snares or by poison set for other animals. To Britain's shame they are not a protected species and to Scotland's shame there the steel trap is legal still. When game preservation became fashionable, in order to provide animals for blood sports, that human predator the gamekeeper, killed many pine martens. Today, pine martens are looked upon more sympathetically.

Perhaps the greatest threat to the pine marten's survival is habitat destruction. Fortunately the Forestry Commission has a far sighted and sensible policy and protects all pine martens in its forests. Martens do no harm to trees but rather help the foresters by keeping a check on potentially harmful animals – squirrels, rabbits, and woodmice which do damage to saplings. The time is long overdue to give legal protection to this fascinating and harmless animal and the Government should be persuaded to give it full protection.

The Stoat

Ian Linn

I heard a faint complaining and whining sound in or close to the hedge, and turning my eyes in that direction caught sight of a stoat, his head and neck visible, peeping at me out of the wood; he was intending to cross the road, and seeing me sitting there hesitated to do so. Still having come that far he would not turn back, and by and by he drew himself snake-like out of the concealing herbage, and was just about to make a dash across the road when I tapped sharply on the wood with my stick and he fled back into cover.

W. H. HUDSON (1841–1922) The Book of a Naturalist

The stoat, *Mustela erminea*, is a member of the weasel family (Mustelidae); it is slightly larger than its close relative the weasel, and is more widespread in the British Isles. It is found not only throughout mainland Britain but in Ireland and on many offshore islands, including Man, Anglesey and Wight. The stoat is absent from Orkney, but has been introduced on to the Shetland Mainland. It is absent from the Outer Hebrides but is present on some of the larger Inner Hebridean islands, including Skye, Mull, Islay and Jura. It is present on Jersey and Guernsey in the Channel Islands. The stoat is widespread throughout Eurasia and North America, from Arctic to Mediterranean latitudes and is present in Japan.

As with many other members of the weasel family, the female stoat is much smaller than the male. Males weigh on average 325g (range 200–450g) whereas females weigh 215g (140–280g). The male measures 400mm from nose to tip of tail (370–440mm), the female 380mm (335–430mm). The tail of the stoat is relatively longer (about 30 per cent of total length) than that of the weasel, which is less than 20 per cent of the total length. The dimensions of the Irish stoat are markedly smaller, being between 50 per cent and 85 per cent of those of the mainland stoat. In their range of sizes, the British stoat and weasel are thought to exhibit the ecological phenomenon of 'character displacement', dividing up the available prey resources so as to avoid competition as far as possible. Thus the female weasel, the smallest of the four, is almost entirely a small rodent specialist, while the largest, the male stoat, commonly takes much larger prey – up to rabbit size. The male weasel and the female stoat fall between these two extremes. In Ireland, with the weasel absent, the stoat straddles the central size range of the British stoat-to-weasel continuum.

In appearance the stoat is a typical 'weasel' and is in fact often called the weasel in Ireland; in America it is called the short-tailed weasel. The body is long, slim and muscular, and the legs short; the face is bluntly-pointed, with small rounded ears; the tail is longer than a weasel's and is well-furred but not bushy. The body colour is brown above, creamy white below, with a sharp, straight demarcation line between the two colours which does not vary from individual to individual. The tip of the tail is black. White flecks on the face and feet are not uncommon. In northern Britain the stoat turns white in winter, except for the black tail tip; in this condition it is known as an ermine (witness the animal's scientific name). This does not happen in southern Britain, but there is a zone in northern England where some stoats turn white, some do not, and some turn white in patches. In the Irish stoat, the upper lip and the margins of the ears are darker, and the light belly colour forms a narrow line, except between the legs.

Stoats are found in many different habitats, from sea level up to high mountains, wherever there is good cover and sufficient food. They are perhaps not so closely tied to dense cover as weasels, and may not uncommonly be seen in fields, ranging well out from hedges and dry stone walls.

Food The stoat will kill and eat anything it can overcome, and its food varies from time to time and from place to place according to what is available. In general it takes about one-third birds, one-third rabbits and one-quarter small rodents, the rest being made up of an assortment of small prey or even of fruit and berries. Prey is killed by a bite on the back of the head. Stoats hunt mainly by scent. They will attract birds by 'dancing' and then, when the proposed prey are close enough, make their attack. This 'dancing' behaviour is not well understood, but similar antics have been observed in stoats whose brains have been damaged by heavy infestations of the worm *Skrjabingylus nasicola* (see below), and there may be a connection. When being relentlessly followed by a stoat, a rabbit will sometimes appear to yield to panic, crouch down and remain still, often squealing, allowing the stoat to approach. This apparently non-adaptive behaviour of the rabbit may be a distortion of the 'freezing' behaviour which is a common response to danger in rabbits and many other animals. Stoats do not suck blood, but eat their prey in the usual way. Despite folklore to the contrary, they will sometimes eat shrews.

Although stoats will occasionally be hunted and killed by larger carnivores, this must be a rather rare occurrence, if only because stoats are by no means common in the countryside compared with, for example, rodents – an alternative and easier prey. Man is without doubt the stoat's most serious enemy.

Stoats move in typical weasel-like manner, usually running quickly with the body held low and straight, but sometimes also using a bounding gallop with arched back. They are very playful; family parties can be seen indulging in rapid acrobatic play, dashing in and out of hiding and making mock attacks upon each other. Family parties may persist into the winter, giving rise to stories of 'packs' of stoats. They swim and climb well. They are active throughout the day and night, but show peaks of activity.

Relationship with man By and large, the stoat is a friend of the farmer and forester because of its predation on rabbits and small rodents, but it tends to be persecuted because it kills some game birds in their breeding season, and because some individuals learn to raid poultry roosts, sometimes killing much more than they can eat (surplus killing)*. The stoat's earlier dependence on rabbits was highlighted when their numbers dropped sharply in the wake of myxomatosis in Britain (1953–56).

Male and female stoats live apart, holding separate territories of varying sizes depending on prey abundance. Stoats have scent

*See also Fox, p.145. Ed.

glands in the anal region, presumably used in territorial scent marking.

Breeding Stoats mate in summer, but normally the embryos do not implant until March of the following year, and the young are born after a gestation of 21–28 days. This mechanism of delayed implantation (see p.20) occasionally goes awry, and winter litters are recorded, presumably as a result of implantation taking place too soon. What determines the moment of implantation is not known. Young females can breed in the year of their birth, but males are not sexually mature until the following spring. A normal litter numbers four to nine, although larger litters occasionally occur. Young stoats eat solid food at four weeks of age, although lactation may last a further three to eight weeks. The young stoat can kill prey when ten weeks old but is not fully expert until about three months of age. The male helps to feed the litter.

There is heavy mortality in early life so that the majority of stoats in a population are usually under one year old, though a longevity of eight years in the wild has been recorded and possibly the life span in captivity is even longer.

Parasites Fleas are not common on stoats, and if present they have usually come from rodent prey. A parasite unique to the stoat is the biting louse, *Trichodectes ermineae*. The nematode, *Skrjabingylus nasicola*, which lives in the nasal sinuses, is common in British stoats (20–50 per cent infestation).

The Weasel

Ian Linn

*She is called Weasel (*mustela*) as if she were an elongated mouse, . . . Weasels are said to be so skilled in medicine that, if by any chance their babies are killed they can make them come alive again if they can get at them.*

Twelfth-century Latin bestiary, translated by T. H. White

The weasel, *Mustela nivalis*, is the smallest of the British Carnivora, but is a very successful species, being widespread on the British mainland. It is not found in Ireland nor on most of the offshore islands, but is present in Skye, Anglesey and the Isle of Wight. It is widely distributed all over Europe, North Africa, the Middle East, the USSR and northern China. It is common on the North American continent, where it is known as the least weasel, and until recently went by a different scientific name, *Mustela rixosa*. It has been introduced into New Zealand.

The weasel is very small and its size is very variable. Females may be as small as 35g or as large as 90g. The total length of a female, nose to tail, averages about 215mm, but may vary between 205mm and 250mm. Males are considerably larger, averaging 120g in weight (range 50–200g) and 260mm in total length (range 205–300mm). There is a persistent story among countrymen of a small kind of weasel, the so-called miniver, finger-weasel or mouse-weasel. There is no doubt that in certain regions, such as northern and mountainous Scandinavia, the Alps and southern Spain, weasels are quite tiny; but bearing in mind the great size variability of the species – north African weasels, for example, are bigger than British stoats – it seems likely that these are local populations of animals whose average size is at the small end of the possible range, and not a separate species. Very small individuals, usually immature females, can crop up anywhere.

Weasels give their name to a family (the Mustelidae) of the Carnivora, and are typical of the group. They have a long, narrow body which is lithe and muscular, with short legs; a small, bluntly-pointed face with small rounded ears, joined to the body by a thick, muscular neck; and a shortish, rather bushy tail. Weasels are bright chestnut brown above, and clear white below. The tail does not have the black tip seen in the stoat, and the margin between brown back and white belly is uneven, and different in every individual. Although in extreme northern climates the weasel turns white in winter, this happens only rarely in Britain. (Colour illustration facing p.162.)

Habitat and habits Weasels are found in any habitat which offers adequate prey and shelter: woods, farmland, scrub land, and open moorland. They can live close to man, in stacks, farmyards and even large towns. They like cover, and in open country prefer thickets, hedges and dry walls. Being so small, they can penetrate mouse holes and mole runs.

Weasels move quickly, either with the body held low and straight, or in a bounding gallop with the back arched. They often stop and stand upright to survey their surroundings. They can swim well, and have been observed eating fish; but presumably they do not hunt in the water regularly, for fish do not appear in food lists based on studies of gut content or scat analysis. Weasels climb well, and will often travel along hedges one or two metres above the ground, presumably hunting birds. They are active throughout the day and night, but show nocturnal tendencies.

Males and females hold separate territories, which vary in size according to abundance of prey. In captivity they have been observed dragging their hind-quarters along the ground, presumably making a scent mark with their anal glands; such behaviour would be a valuable territory marker.

Food The food of the weasel consists of any other animal which it can catch and kill, but tends to vary from place to place according to the availability of suitable prey. The diet of the smaller female weasel consists almost entirely of mice and voles, but the larger male takes a wider range of prey, which can include rats, moles, shrews (despite folklore to the contrary), rabbits, birds and their eggs, frogs and toads, reptiles, crayfish and insects. They are known to raid nest boxes put up for birds. Weasels are agile, fast-moving, and strong for their size; small prey is killed quickly and efficiently by a bite on the back of the head which penetrates the brain. Larger prey, such as rabbits, are killed with greater difficulty by repeated attacks aimed mainly at the throat, or in the case of birds, at the large veins under the wings. Only a predator of considerable strength, stamina and ferocity could succeed as the weasel does in subduing prey so much larger than itself.

Weasels are regarded as vermin by gamekeepers, and it may well be that their destruction is necessary to ensure high (although quite unnatural) populations of game birds, whose eggs and young are at risk in the breeding season. But weasels are the friend of the farmer and forester. A family of weasels could account for 2,000 or more small rodents in a year, a level of predation which could significantly depress rodent numbers and so protect crops. Weasels do not suck blood, as country lore has it, but eat their prey in a normal manner. They are provident eaters, wasting little when hungry, but may, when prey is abundant, kill much more than they can eat, storing the uneaten or partly eaten bodies of their victims in the vicinity of their dens, or even right inside them. Presumably this behaviour increases their effectiveness as a controller of small rodent populations. Weasels will occasionally raid chicken runs or make other depredations on small domestic stock, and because of their small size are difficult to exclude, but this happens rather seldom, and the weasel is not considered a serious pest on this account. They can be caught in various kinds of traps, taking advantage of the animal's love of small holes and crevices. Trapping success varies markedly with the skill and experience of the trapper.

Breeding Breeding is in the spring and summer, and there is no delayed implantation. The first pregnant females are found in March, and the littering peak occurs in April and May. Second litters, or first litters of females born early in the year, prolong the breeding season until September. The gestation period is 34–37 days. Litters consist of three to eight young, with a usual number of five or six. Young weasels stay with their mother in family groups until they are 9 to 12 weeks old, by which time they are able to fend for themselves.

Winter aggregations presumably of several family groups, have been recorded. The males take no part in rearing the young.

Populations of weasels fluctuate widely, a phenomenon which in some cases may be linked with the abundance of small rodents; but not always, for drops in weasel numbers are known even when their prey is numerous. There is heavy mortality in the first year of life, and the weasel's life span in the wild is unlikely to exceed three or four years, with an average of little more than a single year. In captivity a life of ten years is possible.

Enemies Being so small the weasel, despite its fierceness and agility, can be killed by many larger predators, and is brought home not uncommonly by domestic cats. Its numbers in the countryside are, however, small compared with rodents and other alternative prey, so predation by other animals is probably not a very important cause of mortality. Man is without doubt the weasel's main enemy.

Parasites Many kinds of flea infest weasels, and there is a biting louse, *Trichodectes mustelae*, found on no other host. The most remarkable parasite is a nematode worm, *Skrjabingylus nasicola*, which is found in the nasal sinuses of 40 per cent to 100 per cent of weasels. Although it can cause considerable damage to the bones of the skull, it appears to cause neither illness nor death in the host animal.

The Polecat

William Condry

The polecat is in every respect admirably formed for the peculiar mode of life assigned to it by the all-wise Author of Nature.

THOMAS BEWICK (1753–1828) History of Quadrupeds

If you encounter a polecat, *Mustela putorius*, in daylight you see a slender, sinuous animal a foot or two long, low-slung, furry, with a small flattish head and a shortish tail. Apart from being white about the mouth, the cheeks and the tip of its small, rounded ears, it may seem entirely black. But if it turns away from you, causing the dark outer hairs to part, then you see that its thick under-fur is cream-coloured. In fact caught in a car's headlights, the way most live polecats are seen, they can look more white than black. Also recorded is a well-marked colour variety in which the pelage is anything from straw-yellow to a bright fox-red. In the early part of this century many reports of these latter colours came from south Merioneth and north Cardiganshire, but there have been few sightings of this variety since the 1950s.

Adult male polecats usually reach about 60cm in length including the tail, and may weigh nearly 1·4kg. Females are appreciably smaller. Polecats do not turn white in winter and albino polecats are unlikely to be reported because any found would almost certainly be dismissed as albino ferrets. Ferrets are indeed domesticated polecats, long kept in captivity for hunting rabbits.

Distribution Although once widespread in Britain (it was never in Ireland) the polecat was wiped out nearly everywhere in England and Scotland by the gamekeepers of the nineteenth century. However, in the wilder parts of Wales where there were neither game nor gamekeepers, the polecat survived. Then World War I and its aftermath greatly diminished gamekeeping and the polecat began to increase, until now it is common in most of Wales except Anglesey and the industrial districts. From Wales it has edged back into parts of the English border counties, but any further advance eastwards is likely to be slow in the face of all the pheasant rearing and vermin destruction prevalent in so much of the English countryside. 'Polecats' turning up in unlikely localities are almost certain to be escaped ferrets or their descendants. For such ferrets sometimes establish feral communities and their offspring, though often piebald, are quite frequently dark all over and extremely like true polecats. Abroad the polecat is widespread in Europe but is replaced further east by a much paler race, the Russian or steppe-polecat, *Mustela eversmannii*.

Habitat Within its range, the polecat is at home in woods and parkland, in hedgerows and in village gardens, in marshland and in coastal areas; in fact almost throughout the countryside, but probably not above the 400m level. In winter, especially, some polecats frequent villages and even farmyards if dogs are not too much in evidence. By the end of the winter their dens, which are often in hay barns, contain copious remains of food (fur, bones and feathers) and also an accumulation of black, twisted, finely tapered droppings each about 5cm long. Other likely hiding places, summer or winter, are log piles, thick vegetation or holes in the ground. At night polecats evidently travel a great deal for they are frequent road victims – their corpses the chief evidence of their abundance in some places.

In former times when polecats were everywhere common, they were objects of the chase and there were stories of polecats being followed for many miles across country. But sound modern information about their movements and territorial behaviour is lacking and could probably be obtained only by the use of electronic tracking devices.

Habits The polecat is usually nocturnal but I have occasionally seen one in daylight questing along nose to ground, so intent on its pursuit of rodents that it has passed very close without noticing me because I kept still. From this I conclude that although the polecat's senses of smell and hearing must be very keen, its sight, at least by day, may be less acute. Polecats are nearly always seen singly but occasionally whole families appear. A friend of mine once saw five polecats cross a main road near Aberystwyth, one after the other, in mid-afternoon.

Breeding Some polecats, if not all, become sexually mature towards the end of their first winter and mating takes place in the spring (from late March onwards). There is no delayed implantation of the fertilised egg and the gestation period is about six weeks. Polecats normally litter once a year in May or June. Four or five young may be produced and they are nearly full-grown by late summer.

Food The polecat is almost entirely carnivorous, the flesh of rabbits and small rodents predominating. The rabbits are taken mostly in woods, farmlands and sand dunes. Rodents are preyed on not only in the lowlands but also on moorlands and in high-level plantations, especially when the trees are young. Around farmyards and villages in winter, rats, house mice and carrion are probably important in the diet. In summer reptiles including lizards and even adders are reported to be eaten. So are frogs, birds, fish, insects, worms and occasionally wild fruits. Formerly the polecat had a reputation as a slayer of poultry, 'polecat' being derived from 'poulecat' – the cat that attacked pullets. Not being hibernators, polecats need to find plenty of food at all seasons: so they must be competing to some extent with stoats, weasels and foxes all the year round.

Natural enemies Though its young may occasionally be snatched by other predators the polecat can now have few natural enemies in a world from which the larger carnivores have long been banished. For its size it is a strong and fierce adversary, sharp in tooth and claw. It also has an unusual weapon in its armoury, one that was doubtless evolved to discourage attacks by wolves, lynxes and other large enemies. When pursued closely a polecat can produce a noxious smell in the face of its aggressor – a foul emanation released by two

Young weasels playing. Smallest of British carnivores, the weasel is agile and ferocious. In extreme northern climates its coat turns white in winter but this rarely happens in Britain.

The dark coat of the polecat hides a thick cream-coloured undercoat which may show clearly as it moves, making it appear a light-coloured animal.

anal glands. Hence the common saying 'stinks like a polecat'. This power to produce unspeakable stenches gave the polecat its other name of 'foumart' or 'foulmart' to distinguish it from the 'sweet mart' or pine marten. The Welsh for polecat, *ffwlbart*, is evidently derived from 'foumart', a word of French origin, and it is strange that no Celtic name has survived in Wales for such a well-known native animal, whereas other indigenous mammals have retained their ancient Welsh names. Polecats are not very vocal. They sometimes chatter, growl or hiss but the loudest noise I have heard was a repeated screaming by one pursued by a dog. Later the dog went slinking home drenched in so appalling an odour that it could not be allowed indoors for days!

Conservation The world's polecats are grossly exploited for their furs – thousands of these 'fitches' are imported annually into Britain for auction to the trade and then re-exported. The demand for British fitches used to be considerable and, even today, Welsh country newspapers sometimes carry advertisements from furriers offering money for polecat skins. Taking Britain as a whole the polecat is a rarity, just as deserving of legal protection as are the birds of prey. Granted that in so thickly populated a land there is no possible place for wolves or bears, but there seems no justification for the persecution of such small predators as polecats just because they happen to be unpopular with people who want to shoot pheasants.

Down the ages man has dealt destruction to the wildlife which shares his world, exterminating some species completely, reducing others to pitiable rarities, and still the destruction goes on. Is it not time we began to cherish all our remaining wild animals, including the predators, in the belief that each different kind adds to the richness of the natural world and therefore of our own lives? The philosopher Thoreau spoke of wildness as a tonic for us all. The polecat, so beautiful, so shy and in most places so rare, is the essence of such wildness.

The Mink

Ian Linn

In one moment I've seen what has hitherto been
Enveloped in absolute mystery,
And without extra charge I will give you at large
A Lesson in Natural History.
LEWIS CAROLL (1832–98) The Hunting of the Stark

The American mink, *Mustela vison*, has joined the British fauna as a result of escapes from some of the farms where it has been bred for its fur since 1929. Breeding in the wild was confirmed in 1956, in Devon. Since then, the mink has shown that it is well adapted to life in the British countryside, and has become widespread. It is now found throughout most of mainland Britain, with the exception of northwest Scotland, the Lake District, the greater part of Wales and the industrial Midlands. The offshore islands are clear so far, with the exception of Arran in the Firth of Clyde, and Lewis in the Outer Hebrides. In Ireland the distribution is discontinuous.

These mink are native to the temperate forest zones of North America, but have now become established in Iceland, Norway, Sweden, Denmark, Finland, North Germany and the USSR. The related European mink, *Mustela lutreola*, is rather eastern in distribution, its main centres being in Finland and in Russia to just east of the Urals; but populations of this species in France and in the countries of eastern Europe are declining, and may already have disappeared in many cases. It is not known in the British Isles.

The mink is a medium-sized carnivore of the weasel family (Mustelidae). A typical wild adult male will weigh about 1kg (range $\frac{1}{2}$–$1\frac{1}{2}$kg) and measure about 60cm from nose to tip of tail (range 50–70cm). The female is much smaller, weighing only about 600g (430–700g) and measuring only about 50cm (48–54cm). The mink has a bluntly pointed face, with small rounded ears, a thick, powerful neck, short legs, a long narrow body and a bushy tail. The fur is rich, glossy and thick, and very hard-wearing as a garment. Wild mink are usually dark brown (from chocolate colour to almost black) though pale animals similar to the original ranch-bred varieties crop up from time to time. They are the same colour above and below, but the dark animals have a white chin spot and often some other white spots and flecks on the underside.

Habitat and habits The mink is a typical carnivore, well adapted to catch and kill the animals it needs for food. It is agile, strong and active, and has sharp teeth and powerful jaws. It is a waterside animal found mainly near lakes and rivers and sometimes on the seashore, for it hunts both on land and in the water. Its senses are undoubtedly acute, though its vision, which has to work in water as well as in air, is not perfectly adapted for either.

The gait of the mink may be a walk or run with the body held low and level, or it may be the typical bounding gait with arched back seen in other weasel-type animals. Mink climb well, but probably do not hunt much in the trees. They also swim well enough although their only obvious adaptation to swimming is their partly-webbed feet. Their typical splay-footed, five-clawed tracks, sometimes with a tail-mark can be found in sand or mud along the banks of lakes and rivers.

Mink den in holes under trees, in river banks and among stones. They are solitary animals for most of the year, although the young may stay with the mother for some months before becoming completely independent, and family groups are sometimes seen.

Mink hold territories if they can, though a certain number are 'transients', non-territorial animals which move on, apparently in search of a place to settle. In poor quality habitats, where food or some other vital resource is scarce, these 'transients' are the commoner; but in richer habitats the territorial system tends to become stabilized.

Breeding Males travel widely during the spring in search of females, with which they mate promiscuously. Females become pregnant between late February and early April. Gestation lasts a minimum of 39 days, but this period may be extended up to 76 days, by a variable delay in implantation of the developing embryo (see p.20). A period of 45–52 days between copulation and parturition is about average; in ranch mink the peak in littering is towards the end of April.

A usual litter will be five or six, but may be less or even more. The young remain with the mother during the summer, but disperse to find their own territory in the autumn. It seems likely that there is considerable juvenile mortality, and that relatively few young survive to become established adults. The males take no part in the care of the young.

Enemies Mink have few enemies apart from man, but are probably taken, rather rarely, by the larger predators. Other factors, such as parasites, disease and starvation, are likely to be more important than predation in limiting mink numbers – particularly among any juveniles which fail to develop their hunting skills, or fail to find a suitable territory. In many parts of Britain, these seem to be the factors which are keeping mink numbers within the limits which habitats can carry. It therefore seems unlikely that mink will become much commoner than they now are.

Food The diet of mink consists almost entirely of vertebrate animals, mainly fish, birds and mammals. Amphibia (frogs) are taken sometimes, but invertebrates and vegetable matter hardly at all, though in chalk streams crayfish may figure in the diet. Mammals, birds and fish are eaten in approximately equal proportions, but these proportions can vary considerably from place to place and from time to time in any given area, according to the abundance and availability of different kinds of prey. Among fish, eels are preferred, probably because they are easier to catch than midwater fish; but eels are taken less frequently in winter, for they then become torpid and tend to hide in the mud and between stones. Coarse fish and salmonids (trout, sea trout and salmon) are, in contrast, taken more in winter, when they swim more slowly than in summer. Some species are more vulnerable after spawning. Among birds, waterfowl are taken more than other groups. Rabbits, probably mainly young ones, are taken mostly in summer.

serves both as a recognition sign between badgers, and as a type of warning coloration, best seen at night.

One might well ask why a badger needs warning coloration when it has no enemies except man, and with its proverbially strong bite and raking claws is well able to defend itself. Cubs are more vulnerable and can easily be killed by foxes, dogs, and in the past, other animals such as wolves. However, they derive some degree of immunity from having the same coloration as adults, predators being deterred by the resemblance, and when cubs are approached they fluff up their fur to make them look much nearer to adult size.

Badgers are great diggers and are well adapted for a partially fossorial, or burrowing life. The body is thick-set, wedge-shaped and carried low on the ground on short, but very strong legs. The fore limbs are immensely strong and bear long claws which are admirable tools for loosening the earth and winkling out stones, when digging a tunnel. One of the problems when digging in confined spaces is the dust which may get into eyes, nostrils and ears. The eyes, as in other mammals, are protected by eyelids, but badgers can also, by muscular action, close the openings of the ears and restrict the size of the nostrils. They can also blow out air in short blasts to clear dust particles, taken in when breathing.

The average length of an adult male is about 90cm including a 15cm tail; females are usually several centimetres shorter. For their size they are surprisingly heavy, males averaging about 11·6kg and females about 1·4kg less. However, weights vary considerably according to locality and season, and by winter badgers will have accumulated several pounds of extra fat, to be used as a food store when times are hard. Occasionally very heavy badgers have been recorded, in some instances up to 27·3kg in weight.

A badger appears grey from a distance owing to the colour of the individual guard hairs. On the upper parts these hairs are light at the base and tip, with a dark patch between. Hairs on the legs and underside are dark.

There is quite a lot of variation in hair colour. Adults may be reddish (erythristic), almost black (melanistic) and occasionally white (albino). In addition, badgers living in some soils get their fur stained, for example those living in red sandstone regions often look quite reddish.

The badger's home Badgers make extensive underground burrows known as setts. These consist of an intricate system of tunnels and chambers sometimes dug at several levels. The external openings are much bigger than those of rabbit burrows, the minimum diameter being about 24cm, but they are usually much larger. The number of openings to a sett varies considerably according to ease of digging and how ancient the sett is – some are several hundreds of years old. To give some indication of size, one well-established sett in Gloucestershire which was surveyed accurately had twelve entrances, its 94 tunnels totalled 310m in length and the excavated soil was estimated to have been 25 tonnes.

The spoil heaps outside the entrances characteristically have a lot of vegetable material incorporated with the soil. This is old bedding which was used to line the chambers. Bedding consists of any available vegetation which is near the sett, but coarse grass or bracken is preferred. Usually it is brought in during spells of dry weather, particularly in the autumn, but bedding collection can take place during any month of the year. In May, bluebell and dog's mercury leaves are brought in green. When there are signs of bedding near a sett entrance during January it is a good indication that cubs are likely to be born there within the next few weeks.

When gathering bedding a badger will rake up the vegetation with its claws, or bite it off if it is too tough. It then makes it into a large bundle and hugging this to its chest shuffles backwards to the sett, keeping the bundle in position with chin and fore legs. Sometimes it will bring back bedding from 50m or more away, a journey which might involve crossing a lane and surmounting numerous objects, such as banks or tree roots, before reaching the sett entrance. The badger finds its way with unerring accuracy in spite of going backwards, and disappears in the same manner still clutching the bundle under its chin. On some nights as many as 30 such bundles may be brought back in this way.

Habitat Badgers live in many kinds of habitat. Their preference is for deciduous woodland, but hedgerows, scrub, moorland, sea cliffs and open fields are commonly used. They will also use embankments, quarries, mines and even rubbish tips and occasionally they will burrow under buildings.

The ideal site from a badger's point of view is one where there is adequate cover around the entrances so that they can emerge unseen, where the soil is well drained and easy to dig, where there is a plentiful supply of food nearby which is available in one form or another all through the year, and where disturbance from man or his animals is at a minimum, especially at night.

Signs of badger activity Much can be found out about badgers by visiting a sett during the daytime although the badgers themselves are unlikely to be seen for they are mainly crepuscular and nocturnal, except in very secluded places. If the large heap of excavated soil outside one of the entrances is examined, the type of bedding used can easily be determined, and if some of the lumps of earth are broken up, badger hairs will probably be found. You may also sometimes come across the skeletal remains of a badger which had died below ground some years before, and which have been thrown out during digging operations. Old badger skulls are often found in this way.

You can usually tell an occupied hole by signs of recent digging, the five-toed pad marks near the entrance, the presence of flies near the hole, and the absence of old leaves and spider webs.

Leading away from the sett will be several well-marked paths, some of which may be traced for very long distances. These lead to important feeding grounds, drinking places, alternative setts, playing trees or dung pit areas.

Dung pits may be situated quite near a sett; they are conical and occur in groups. The droppings are not covered up, and their consistency depends on the food eaten: they always appear muddy after a meal of earthworms for instance.

There is often a scratching tree (usually an elder) near one of the sett entrances. When using such a tree a badger goes up to it, gets on to its hind legs, reaches up with its fore legs and scrapes the bark with a downward action, cleaning its claws in the process. They also sometimes climb trees, gripping the bark like a bear. A scratching tree may show marks on the bark up to a height of about 3m.

The common occurrence of elder bushes near a sett might suggest that badgers chose the site accordingly, but this is not so. On the contrary, the elders are there as a result of badger activity. Badgers are fond of elder berries, but elder seeds pass through their bodies unchanged and are deposited with the droppings. As the dung pits are often near setts the elders germinate at these places. Elders also grow well in disturbed soil and where the nitrogen and phosphorus content is high, so they flourish near setts.

Senses and general behaviour Sight is the poorest of a badger's main senses and badgers probably see best in light of low intensity. They use their eyes largely for detecting movement and the outlines of larger objects, rather than for obtaining more detailed information. The cubs in particular are short sighted.

By contrast, hearing is very acute and badgers can detect a wide range of frequencies. It seems probable that they often locate the position of prey by the sounds they make. Hearing also plays an important part in communication between badgers as they make a variety of vocal signals. When excited, cubs make a continuous whickering, a variable high-pitched chatter interspersed with rather staccato single notes. Adults make a number of threat sounds including a muffled growl which serves as a serious warning, and a staccato bark which means, 'keep off'. A single staccato note rather like that of a moorhen, when made by a sow, may cause her cubs to run towards her. It may also serve as a contact call. Adults also make a kind of whinnying purr. A sow uses a very quiet form of this when nursing cubs: it probably expresses affection and pleasure. The boar can make a much deeper and more vibrant vocalization which is very evident at the mating season. It is uttered when patrolling a territory and in the act of mating. Badgers also make a hair-raising scream. They certainly do this when badly frightened or hurt, but it may also be used as a type of challenge.

The sense of smell is extremely well developed in badgers and is by far their most important sense. It is used for recognizing individuals, for detecting their sexual state, for locating food, finding their way about and for warning themselves of danger.

When a badger first emerges from its sett it scents the air carefully. This may warn it of any danger, such as the presence of man, and help it to determine what it will do and where it will go. Later when satisfied that all is well, the badger will leave the vicinity of the sett and follow a path which is in fact a scent trail. It will move at an ambling trot, nose to ground and with its hind quarters swaying from side to side. It is by scent that it will recognize landmarks *en route* and, when it reaches a feeding area, many of the food items will also be detected by smell.

Badgers not only collect information about their environment from the scents they detect, but they also produce their own smells and recognize scent signals made by other badgers.

The scents badgers use for communication come from various sources, such as urine, sweat and other glands of the skin, but the most important are the secretions of the sub-caudal and anal glands. The former are a pair of skin pouches just below the tail which secrete a pale yellow, fatty substance with a faint, musky smell. The anal sacs are internal, but pour their secretions down ducts into the anal cavity.

When a badger is travelling it often squats for a moment and leaves a drop from the sub-caudal glands on a path, tree root or any other suitable object. This musking is a means of signposting a route. They will also musk objects around a sett, and members of the same social group will do so repeatedly on each other. Boar will musk on sow, sow on boar, adults on cubs and cubs on each other. It is thought that this secretion is slightly different in each individual and serves for personal recognition, and that by musking on each other, the social group acquires a composite smell which is characteristic of that community and differs from that of neighbouring groups.

Anal gland secretion, on the other hand, when mixed with the faeces, is mainly used for marking out territory. Each social group of badgers may occupy and defend an area of about 50 hectares in good badger country where food is plentiful. The territory is marked out by dung pits, dug at strategic places especially round the perimeter. They act as 'trespassers will be prosecuted' notices. During the period February to May in particular, these dung pits are visited regularly and the scent notices reinforced. Dung pits are also dug by the sides of main paths and near conspicuous geographical features within a territory, such as hedgerow, bank or road. A dominant boar may spend much time patrolling the boundary of his territory and if another badger from a neighbouring group trespasses, a fight may develop. Sometimes fights can be very severe with serious bite wounds inflicted.

Each social group occupying a territory may consist of as many as 15 badgers although such a high number would only occur if there were several litters of cubs present. One or more adult boars and several adult sows may be in the social group as well as sub-adults and cubs.

Play is a very characteristic activity of social animals and among badgers, can be observed especially between April and July when the cubs are developing rapidly. Although cubs play more frequently the adults often join in. Cubs indulge in games similar to 'king of the castle' and 'tag'. The ground around setts and particular playing trees often are denuded of all vegetation by their play.

Food Although badgers belong to the order Carnivora, they are truly omnivorous in their diet. They feed on a great variety of animal and plant products, their choice depending largely on availability.

The badger is a forager, not a hunter. Nose to ground, it searches persistently for small prey. Many items are found accidentally and, if food is not abundant, a badger may spend many hours foraging, before finding enough for its needs.

Although a badger's menu is so wide it certainly has its preferences and relies much more on certain categories of food than on others. The importance of eathworms cannot be overestimated. Whenever the weather is sufficiently mild and damp for earthworms to be available, badgers will take them in large numbers – often to the exclusion of anything else. Several hundreds may be taken in a single night. A great variety of insects are also eaten, particularly dung beetles, wasps, bumble bees, caterpillars and the larvae of crane flies and cockchafers. They also take mammals, especially their young, including rabbits, rats, mice, voles, shrews, moles and hedgehogs. Amphibians may also be of importance in some districts, and slugs and snails taken when readily available. Carrion is eaten, particularly in winter.

On the plant side of the menu, cereals and fruit are the most important. Oats and wheat are regularly taken, particularly in dry summers, some when still on the stalk, but mainly from gleanings after harvesting. In the autumn badgers will eat much fruit, including blackberries, bilberries, acorns, beech mast and windfall apples, pears and plums. They will also dig out the storage organs of such woodland plants as wild arum and pignut.

Breeding Cubs are born mainly between mid-January and mid-March, with a peak during the first half of February in southern and south-western Britain. The number in a litter ranges from one to five, but three is the most usual. Typically, the cubs are born below ground in a special breeding chamber containing plenty of dry bedding. At birth they are about 120mm long, plus a short tail. They have a pinkish skin covered with greyish fur; the facial stripe is usually just visible. For the first five weeks the eyelids are fused, but at first when their eyes have opened the cubs have little cause to use them, for cubs seldom come above ground until eight or nine weeks old.

Badger cubs are suckled for at least three months, by which time they are well grown and quite active. They remain with the mother at least until the autumn and usually well into the following year. Female cubs usually become mature at 12 to 15 months, but males take up to two years.

Mating may occur during any month of the year from February to October, but the main mating period is between February and May. This coincides with the time when the young sows are becoming mature and when many older ones come into oestrus following the birth of a litter. A further, but less important, peak of mating activity occurs in the late summer and autumn.

It would be reasonable to expect that with such a variable mating season, birth times would be correspondingly varied. The reason that this is not so is because of delayed implantation (see p.20). Although fertilization can occur after any mating, the blastocysts which develop from the fertilized eggs do not implant in the wall of the uterus until about mid-December. A placenta is then formed and there are about eight weeks of normal gestation before the young are born. So, by delaying implantation, the majority of cubs are born at the best time of year for survival. Early February may not appear at first sight to be ideal, but the cubs are kept warm thanks to the insulation of the bedding, and by the time they are weaned there is plenty of food available and they have the rest of the year to grow strong and put on fat, before the winter sets in.

Badgers do not hibernate although they do become lethargic during December.

Man and the Badger From time immemorial badgers have been looked upon as creatures of mystery and superstition. This is aptly illustrated by some verses found nearly 200 years ago on the fly-leaf of an old bible:

Should a badger cross the path
which thou hast taken, then
Good luck is thine, so it be said
Beyond the luck of men.

But if it cross in front of thee,
Beyond where thou shalt tread,
And if by chance doth turn the mould
Thou art numbered with the dead!

Superstitions are not dead, even today, but now man's thoughts usually turn to such mundane questions as 'are they useful or harmful?' This kind of question is not easy to answer in categorical terms for any animal as large as a badger is bound to conflict to some extent with man's interests. It is all a matter of balance.

The poultry farmer has nothing to fear if his birds are properly housed, although badgers certainly kill poultry occasionally, but not typically. Usually this happens when normal food is short, or when a badger is old and has very worn teeth.

Although some gamekeepers still persist in killing badgers, the

Game Conservancy considers that damage by badgers in relation to pheasant rearing is insignificant and calls for no repressive measures.

Badgers may be a nuisance if they knock down cereals and consume grain, but again losses are small. To the dairy farmer, badgers are no problem except in localities where bovine tuberculosis has become endemic in the population. Fortunately over most of Britain, badgers are free from this disease, the problem being largely confined to parts of the south west.

As far as forestry is concerned the badger is looked upon as a friend, for it reduces the rodent population and other pests, but badgers may dig under wire netting and let rabbits into young plantations. This problem has been overcome by putting in special gates where badger paths cross the boundary. These gates have heavy swing doors through which badgers readily pass, but which keep rabbits out.

In a few localities badgers damage root crops such as carrots, and they may also be a problem in places where soft fruit is grown extensively if these are in the vicinity of a sett.

On the credit side badgers certainly destroy large numbers of mammalian and insect pests, and they give much pleasure to many people. So on balance it is fair to say that some badgers do a little harm, and can occasionally be a nuisance, but they also do a little good. In most ways they conflict very little with man's interests.

Badger control For centuries badger numbers have been controlled by direct human action. Badger digging, hunting, snaring, trapping, shooting, and more recently gassing have all been used to destroy them. Fortunately, the abolition of the gin trap and the passing of the Badgers Act has reduced some of the cruelty inherent in these practices. Without a special permit from the Ministry of Agriculture, Fisheries and Food, it is now illegal to hunt, dig out or gas badgers. Digging still goes on, but to a lesser extent now and gassing is still practised on some farms and shooting estates. These are matters against which there must be continual vigilance. *

Even more important is that there is no law against snaring and in recent years there has been an increase in the use of snares to catch both foxes and badgers. Some snares are put down deliberately for badgers, but often the snare is set for a fox and a badger is caught instead. Snaring can be extremely cruel as a badger is very strong and may tear out the peg fixing the snare and go off with the wire

*For the RSPCA view see *Badgers & Bovine Tuberculosis*, a special report published in 1980.

deeply embedded in its tissues. This may lead to a very painful and lingering death.

Many badgers are also killed on the roads. Traffic accounts for an ever-mounting toll of casualties and must be one of the most important causes of badger deaths.

To conserve the badger everything possible should be done to reduce these pressures. In some places losses on the roads have been reduced by putting underpasses in places where, in the past, badgers have habitually crossed them. Many of these tunnels and culverts are regularly used.

If badgers need to be excluded from areas which need special protection, an electrified wire, as for cattle, can be used effectively. It should be supported at a height of about 10cm from the ground. Badgers will try to pass under such a wire rather than jump over it. Rope soaked in a smelly deterrent such as old diesel oil pinned out at a similar height, can also be effective. But it should be stressed that these techniques are best applied *before* damage is done, for once badgers have learnt that there is an abundant food supply in a certain place, it takes a lot to keep them out. A further method of protection, particularly where the point of entry is limited, is to attach strong sheep netting to a fence and bend it outwards at ground level, lightly turfing it on top. The badger tries to burrow under it, but comes up against the bend in the netting and cannot force an entry.

The Otter

Paul Chanin

Underwater eyes, an eel's
Oil of water body, neither fish nor beast is the otter.
TED HUGHES (1930–) An Otter

The retiring habits of the otter, *Lutra lutra*, ensured that it was rarely seen even when it was to be found on most rivers in Britain. Now that the otter is absent from many rivers, the number of people who have seen one in the wild is very small indeed, and it is hardly surprising that many reports of otters turn out to be sightings of water voles or mink. Otters are, in fact, much larger than these species, males reaching a length of 1·2m including a tail of 40cm and weighing about 10kg. The females are a little smaller, weighing about 7·5kg. The short legs and long, sinuous body of the otter clearly indicate its membership of the weasel family, although, unlike the other British Mustelidae, it has a large tail which is broad and stout at the base and flattened along its length. The otter's head is blunt and flat-topped, with a broad muzzle formed by fleshy pads on either side, which carry the magnificent set of whiskers. The eyes and ears of the otter are quite small. The coat varies in colour from a fairly pale to a very dark brown. The underside may be paler than the back and sometimes the chin and throat have a distinctly pale, almost white patch.

We must remember that the otter is not a water animal but a land animal that spends much of its time in the water, particularly when feeding. Although the otter has become adapted to hunt better in water than on land, the most important changes that have taken place in its evolution have been in its behaviour – most of the structural changes being a matter of degree. Thus, the coats of most mammals are waterproof, but the otter's is more so. The underfur is dense and the long guard hairs keep it dry and trap a layer of air to insulate the body from the cold of the water. When an healthy otter leaves the water, the guard hairs clump together to give a spiky appearance, and after a few shakes, the coat is almost dry. If an otter is in poor condition or the water contaminated, its coat may become waterlogged, its body chilled and the otter may die.

The webbed feet of the otter are mainly used for slow swimming in a dog-paddle fashion. For greater speed, the otter lays its legs alongside its body, so that the hind feet, the end of the body and the base of the tail, together form a broad surface which is flexed up and down like the flukes of a whale.

Hunting under water poses problems for the otter. Most of its close relatives hunt mainly by smell, but this is impossible in water and, although sound carries very well there, it seems unlikely that otters could hear a fish swimming in still water, let alone in a fast flowing stream! This leaves the otter with sight and feeling and, in clear water and with a source of light, the otter undoubtedly hunts by sight. In turbid water or on a dark night, the otter seems to use its whiskers to detect the vibrations made by fish as they swim.

Habitat and distribution Otters inhabit every continent except Australasia and Antarctica, and our own Eurasian otter has one of the widest distributions of the group, stretching from Ireland to Japan and from North Africa to the Arctic tundra. Within Britain, the otter is still widespread but is now scarce or absent from much of central England and is much less common in the rest of England than it was before 1950. In Wales, otters are still to be found over much of the country except in Glamorgan and Gwent. Otters are probably fairly common throughout most of Scotland but scarcer in the east and south than formerly. The west coast of Scotland together with the Islands (including Orkney and Shetland) is the stronghold of the otter in Britain today.

Otters may be found beside rivers, streams, marshes, lakes and on the coast – anywhere in fact that provides an adequate supply of food and freedom from disturbance. Insufficient supplies of food mean that the smaller hill streams and sandy or shingle beaches form the least suitable habitats and, were it not for the activities of man, the densest populations of otters would be found on lowland rivers and rocky coasts. Increasing human population has driven otters from their preferred habitat and restricted them to places where there still is little disturbance and plenty of cover to conceal their dens.

Behaviour and breeding As the otter is so shy and retiring our knowledge of its day-to-day life is limited. Many people think of otters as carefree, playful creatures, but in fact a great deal of an otter's active time is spent in foraging, hunting or travelling round its range. Diurnal or crepuscular by nature, yet nocturnal when disturbed by man, otters are most easily seen on the remote lochs and rocky coasts of Scotland and most observations of their behaviour have been made there. Contrary to some suggestions that otters can stay under water for at least five minutes, careful timing of feeding otters shows that they usually spend 16–40 seconds in a dive and then return to the surface for air. In fact, it would be surprising if the body of an animal of an otter's size could contain enough oxygen to last for more than a minute or so. While hunting seriously, the otter will make repeated dives, often from the same spot and sometimes with scarcely a pause on the surface. Sometimes an otter will catch a fish every few minutes, while at others it may only average one every 45 minutes or so. Small items of food are eaten in the water but the otter will swim to the shore with larger prey, or if it is feeding cubs.

Otters are solitary creatures. If more than one is seen at a time they are most likely to be a family group – that is a female with her young – for the male usually associates with the female only when she is in breeding condition. In England this may be at any time of the year, but in Sweden where the winters are harsher, and where much work on otters has been done, it is so timed that the young are born in the spring, after a gestation period of two months. At birth the cubs, usually two or three, are blind and helpless. Weaning begins at eight to nine weeks. By the time the cubs are four months old they will have been introduced to the water and will be learning to swim. Possibly a cub sometimes makes its own way into the water, following its mother or siblings, but female otters have been observed to drag their cubs into the water the first time, and even to dive while holding one of them by the ear. After a few days of this, the cub finds it preferable to follow under its own power, but may still try to climb on to its mother's back.

The cubs remain with their mother for a considerable time. Observations made in both Sweden and Shetland have shown that they may stay for periods of a year or more. Eventually however they must depart. When they have gone the female may mate again, although in some parts of Sweden females seemed to breed only every other year. Meanwhile, the juvenile otter will be forced to leave its birthplace and will travel until it finds another suitable area which does not 'belong' to another otter. Otters are usually territorial and will not tolerate the presence of other adult otters of the same sex within their territories although there may be some overlap on the edges of ranges. The size of ranges and the amount of overlap seem to depend on the availability of food, the density of the otter population and the habitat. However, otters of the opposite sex are tolerated and, since the range of a male may be two or three times that of a female (sometimes 15–20km across), one male otter may share his range with two or more females and mate with any of them.

Food Usually, 70–90 per cent of the otter's diet consists of fish and it tends to take eels and other coarse fish in preference to trout and salmon, because they are the easiest to catch. For the same reason the bulk of an otter's diet usually consists of fish 10–30cm long, although it will occasionally take larger fish. The rest of its food varies according to the availability of other kinds of prey and the season, but crayfish, mussels, frogs, waterside birds and rabbits may be included.

The diet of coastal otters is very different from those living in freshwater habitats but, here too, fish are the main item usually with shellfish, particularly crabs, constituting a large proportion.

Otters and man The otter has no natural enemies in Britain except man, and although man has been killing otters for centuries, it is only recently that he has caused a substantial decline in the otter population, and that inadvertently.

As a predator of fish and, in particular, as a raider of manorial and monastic fishponds, the otter has been persecuted from the earliest times. King Henry II and King John each had a royal pack of otter hounds although, initially at least, otter hunting must have been intended as a means of control rather than as a sport. Three and a half centuries later otters were still regarded as vermin and an Act was passed enabling bounties to be paid on otters, as well as on a number of other mammals.

There is no indication of any changes in the otter population until the eighteenth century, when the industrial revolution brought people and pollution to many of the larger rivers, particularly in northern England, and so drove the otter away. During the nineteenth century, improvements in firearms combined with the increased keepering associated with the development of large sporting estates, led to marked declines in the populations of a number of carnivores, notably the polecat, pine marten and wildcat. Although the otter's range was probably not decreased by this, it is likely that its total population did decrease, for when, at the beginning of the present century, these pressures began to lessen, the otter population began to rise. In the Otter Report published in 1957 by the Universities' Federation for Animal Welfare, Marie Stephens makes it clear that there were then no grounds for concern about the status of otters. They were flourishing throughout Britain, except in urban and industrial areas. Twelve years later, a report by the Mammal Society based on otter hunting records showed that the otter had dramatically declined over much of England and Wales. The reasons for the decline have not been easy to determine, not least because even the earliest investigation took place ten years after the decline had started. But a detailed study of the hunting records from 1950 to 1971 shows that the decline started in 1957 or 1958. This means that it is possible to eliminate many factors previously considered important and shows that the otter, like the peregrine and the sparrowhawk, was probably very badly affected by the introduction of the dieldrin type of pesticide. What is perhaps most disturbing is that, although the use of dieldrin has been increasingly restricted in recent years, the otter population has not only failed to recover but is apparently continuing to decline in most areas. The reasons for this are not yet fully understood but are probably mainly connected with the dramatic changes in riparian habitats. If the otter population is to be restored, it must re-invade areas which have greatly changed, and these changes may well have reduced the otter's powers of recovery.

In 1976 the Joint Otter Group was formed, including officers of the Nature Conservancy Council, the Society for the Promotion of Nature Conservation, the Institute of Terrestrial Ecology and the

Mammal Society. Its Report (Otters 1977) listed ten possible pressures on otters of which two – human leisure activity and riparian clearance – have been increasing. Two others, which may have become more important as the otter population declined, were the accidental killing of otters on roads or in fish nets and their deliberate killing either to protect fisheries or for pelts.

The Group recommended measures to alleviate these pressures and one of them, that the otter should be legally protected, was effected on 1st January 1978, when the otter was added to Schedule I of the Conservation of Wild Creatures & Wild Plants Act 1975. Other recommendations require lengthy and co-operative effort between conservationists, riparian owners, recreational organizations and Water Authorities. These latter recommendations were concerned with preserving the otter's habitat and with measures to halt, and eventually reverse the otter's decline. The Group also made general recommendations on the management of waterways to ensure minimal disturbance and that, as far as possible, they should be managed in sympathy with the needs of the otter. On some river systems a series of stretches should be set aside as sanctuaries or havens, within which the otter should be given priority. Otters would not be restricted to these sanctuaries but they would provide a secure retreat both for lying up during the day and, of particular importance, for breeding.

Hunting and control Even though otter hunting originated as a means of controlling otter populations, it eventually became a sport, and it is not surprising that when, in 1965, the hunts became aware of the decline in otter populations, they severely restricted their killing of otters. Furthermore, although evidence showed that the numbers of otters killed by the hunts was having little or no effect on otter populations, many people felt that the disturbance caused by the hunts was detrimental to otters and should be stopped and a recommendation to this effect was made in the report of the Joint Otter Group. This recommendation was made on conservation grounds and not because otter hunting as practised today was considered to be cruel. There is no doubt that in earlier times some aspects of otter hunting involved unnecessary cruelty, but more recently the otter hounds have hunted under a strict code of conduct laid down by the Master of Otter Hounds Association. It was this body that in 1978 decided that otter hunting in England and Wales should cease.

Under natural conditions otters do not adversely affect fish populations and may even improve them by selectively taking diseased and damaged fish, by reducing competition between the fish for food and by removing supposedly undesirable species such as eels. In Scotland otters are still being killed for taking salmon, but it has not been shown that they take sufficient to decrease the yield for man. Similarly, allegations of lamb killing have not been substantiated.

The only situation in which otters could conceivably be a serious nuisance are those where artificially high concentrations of fish are kept in fish farms and fish ponds. Here, one otter could in a short time do a considerable amount of damage. In fact, fish farmers do not consider that otters are a problem. Whether this is because otters are scarce or because adequate precautions are taken is not clear. Should an otter prove to be a nuisance, the only satisfactory remedy is to take steps to exclude the animal from the premises. Killing an otter, even if it were not likely to be extremely difficult, would only leave a vacant range which would eventually be filled by another otter.

The future Although public opinion is now firmly in favour of the otter, its future in Britain, particularly in England, is still in doubt. Whether or not the otter remains a member of the English fauna will depend on the success or failure of man's efforts to retain and to restore its habitat.

The Wildcat

L. K. Corbett

> *The Cat is surely most like the Leoparde, and hathe a great mouthe, and sharpe teeth, and a long tongue, plyante, thin and subtle. He lappeth therewith when he drinketh. . . . He is a cruell beaste when he is wilde, and dwelleth in woods, and hunteth there small beastes as conies and hares.*
>
> 'De Proprietatibus Rerum' translated by Thomas Berthlet (1498)

The wildcat, *Felis silvestris*, is perhaps the least known of all British carnivores. Until recently most recorded information was derived from anecdotal or speculative reports, although information from corpses, occasional sightings and signs of wildcat activities, such as tracks in snow, dens and kills, gave more reliable information on taxonomy, breeding and feeding habits.

The reasons for such scant knowledge are clear. Wildcats are uncommon, shy, cryptic, mostly nocturnal and hence difficult to study. Only in recent years, with the development of sophisticated study tools such as radio-tracking equipment and night viewing devices, has it been possible to gain some understanding of how wildcats really live.

Description The typical and fairly consistent coat of wildcats is tabby, coloured grey or yellowish-brown, with eight to eleven dark body stripes (sometimes broken on the underside), and four to seven strong black leg bands (often incomplete). There are four distinct black stripes running from the forehead to the back of the head which then merge into a thin back stripe. The cheeks show three black stripes (one separate and two joined). Black hairs on the soles of the feet make a typical 'sole-patch'. There is always a patch of white hairs in the umbilical region and occasionally on the chest or throat; the chin is usually of an off-white colour. Adults have orange or rust-red hairs in the groin region extending down the insides of the back legs and underside of the tail base. Wildcats have a pink nose, black pads, horn-coloured claws and amber eyes, and most of their whiskers are white. Occasionally, in old cats, there is a silvery-grey infusion over the back and neck. Wildcat kittens show stronger and more distinct body stripes than adults, especially on the trunk.

The chief feature by which the wildcat may be distinguished from its domestic relative is its tail, which is encircled by about five completely separate, broad, black rings and has a rounded, or blunt, black tip. In contrast, striped domestic tabby cats have tapering tails and the bands are often less distinct, incomplete and connected by a stripe on the top of the tail. Other differences which have been recorded are variations in skull bones, the shape of the lower jaw, and the length of the gut. Hybrids are difficult to identify since so few if any, have been authenticated. In the few cases of suspected hybrids the tail resembles that of domestic cats rather than of wildcats. (Colour illustration facing p.179.)

Distribution and population The wildcat, *Felis silvestris*, occurs from Scotland eastwards through central Europe to Asia Minor and the Caucasus, and southwards through the Mediterranean countries to southern Africa. There are about 21 sub-species but even these can be lumped under three main types, one of which *Felis silvestris lybica* is presumed to be the ancestor of domestic cats.

The sub-species found in Scotland, *Felis silvestris grampia*, is distinguished from the central European wildcat by its darker colour.

Wildcats were formerly distributed throughout the British Isles, except Ireland and the outer islands (Hebrides, Orkney, etc.) but they had disappeared from England, Wales and southern Scotland by the mid-nineteenth century. Even in the Scottish Highlands their numbers were then very low, but there has been a considerable and continuing recovery over the past 60 years. They now are most numerous in Inverness-shire and parts of Aberdeenshire, Angus, Moray, Nairn, Perth and Argyll.

Habitat Wildcats have been seen in almost every type of country, from moorlands to cultivated farmlands, but the preferred habitat is forest, especially dense forests with broom and gorse scrub associations. Here are good supplies of food, cover for hunting and refuge against bad weather and predators.

Reproduction In Scotland, most wildcats mate in March and kittens are born in May. However, litters have been recorded from April through to September, but it is not known whether this is due to an extended breeding season with a peak of births in May, whether females have a second oestrus or whether hybrid wildcats are involved. Males are sexually active from the end of December to the end of June. Captive studies have indicated that the gestation period is about 66 days and that litter sizes range from one to eight, but two to four is the most frequent litter size in the field. The kittens are usually born in dense forest, but soon after they become mobile are frequently shifted to temporary dens often in more open situations, including moorlands. These dens are usually in usurped rabbit warrens or badger setts, in rocky cairns or among fallen debris. The kittens are abandoned quite early, possibly as young as four to five months old, and reach adult size at 12 months, although they increase in weight until they are two or three years old. They reach sexual maturity during the year after birth.

Food The staple diet of wildcats in north-eastern Scotland is rabbit, especially young rabbits and rabbits with myxomatosis. In western Scotland more rodents are taken and rodents probably become the major food source in all areas when they are in the peak stage of their cycle. Birds, chiefly game birds and small perching birds, are also taken to a lesser extent, as are hares of both species, insects and shrews. Grass is also deliberately eaten. Wildcats usually hunt at night especially at dawn and dusk, mostly within or on the edge of forest and scrub. Their basic hunting strategy is stalking, or lying in wait and leaping on prey. This method of hunting implies keen vision, but the wildcat's senses of hearing and smell must be extraordinarily well developed also. In a recent study, one radio-collared female who for two weeks during late winter was blinded by disease, still managed to traverse her home range and survive in reasonable condition.

Wildcats usually eat their prey where it is caught but sometimes carry it into cover. Occasionally they cache their prey by scraping debris over it or even by depositing it in trees.

Home ranges and movements Wildcats occupy home ranges of about 120 hectares which vary with sex, age and season. Adult females are relatively sedentary but will make an occasional brief foray into adjacent moorland and then return to their original range. Adult males occupy the largest home ranges, averaging 176 hectares but their location is only fixed in winter; in early spring once the snows melt, they travel large distances, probably in search of a mate. One radio-collared male travelled approximately 35km in six weeks, before contact with him was lost. Juvenile females occupy the smallest home ranges, average 77 hectares. They are fixed in location and normally within areas occupied by adults. On the other hand, juvenile males are highly nomadic and do not hold a regular home range. They stay in a particular valley for some days only and then move on to the next – possibly because of resident adults.

Large rivers appear to be a barrier to nomadic wildcats since the general line of their travels is deflected by them. But wildcats will readily cross smaller watercourses via bridges, fallen trees, or stepping stones.

Social organization and territoriality Although wildcats may have overlapping home ranges, they are basically solitary and hunt and camp by themselves. Even during the mating season contact between the sexes is brief and pairs meet only occasionally, over about two or three weeks. Wildcats do not cover their faeces (as most domestic cats attempt to do) but deposit them on conspicuous grass tussocks and heather clumps along trails within their home ranges. Faeces and presumably urine also, are probably used to advertise the presence of a resident wildcat. Whenever nomadic wildcats pass through a resident wildcat's home range, the rate of faeces marking tends to increase.

Mortality Wildcats have few natural enemies. Eagles have been recorded taking wildcat kittens and foxes may also do so, since foxes have been seen eating feral domestic kittens. Long severe winters, and predation by man are the chief causes of wildcat mortality. Adverse weather conditions, especially snow, decrease both prey populations and the time during which wildcats are able to hunt efficiently; many then die of starvation. Others are killed by vehicles in winter when they move to lower ground to scavenge along roadways.

In Scotland wildcats have always been regarded as vermin and even today at least 200 wildcats are snared, caught in Fenn traps or shot each year.

Conservation Wildcats are increasing both in numbers and distribution and this is probably related to the large-scale afforestation schemes undertaken recently by the Forestry Commission and by private landholders – which produce good habitats, plentiful prey and refuges in bad weather. Many gamekeepers now have a more enlightened attitude towards wildcats and realize that the number of rabbits they kill more than compensates for the loss of gamebirds. It is inevitable that many wildcats will continue to be killed in snares set for rabbits, since both gamekeepers and farmers have to protect their livelihood from rabbits, but the wildcat's future seems to be assured. Perhaps the greatest danger to wildcats is the eventual risk of having their gene pool swamped by hybridizing with domestic cats.

The Seals

ORDER PINNIPEDIA

C. F. Summers

The order Pinnipedia, the seals, is a group of animals which lives in the sea. The current explanation of their evolution, based upon fossil evidence, suggests that two groups underwent convergent evolution in adapting to life in the sea. One group, the Otarioidea, has descended from bear-like ancestors which entered the sea over 20 million years ago. The other, the Phocoidea, has descended from otter-like ancestors which entered the sea rather less than 20 million years ago.

The modern representatives of both groups show marked similarities. Their streamlined body-form has been developed by partial retention of the limbs within the contour of the body, so that they now form paddle-like flippers for swimming, and by the acquisition of a thick subcutaneous layer of fat (blubber) which smoothes out irregularities in shape and provides thermal insulation. Modifications to the vascular system allow the animal to dive to well over 50 fathoms (90m) or to remain submerged for 20–30 minutes. There is a disproportionately large blood volume and there are large amounts of the oxygen-carrying pigment myoglobin in the muscles. At the start of a dive the seal exhales and closes the nostrils. This has the effect of slowing down the heart-rate from over 50 per minute to less than 15 per minute. During this response to diving, called bradycardia, the blood supply to the brain is maintained, but that to the rest of the body is restricted. Residual air in the lungs is kept in the more rigid, less absorptive part of the respiratory system, so that very little nitrogen goes into solution and nitrogen narcosis, the bends, is avoided. Elevated concentrations of carbon dioxide in the blood are tolerated and, during the course of a dive, muscle respiration may become anaerobic. Nevertheless, despite these morphological and physiological adaptations to life in the sea, none of these animals is completely independent of the land. All come ashore to breed, moult and rest.

The order contains some 33 species, in three families. The family Otariidae, or eared seals, contains five species of sea-lions and nine species of fur seals; the Odobenidae contains a single species, the walrus. The remainder are the true or earless seals, the Phocidae. The main difference between the groups is related to their method of locomotion. The eared seals have hind limbs which can be turned forward under the body and used in four-footed locomotion on land. The true seals cannot use their hind flippers in this way and these play no part in locomotion on land; they are further distinguished by their lack of any trace of external ears and by the internal, as opposed to scrotal, position of the testes. The walrus displays some of the features of both groups but also has very specialized dentition.

Seals vary in size from around 1·5m in length and 50kg in weight for some female fur seals, up to more than 6m in length and 350kg in weight for male elephant seals. Males are not always larger than females – it is not so among Antarctic phocids – but it is a feature of those seals which are polygynous, a condition in which one male monopolizes a number of females during breeding. This trend is well developed in the otariids where each breeding male holds a territory containing a harem of many females. Phocids may be monogamous, as in the ringed seal and the hooded seal, or to a greater or lesser extent polygynous, as in the grey seal. Phocid males however, do not hold territories although they do maintain a position among oestrus cows from which rival males are excluded. Longevity and age at maturity differ from species to species and also within species. Female elephant seals may mature at two years of age. Female grey seals may live for over 40 years. Males normally mature later and die younger than females.

Food and predators While some species feed predominantly on a particular prey (for instance, crabeater seals and Antarctic fur seals feed on krill, leopard seals on penguin, and walruses on benthic invertebrates) most are both catholic and opportunistic in their choice of prey, taking a wide variety of fish and invertebrates.

Sharks may be important predators on sea-lions, fur seals, elephant seals and monk seals. Killer whales also take seals. A significant proportion of Cape fur seals may fall prey to jackals, and of ringed seals to polar bears and Arctic foxes, but the most important predator, especially in the northern hemisphere, probably has been man, although with the advent of protective legislation some species, such as the grey seal, have virtually no natural enemies.

Distribution and exploitation Otariids are widespread in the southern hemisphere and in the Pacific, whilst most phocids have a circumpolar distribution. In total the group contains around 30 million individuals but the abundance of species is very different. Crabeater seals form almost half the total and, at the other extreme, the Hawaiian and Mediterranean monk seals number just a few hundred individuals. The species which have been studied well enough to allow trends in population size to be established are those which have been most recently exploited by man. Seal products such as oil from elephant seals, hides from fur seals and phocid seal pups, ivory from walrus tusks and meat from many species, have been traditionally important to man and have been obtained with relative ease – even by primitive hunters. Consequently, with the exception of the Antarctic phocids, most species have been exploited to some extent.

The earliest examples of wildlife management are provided by the controlled exploitation, during the nineteenth century, of the South American and North Pacific fur seals. Under more recent controls, severely depleted stocks of Antarctic and Cape fur seals and of elephant seals have recovered to levels which can sustain limited exploitation. Some species, though now less abundant than in earlier times, have never been endangered and continue to be exploited on a sustainable basis, for example the harp and hooded seals and the walrus. The Convention for the Conservation of Antarctic Seals will, if ratified, ensure close seasons and catch limits for the leopard, Weddell, Ross and crabeater seals, in advance of a commercial scale exploitation of this very considerable resource. However, legal protection is unlikely to change the fate of the Mediterranean monk seal (whose Caribbean relative is probably extinct) because of the difficulty of enforcing protection of such a small stock in the many countries where that seal occurs. Neither will it help the ailing stock of grey seals in the Baltic where the population, depleted to a few hundred by over-hunting, cannot recover because of female sterility caused by marine pollution. But these are exceptions to the generally healthy state of seal stocks. Future threats to their well-being may arise from indirect contact with man, such as disturbance and habitat destruction caused by offshore drilling and by competition for important marine resources such as krill.

British Seals

C. F. Summers

Common seal

. . . That sunset, shrug after shrug,
The seals abandon the shore.
Across the sacrificial rock
Drifted a delicate smirr,
Tresses of haar, a fleece of fog.
It scarfed in one cold weave the selkie-flight. . . .

GEORGE MACKAY BROWN Winterfold

The two species of the order Pinnipedia which are native to the British Isles are both phocid seals – the common seal, *Phoca vitulina*, and the grey seal, *Halichoerus grypus*. Common seals measure about 1·5m in length and weigh up to 85–90kg (males may be slightly larger). Grey seals show marked sexual dimorphism. Females measure up to nearly 2m in length and weigh up to 220kg whereas males measure up to 2·3m in length and weigh over 300kg. Pelage pattern is similar for common seals of both sexes – numerous dark spots on a light ground. Grey seals have fewer, larger spots and the pelage pattern is darker than the background in the female and *vice versa* in the male. However, neither size nor pelage are good field diagnostics for these species, especially when the animals are in the sea. A better character is the shape of the head. In the common seal this is round and cat-like with a short concave snout with V-shaped alignment of the nostrils. The grey seal has a flatter horse-like head with a straight-profiled snout and nostrils in parallel formation. The dentition provides positive indentification – common seals have clearly tricuspid post-canine teeth while grey seals' post-canines have a single large cusp with additional rudimentary cusps.

Breeding Since seals come ashore to breed it is not surprising that this part of their life-cycle has been well studied in comparison with their activities in the sea. When ashore they are especially vulnerable to predation. The common seal is better adapted than the grey seal in this respect, since its pup is able to swim within a few hours of birth whereas grey seal pups are born above high water level and are more or less confined to land for several weeks after birth. This is reflected in the choice of breeding habitat. Grey seals congregate, often in many hundreds, at breeding assemblies on remote, often vegetated islands such as North Rona, the Monach Isles (Hebrides) and the Farne Islands (Northumbria), on exposed coasts such as the cliff-bound beaches of South Ronaldsay (Orkney) and Hermaness (Shetland) or on cave-beaches such as those scattered along the coasts of Cornwall and Pembrokeshire. During the autumn breeding season, which coincides with the period of equinoxial gales, these areas are particularly inaccessible from land. Common seals, which pup in the summer, exploit much more sheltered localities such as tidal skerries which abound on the west coast of Scotland, and tidal sandbanks which occur in many of the east coast estuaries such as the Wash, the Tay and the Moray Firth. These sites, which are totally immersed at high tide, must be close to deep water when exposed at low tide. Apparently suitable sandbanks which do not have rapid access to deep water, such as occur in the Solway, for example, are not used by seals.

At birth the common seal pup weighs about 10kg and has already shed its pale infant fur (or 'lanugo') in the uterus. It takes to the water on the first high tide after birth and is closely attended by its mother for several weeks. In contrast, the grey seal pup is born in its white infant fur and is attended by its mother on land for only 17 or 18 days. After this time the cow mates and returns to the sea. During lactation, the pup will grow rapidly from its birth weight of about 15kg to a weaning weight of up to 50kg. At about this time, some two or three weeks after birth, the pup moults its natal coat for the darker adult pelage and then spends a further period ashore before going to sea to feed itself for the first time, at about five weeks of age.

There is a dispersal of young pups of both grey and common seals from the birth site but it is not known whether this is an active process or if the young animals are carried, in some cases distances of several hundred nautical miles, by storms and currents. Nevertheless, it is usual for individuals, when mature, to enter the breeding population of their origin.

Grey seal cows enter the breeding stock at about five years of age but the bulls, although mature at more or less the same time, do not take part in breeding until they are about twice this age. The species therefore, is polygynous and has a bull:cow ratio of between 1:5 and 1:10 on the breeding grounds. Bulls do not have territories or harems in the strict sense but they do participate in ritual fights to maintain a presence near oestrus cows. The success of an individual bull is largely dependent on the length of time spent ashore during the breeding season. Young bulls, attempting to join the breeding stock, may spend only a few days ashore during which time they may be repeatedly put to flight by older bulls and may return to the sea without having achieved a successful mating. The most successful bulls may spend six to eight weeks ashore and mate several times with a number of different cows. As in all seals, and a number of other quite unrelated mammals, grey seals exhibit delayed implantation (see p.20). This delay before the start of a gestation period of about eight months is a mechanism to bring the development and birth of the entire new generation of grey seals approximately together. Because the females all give birth at approximately the same date the breeding stock has to spend only a comparatively brief period on land exposed to the predation of man.

There is no comparable social organization among common seals. They do not congregate into large assemblies to breed but remain more or less dispersed throughout the year, in groups which range in size from tens to hundreds, depending on the habitat. They mature at the age of four to six years, have a sex ratio of about 1:1 in the breeding groups and are thought to mate promiscuously. Nevertheless, female common seals tend to live rather longer than males (up to 30 years and 20 years respectively) just as in the polygynous grey seal (up to 35 years for cows and up to 25 years for bulls).

The breeding season imposes a considerable drain on the fat reserves of grey seals since both sexes fast while ashore. On returning to the sea the breeding group disperses over a wide area for a period of feeding to replenish these reserves before segregating into sexes towards the end of the winter, when they come ashore in large herds to moult. These moulting haul-outs contain seals of all ages and are found in different places from the breeding sites. After the moult the population disperses during a further feeding phase, before converging once more on the breeding grounds towards the end of the summer.

Distribution Seals have a generally northerly and westerly distribution in the British Isles. Both species occur in significant numbers in Shetland (4,000 common; 3,500 grey) Orkney (3,000 common; 15,000 grey) and the Hebrides (6,000 common; 40,000 grey) with smaller stocks in Ireland (2,000 common; 2,000 grey) and south-west Britain (3,000 grey). Two exceptions to this general pattern of distribution are the large populations of grey seals (8,500) at the Farne Islands – thought to be a separate breeding population from the Scottish stocks – and of common seals (6,500) in the Wash (probably more closely related to the German Bight stock, which extends from the Dutch Wadden Sea to west Jutland, than to those in Scotland). In total these figures represent about two thirds of the world's grey seals (the remainder occurring in Eastern Canada and Scandinavia) and somewhat less than one third of the European subspecies of the common seal (the remainder occurring in Iceland, Norway and the German Bight). Other sub-species of the common seal occur on both sides of North America, where it is called the harbour seal, and on the Asian coast of the North Pacific.

From neolithic times to the present century, seals have been hunted by man. Their carcases provided blubber for oil, pelts for clothing and meat for food. Although there are no reliable estimates of abundance in former times it is probable that, at the beginning of the present century, because of hunting by man, grey seals were fewer than common seals and that both species had previously been more abundant. At about this time, changes in the economies of remote areas, especially in Scotland, had already rendered seal hunting unimportant and this probably arrested the downward trends in their numbers. However, because of the publicity given to the grey seal pup hunting in the Hebrides, coupled with the unauthenticated claim that the species numbered only about 500 individuals in Great Britain, the first Grey Seal Protection Act was passed in 1914. As might have been expected the species thrived under this protection and that afforded by the second Grey Seal Protection Act passed in 1932; so now grey seals number approximately 70,000 individuals in the British Isles (compared with just over 20,000 common seals). Current disparity between the relative abundance of the two species, reflects the rapid recovery in grey seal numbers, rather than a continuing exploitation of common seals which have probably changed little in abundance during this period. A boom in common seal pup hunting during the 1960's did, however, give rise to some concern about over-exploitation of seals in Shetland and in the Wash and led to the passage of the current legislation, the Conservation of Seals Act, 1970. This Act, which applies to both species, was drafted not merely as a third protection act, but as a flexible legal instrument for implementing management policies which would take account of the various conflicting interests relating to seals. It gives the Secretary of State (for the Home Office in England and Wales and for the Scottish Office in Scotland) power to grant licences to kill seals for research, for the protection of fisheries, for commercial exploitation or for management purposes, as well as the power to enforce complete protection wherever this becomes necessary.

Food and exploitation Seals eat a wide variety of food including a number of invertebrate species but fish predominate in their diet and salmonid (e.g. salmon) gadoid (e.g. cod) and clupeoid (e.g. herring) species often form the bulk of the remains found in seal stomachs. In addition to feeding directly on commercially important fish species at sea, seals raid fishing gear, particularly set nets. They eat fish already caught, allow others to escape and sometimes damage the nets as well. A third effect of seals on fisheries is that the grey seal is the primary host for codworm, *Terranova decipiens*, a nematode parasite which matures in the seal stomach and is transmitted via an intermediate crustacean host to several species of gadoid fish. The larvae migrate from the fish gut into the musculature and have to be removed from fillets by hand before marketing. While it is very difficult to quantify precisely the impact of seals on fisheries, and even though this impact is probably less than, for example, the effects of over-fishing, it is clear that as seal stocks increase, their impact on the dwindling fish stocks in British waters is progressively damaging. The interests of the fishing industry would be best served by reducing the number of seals in British coastal waters. Since the early 1960's committees set up to advise ministers on seal stocks management issues have been recommending that grey seal numbers be controlled. But fishery protection grey seal pup culls, carried out since 1962 in Orkney, have been ineffective in reducing that stock, although they have to some extent checked its rate of increase.

It is doubtful if anyone has ever made a full time living from seal hunting in the British Isles. However, a handful of people scattered through the offshore islands of Scotland obtain an essential part of their livelihood by hunting seal pups during the breeding season.

The chief differences between these hunters and their neolithic counterparts are that the numbers of pups now taken are controlled by licence, rather than by the efficiency of the hunter, and that the products obtained are traded, rather than consumed by the hunter's community. In recent years these hunters have exploited common seals in the Wash, Shetland, Orkney and the Hebrides and grey seal stocks in Shetland and the Hebrides. The interests of pup hunters are best served by maintaining high stock levels which will sustain large scale cropping of pups.

Seals are seen from a third viewpoint by the 'nature lover' who, in general, is opposed to killing any wild animal, particularly one as appealing as a young seal. Among some conservationists there is a commitment to 'leaving nature to take care of itself'. This is exactly what was happening until, in 1914, the grey seal's only natural enemy, man, was legislated out of effective existence. One of the consequences of this was illustrated during the 1960's, at the Farne Islands where the density of seals on the breeding grounds was so high as to initiate a chain of events that started with changes in floristic composition and progressed through soil erosion to destruction of puffin burrows. By constructing new burrows in the following year the puffins exacerbated the soil erosion process, and so the whole situation deteriorated. The National Trust, which manages the islands as a nature reserve, responded by initiating a programme of adult culling in an attempt to prevent seals from pupping on the more vulnerable islands. This situation, which had arisen by applying a management regime of total protection over a long period of time, illustrates the complexity of conservation problems and the need for a positive attitude towards stock management.

Public interest in seal culls has been extraordinarily high and inconsistent with its apparent lack of interest in the use of myxomatosis against rabbits and culls of red deer – to take two examples which might be regarded as comparable. A great deal of controversy is, no doubt, fuelled by the emotional reporting by the media, particularly on the cruelty aspect. The Conservation of Seals Act 1970 specifically bans, except under licence, the use of poisons and inappropriate firearms for killing seals, and outlaws strychnine in any circumstances. In issuing licences the Secretary of State has the power to specify the means of killing, to ensure that it is humane.

The pelts of all pups killed under licence in the UK are inspected by representatives of the Secretary of State to ensure that the specified method of killing has been used. Adults are most humanely killed by a high velocity rifle used at close range. Culls of adult seals in the UK have always been observed by representatives of the RSPCA (at the Farne Islands) and of the Scottish SPCA (in the Hebrides). However, to avoid causing unnecessary suffering some indirect effects of grey seal culls have to be taken into consideration. The disturbance of killing adults in a breeding assembly causes some of the surviving mothers to desert their pups. In addition, pregnant cows which are forced by the activities of the marksmen to pup in unsuitable sites may subsequently fail to rear their pups successfully. It is necessary to build into adult culling programmes a provision for locating and destroying any ailing pups, but natural mortality at big breeding assemblies, such as North Rona, is so high that about a third of the pups born each year die before they are old enough to go to sea. The reduction of this level of mortality is not a simple consequence of reducing the size of the assembly by adult culls. Grey seals are highly gregarious and crowd into preferred parts of a breeding area. For example, at the Farne Islands the number of cows taking part in breeding was reduced from over 2,000 in 1971 to about 1,400 in 1976; yet the number of pups born on Staple Island, the preferred island in the group, remained the same throughout. This behaviour mechanism ensures that bulls maintaining a position in a densely populated part of an assembly will fertilize a large number of cows, and that a cow which pups in such a place will be fertilized by a successful bull. It also shows that culling seals because they are 'too over-crowded for their own good' is clearly nonsensical. The issues affecting seal stock management are sufficiently complex without being obscured by anthropomorphism.

Artiodactyls

ORDER ARTIODACTYLA

Michael Brambell

The Artiodactyls are ungulates – that is hoofed animals which carry their weight on the hardened ends of the digits of their fore and hind legs. The order includes pigs, deer, sheep, antelopes and many other animals. They are also known as the even-toed or cloven-hoofed animals – as distinct from the odd-toed Perissodactyls which consists of the horses, tapirs and rhinoceroses. This distinction between the two orders may seem trivial, but really it is fundamental for it reflects the whole history of the Artiodactyls, a group of species descended from a common ancestral population living over 60 million years ago, by which time it had already diverged from the Perissodactyls.

Locomotion The name Artiodactyla suggests that the feet are important to the group's success, and the fact that they walk on the tips of their toes is part of the reason for it. That single adaptation effectively lengthens the leg without any other change in the anatomy. An animal on tiptoe can reach higher and run faster, for the same effort, than can any plantigrade animal. On hard, flat ground the single hoof of the horse's foot may have an advantage, both for speed and for wear, but there are few habitats where the ground is consistently even and hard, and where there is also abundant food, rich in energy. If the ground is not flat and hard the split hoof of the Artiodactyl has a further advantage – it can spread out so that the load-bearing surface is increased.

Some Artiodactyls have become adapted to life on consistently soft surfaces. In these the two outer digits, the dew claws, have also developed hard tips, so that, as the two main digits sink into the ground, the dew claws take a large share of the animal's weight. Thus, at one extreme, we find such animals as the Asiatic or water buffalo with large splayed digits and well-developed dew claws, living in marshy areas, and at the other, animals like chamois with petite hooves and vestigial dew claws, living on the most rugged of mountain sides. Meanwhile the vast majority of Artiodactyls live in the tropical and temperate savannahs and woodlands, with feet intermediate between these two extremes.

Spread of the Artiodactyls Until man began to have such a dramatic effect upon the earth's surface, disrupting every habitat so far colonized by other mammals, the Artiodactyls were still successfully expanding, as, for example, were the marsupials, bats, rodents, carnivores and whales. But this expansion was at the expense of other mammal groups such as the rabbits, elephants, horses and rhinoceroses. All of these were on their way out – on their way to join other once-successful animal groups which had flourished, faded and become extinct. The Artiodactyls were so successful because they were able to exploit the green foodstuffs which abounded in the grasslands and forests of all continental land areas, except Antarctica. Had they reached Australia without man's help, they might have ousted the kangaroos and wallabies from the energy-rich niche provided by that continent's grassland and bush.

Digestion Artiodactyls feed directly on green plants but, like all other mammals, they lack the kind of enzymes capable of breaking down the cellulose of which so much plant material consists. To overcome this they give space and support to myriads of micro-organisms which do have the right enzymes, and are thus able to convert the cellulose into their own body tissue. The micro-organisms grow and multiply until they overflow from their haven and meet the harsh realities of the rest of their host's digestive tract. There they are attacked by the hosts own enzymes which are well capable of digesting the materials into which the cellulose has been changed. So the host mammal is really feeding not on the food that it itself eats, but on the micro-organisms which it has harboured. Both the Artiodactyls and the Perissodactyls deal with cellulose by this microbial digestion, but in the Artiodactyls the first step takes place in the forepart of the stomach, which allows the product to be subjected to the whole length of the digestive tract before being voided. In the Perissodactyls only the terminal part of the gut is involved in microbial digestion, so the Artiodactyl can make more efficient use of the energy locked up in green food, than even the horse is able to do. The fore-gut adaptations are most advanced in the deer, giraffes, antelopes, cattle, goats and sheep. Nevertheless the hippopotamuses and camels have sufficient adaptations for some microbial fermentation to be complete, before the food reaches the true digestive areas of the gut; only the pigs retain a simple digestive system.

Classification The order Artiodactyla consists of nine Families: the pigs and peccaries, closely related to each other; the hippopotamuses, fairly closely related to the pigs; the camels in north Africa and western Asia, with their close relatives in South America, the llamas and their cousins; the little chevrotains or mouse deer; the deer family; the giraffe and the okapi; the pronghorn; and lastly the great family of bovids containing cattle, antelopes, duikers, gazelles, goats and sheep.

Wild British Artiodactyls now include only two indigenous species – the red deer and the roe deer – but there are several introduced species of deer. In the past at one time or another, wild boar, hippopotamuses, 'Clacton' fallow deer, Irish giant deer, reindeer, moose, wisent or European bison, aurochs, gazelles, saiga, musk ox and a wild sheep have lived in Britain, reflecting both warmer and colder phases in the history of these islands.

British Deer

D. I. Chapman

Roe deer

We do not discern those eyes
Watching in the snow;
Lit by lamps of rosy dyes
We do not discern those eyes
Wandering aglow,
Fourfooted, tiptoe.

THOMAS HARDY (1840–1928) The Fallow Deer at the Lonely House

The deer family, which comprises about 40 species, occurs throughout the Americas, Asia and Europe – some members have been introduced into Africa and Australasia. Six species live wild in Britain and deer are probably more numerous here today than they have been since Elizabethan times: there are certainly more species in the wild and they are continuing to spread. Roe and red deer are indigenous. Fallow deer died out during the last Ice Age which ended some

10,000 years ago and were reintroduced by the Normans. The other three species – Chinese muntjac, Chinese water deer and sika deer – were introduced in the latter half of the nineteenth century or early this century. Reindeer were present in Britain in the postglacial period but probably had become extinct by Roman times. Domesticated reindeer were reintroduced to Scotland in 1952, but the herd is managed and cannot be regarded as wild or even feral.

Indigenous and established introduced species.

	Shoulder height cm	*Weight kg*	*Status*
Chinese muntjac			
male	up to 48	av: 14	Introduced late 19th
female	up to 45	av: 12	or early 20th century
Chinese water deer			
male	up to 60	11–14	Introduced about 1900
female	up to 50	9–11	
Fallow deer			
male	90–95	46–80	Reintroduced by the
female	70–85	35–52	Normans
Red deer			
male	up to 122	93–122	Indigenous
female	up to 114	68–90	Measurements in Scotland
Roe deer			
male	64–67	av: 26	Indigenous
female	63–67	av: 24	Measurements in Dorset
Sika deer			
male	av: 81	av: 64	Introduced 19th century
female	av: 73	av: 41	Measurements in Dorset

The six species of British wild deer vary widely in size, from the diminutive muntjac to the mighty red deer – Britain's largest land mammal. The shoulder height and weight of adult deer are given in the Table above. Weight in particular, varies greatly with age, condition and locality and the values given must be regarded as no more than a guide. For example, a mature male red deer in southern England where food is plentiful and the climate mild, may weigh 180kg but in the harsher Scottish Highlands, the average is about half this weight (see Table, weights are of the complete animal).

During the evolution of deer, elongation, fusion and loss of bones have resulted in the ankle being situated half way up the hind leg as the hock, and the wrist becoming the 'knee' of the front leg. Thus deer walk on their toes only, rather than on the whole foot. Similarly an athlete runs not on the flat of his foot but on his toes, bringing the bones of the sole temporarily into line with the rest of the leg. Thus he adopts the condition which has evolved as the normal arrangement in the fleet-footed and agile deer.

Apart from Chinese water deer, the adult males of deer are characterized by having on the skull just above the eyes, a pair of permanent, hair-covered, bony outgrowths called pedicles. Pedicles, which develop at puberty, support the bony antlers which are cast and regrown annually. Whilst growing, antlers are covered with soft furry skin known as 'velvet'. This velvet dies and is shed when the antlers are fully grown and have become dead bone.

Hearing, sight and smell are all very important to deer. Their large ears, situated high up on the sides of the head, can be moved independently of each other through 180°. They have large eyes situated on the side of the head which give them a wide field of view. Smell is probably the most important of the deer's senses. A deer which has been disturbed but is not quite sure of the cause, may be seen to raise its head and sniff the air. Deer have specialized areas of skin which contain much greater numbers of both sebaceous and sweat glands than does 'normal' skin. These areas, which produce an oily secretion, are known as scent glands. Depending upon the species of deer, scent glands may occur on the forehead, at the corner of the eyes, between the toes of the hind feet, on the hind legs just below the hocks and, in the males of some species of deer, on the prepuce. Scent from these glands is deposited on the soil and vegetation. This may be done either casually as the deer walks or as the animal purposefully rubs its glands on trees and bushes. Scent may also be deposited when deer urinate. Some male deer develop a very pungent odour at the time of the rut and mark their territories with scent. Although the purpose of scenting is almost certainly communication, and even to the relatively insensitive human nose there are differences in odour between the different glands, the language of the deers' various scents still has to be deciphered by man. Odour may also be important in food selection, enabling the animal to choose suitable plants and fruits.

Almost nothing is known about the enemies of deer in Britain other than man. Dogs and foxes are frequently cited as taking weak or young animals, but most of the information is anecdotal. Deer no longer die in their hundreds from the 'murrain' as they did in past centuries, although pneumonia caused by parasitic lungworms is reported to kill large numbers of young roe deer in Cranborne Chase, Dorset.

It is often said that man is the deer's worst enemy and certainly those who set snares or take 'pot shots' at deer with unsuitable weapons are frequently guilty of cruelty. Nevertheless, deer are still spreading through the countryside. Sooner or later this increase brings deer into conflict with agricultural, forestry or horticultural interests. So, because of the absence of effective wild predators, man has to keep the number of deer in check. A sensible balance, fair to man and beast, must be found.

Deer control Fallow and red deer used to be widely hunted by hounds but only a few packs still survive. The New Forest Buck-hounds take about ten fallow deer a year but on occasions, particularly in early spring, aim only at disturbing deer from agricultural land. There are over 1,000 fallow deer in the New Forest area and 300 or 400 have to be killed each year. Obviously therefore, hunting with hounds cannot be regarded as an effective method of deer control.

Undoubtedly the best and most humane method of deer control is shooting by an experienced marksman with a rifle. The killing of most species of deer is covered by legislation which stipulates close seasons (Table p.207), the times of day when deer must not be shot, and the type of weapons permitted. Deer may not be killed during the appropriate close season except to prevent suffering, or serious damage to crops including growing timber. At present there are no close seasons for Chinese muntjac or Chinese water deer. The close seasons do not, unfortunately, always take account of the biology of the animals. Female fallow deer, for example, may be killed legally from 1st November onwards, although they may still be lactating and their fawns only four or five months old. So, as lactation frequently continues into January, many fawns whose mothers have been shot will be deprived of this nourishment, with unknown effect upon their ability to survive the winter. On the other hand, the close season starts again on 1st March (in England and Wales); but for this there is no sound biological reason, because fallow fawns are not born until the latter part of May, at the earliest. Until more is known of the effects of being orphaned, it would be far better, for the fawns' well-being if the close season for female fallow were extended to 31st December and started again on 1st April. A similar case can be made for altering the close seasons for females of the other species of deer, although not necessarily to the same dates.

When a young fawn is found alone, the mother's habit of leaving

Close seasons for deer

	England & Wales	Scotland
Fallow deer		
male	1 May–31 Jul.	1 May–31 Jul.
female	1 Mar.–31 Oct.	16 Feb.–20 Oct.
Red deer		
male	1 May–31 Jul.	21 Oct.–30 Jun.
female	1 Mar.–31 Oct.	16 Feb.–20 Oct.
Roe deer		
male	1 Nov.–31 Mar.	21 Oct.–30 Apr.
female	1 Mar.–31 Oct.	1 Mar.–20 Oct.
Sika deer		
male	1 May–31 Jul.	1 May–31 Jul.
female	1 Mar.–31 Oct.	16 Feb.–20 Oct.

The dates are inclusive. There are no close seasons for Chinese muntjac or Chinese water deer.

it is frequently misinterpreted as abandonment, so the fawn is 'rescued' and taken home. This well-intentioned but misguided action usually leads to distress and even to cruelty, because few people have facilities for feeding and housing deer. Furthermore, hand-reared male deer can become extremely aggressive and dangerous. Such 'lost' fawns should be left alone: the mother is unlikely to return while human visitors are still present.

The Chinese Muntjac

The adult Chinese muntjac, *Muntiacus reevesi*, is a small, unspotted, reddish-brown deer slightly duller and darker in winter than in summer. Its head is a ginger-brown and females have a black triangle on the forehead. The males' antlers consist of a single beam which curves downwards and inwards at the extremity and there may also be a very short brow tine. The muntjac's legs are slender and pale on the inner sides. Its tail is about 10cm long, ginger on top and white underneath. When running the muntjac carries its head lower than its rounded back, presumably an adaptation to its life in thick vegetation.

The Chinese muntjac is a native of China and Taiwan. It was introduced early in the present century by the Duke of Bedford on his estate at Woburn Abbey in Bedfordshire. It now occurs over much of southern England from Devon to Sussex, and as far north as Lincolnshire. It has not been recorded in Northern Ireland, Scotland or Wales. The Chinese muntjac's closest relative, the Indian muntjac occurs in India and adjacent parts of Asia.

Food The diet of muntjac is entirely vegetable and they are browsers rather than grazers – eating ivy, brambles and other shrubs and trees, in preference to grasses. Fruits are also readily eaten. They appear to do little damage to crops and trees, probably because of their small size and numbers. Their fraying of tree seedlings and fondness for roses and other shrubs can bring them into conflict with man.

The diminutive muntjac, introduced from China, is not much larger than a fox. The male has small, simple antlers which point backwards from permanent projections. The female has a black triangle on the forehead.

Breeding and territoriality Muntjac, unlike other species of wild deer in Britain, do not have a well-defined rutting period. Females breed throughout the year and consequently newborn fawns may be found at any time. Female muntjac come into season within a few days of giving birth, so they can be pregnant almost continuously. After a gestation period of seven months, a single fawn is born, weighing 100–150g. The young are spotted at birth but at about six weeks the spots begin to fade, and by three months of age, the adult coat is attained.

Muntjac have a characteristic, single bark which may be repeated at frequent intervals, often for many minutes. Barking is particularly common around the time a fawn is born and when a doe is in season, although it also occurs when the deer are alarmed. Both fawns and adults also squeak and, if caught or injured, give a piercing shriek.

Muntjac are thought to live in family groups of male, female and young. Mutual grooming between the sexes is common and adult males as well as females groom young fawns.

Muntjac mark their home ranges by stripping the outer layers from small shoots and plants such as thistles using their teeth to do so. Afterwards the vegetation is anointed by scent glands, situated on the head both between and below the eyes. Muntjac droppings, which accumulate in well-marked latrines, are small, shiny, black, cylindrical pellets, each with a point at one end and a depression at the other. As aggressive behaviour occurs among muntjac, particularly between adult males, droppings and the fraying of stems may be territorial markers warning others not to intrude.

Control Muntjac may be shot throughout the year. As the female may give birth at any season it is difficult to decide the right time to cull them, should this become necessary. It is probably better to shoot females in the summer than in the winter, because orphaned fawns will have a better chance of survival.

The Chinese Water Deer

Our knowledge of the Chinese water deer, *Hydropotes inermis*, is extremely meagre and is based almost entirely on observations of captive animals. Chinese water deer are slightly taller and more

A male Chinese water deer with the distinctive protruding canines in the upper jaw, which are not usually apparent in the female.

leggy than muntjac, but with similarly elevated hind quarters. They have round, beady, black eyes, a pale chin and a black nose surrounded by an area of white. The ears are large, rounded and situated high up on the head. The tail is short. Adult males have large upper canine teeth (5cm long) which protrude as tusks from the sides of the mouth. The upper canines of the females are much smaller and do not usually project below the upper lips. In summer, adults of both sexes are a uniform reddish-sandy colour with paler underparts. In winter the adults have a very thick coat which is of a brownish-sandy colour, flecked with grey. Newborn animals are browny-fawn with rows of white spots along each side of the body. As the fawn grows up the spots fade away.

Distribution In spite of their high fertility, Chinese water deer are uncommon in England, perhaps because of high mortality and unsuitable habitats. In their native countries, eastern China and Korea, they inhabit reed beds and estuarine swamps. In England they are confined mainly to parts of Bedfordshire and Hertfordshire near Whipsnade and Woburn Park from which they originally escaped, but they are present also in Woodwalton Fen in Cambridgeshire and in some of the reed beds of the Norfolk Broads. Chinese water deer have no close relatives.

Food Chinese water deer are grazing animals – grasses and other small plants forming the main part of their diet.

Breeding Chinese water deer rut in November and December, followed by the birth of fawns in May and June. Females attain puberty and become pregnant at their first rut when about six months old and give birth for the first time when one year old. They are prolific animals and may have five or so fawns at a birth, although from one to three is more usual. Males are territorial at the time of the rut, marking their areas by scrapes in the soil and fraying plant stems with their teeth.

The European Fallow Deer

The fallow deer, *Dama dama*, is common throughout England and is found in many areas of Northern Ireland, Scotland and Wales. It is the species most favoured in deer parks. Fallow deer are long-legged, similar in size to a domestic goat, and occur in a wide variety of colours. Adult males are characterized by antlers which are broader at the top than at the base, unlike those of any other species of wild deer in this country. In well-developed individuals, the antlers are palmate, resembling a hand. Fallow deer can be divided into four main colour varieties: common, menil, white or black.

The summer coat of common fallow is a rich reddish-brown over the head, upper side of the neck, back and flanks. The back and upper flanks are splattered with white spots. A black stripe runs down the middle of the back from the nape of the neck to the end of the tail. The underside of the head and neck and the lower legs are pale, almost white, and the chest, belly and underside of the tail distinctly white. The buttocks are also white but bordered by a black line shaped like a horseshoe. In winter, this variety assumes a darker, duller, grey-brown appearance with the spots becoming barely detectable. The belly and tail retain their summer coloration.

A male fallow deer, in winter coat, rubs his antlers against a tree, marking his territory.

The menil variety is a paler form of the common fallow. White fallow deer are not total albinos because their eyes, and often their noses, have normal pigmentation. At close quarters they may be seen to be very slightly dappled. The black variety has a glossy summer coat, black or dark brown on the head, back, flanks, buttocks and tail, with a barely detectable paler dapple. The underside of the neck, lower flanks and belly are mushroom colour. In winter, the coat is duller and browner. There are many variations in these colour varieties, particularly intermediate between the common and the menil. Wild herds of fallow deer of mixed varieties are not uncommon. (Colour illustration facing p.195.)

Distribution For centuries, fallow deer have provided food, sport and pleasure for man and the same is true today. They are widely spread throughout the British Isles, especially in the south. Happily they can co-exist with man: wild fallow live on the edge of at least two large housing estates within 40km of the centre of London.

The European fallow deer has been widely distributed by man and occurs now in 36 countries spread over six continents. Its closest relative, the Persian fallow deer, *Dama dama mesopotamica*, which now occurs in the wild only in one small area of south-west Iran, is on the verge of extinction.

Food Fallow deer are predominantly grazing animals, feeding in fields, meadows and pastures but usually near woodland. They eat a wide variety of plants and fruits as well as grasses; the remains of over 110 plant species have been found in the stomachs of fallow deer from the New Forest.

Breeding Fallow deer are gregarious and, with the exception of adult males, spend much of their time in herds. These herds usually comprise adult females, yearlings and fawns. For most of the year the adult males form small bachelor groups and live apart from the main female herds, returning in August and September, before the rut.

The rut, which occurs in October and November, is a period of tremendous activity. A rutting male parades up and down his territory, groaning frequently and chivvying the females which have been attracted to him. Both males and females attain puberty in their second year but, whereas the latter become pregnant as yearlings and give birth for the first time when two years old, the mature males probably prevent most yearling males from breeding. Fawns are born in late May and June after a gestation period of about eight months. Male fawns weigh about 4·6kg: females slightly less.

The Red Deer

The red deer, *Cervus elaphus*, has been immortalized in Landseer's famous painting 'The Monarch of the Glen' beloved by our Victorian ancestors, and much of our knowledge of red deer in Britain comes from studies made of those in the Scottish Highlands. Little is known of their behaviour in lowland, woodland habitats. The summer coat of adults is usually a sleek reddish-brown with a dark brown line running down the nape of the neck and along the back. The throat, underparts and legs are paler. They have a small tail, 15–20cm long, and a buff rump patch which extends above the tail. Occasionally a faint dappling is seen on the sides and rumps but distinct spots do not occur. The winter coat, which develops from September to November and is shed in the following April and May, is generally brown and much coarser. Adult males carry large branching antlers and, in winter, a coarse mane. The antlers are cast from March to June. New antlers are grown during spring and summer and become fully developed from July to October. Newborn calves are reddish-brown and have numerous white spots over the back, sides and rump. By two or three months old these spots have faded away and the colour of the calf's winter coat becomes similar to that of the adult.

A male red deer, surrounded by his harem of females during the rutting season, throws back his head to make the loud, deep, drawn-out roaring mating call of the species.

Distribution The main area for red deer in Britain is in northern Scotland where the population is estimated at over a quarter of a million animals. Small populations occur on Dartmoor and Exmoor, and in the Lake District, the New Forest, the Roches and Thetford Chase (Norfolk). A few are present in Wales and in Ireland. Red deer of various forms are distributed widely over Europe, the Middle East, the USSR and Asia as far east as China. They have been introduced into Australasia and South America. In New Zealand where, owing to the absence of indigenous browsing mammals, the endemic vegetation has developed no prickles or other resistance to their depredations, the introduced deer have devastated large areas and pose a very difficult problem. The wapiti of North America is closely related and is probably best regarded as a large sub-species of red deer.

Food Red deer eat a wide variety of plants depending upon what is available. On open hill ground, grasses and sedges together with heather, form most of their food but they will browse seedlings and trees and shrubs wherever available. Browsing and stripping of bark frequently brings them into conflict with foresters. This is a particularly serious problem in parts of Scotland where the deer's traditional wintering areas have been planted with trees. At its worst, plantations are ruined and natural regeneration ceases. When hard weather sets in, red deer may start raiding crops and so bring themselves into conflict with farmers as well as foresters.

Habits Red deer may be found in both deciduous and coniferous woodland, fields and open moorland. In summer, in the Highlands, deer move to ground above the tree line but in winter descend to lower ground, where there is more food and shelter. There is also a daily pattern of more limited movement, the deer moving to higher ground for the day and descending in the evening to feed. They are sociable animals but the sexes live apart, except during the October rut. The matriarchial female herd is composed of a mature animal, her adult relatives and their dependent young of both sexes. Herds of adult males are based upon a linear hierarchy which is related to the size and state of the animal's antlers. A dominant male will fall in the hierarchy when he casts his antlers and, when all the males have cast their antlers, a fluid situation develops. As the antlers grow again the hierarchy re-develops.

Breeding Red deer are seasonal breeders and although males are fertile from about September to March, most conceptions occur during the rut which is a period of hypersexual activity. Adult males feed little during this period but spend much of their time roaring, wallowing in muddy hollows, rounding up groups of females and attempting to fend off rivals.

Relationship with man The hunting of red deer by man for food, clothing and implements has occurred from time immemorial but the sport of stalking probably reached its heyday only in the late nineteenth century with the rise of the traditional Scottish 'deer forest'. Red deer have been culled by stalking for many years and if done properly with a rifle it is humane, even if it is done for sport. Apparently however the shooting ability of many stalkers leaves much to be desired, for a recent report on red deer in South Ross states 'Inexpert shooting, principally on the part of guests (of owners of deer forests), results in many wounded and badly shot beasts'. One venison dealer estimated that 25 per cent of male red deer that he received were damaged in the haunch or saddle. Stalking is still extremely important in Scotland and over half a million hectares of open hill land are designated as 'deer forest' where 25,000 to 30,000 red deer are killed annually. Red deer are thus a valuable resource, providing an important source of income from the rough land they occupy.

The Roe Deer

The roe deer, *Capreolus capreolus*, is a smallish, unspotted, brown deer, almost tail-less and with a distinctive black nose and a white chin. When alarmed the pale buff or white hairs of the rump patch are erected to form a 'powder puff'. Roe cast and re-grow their antlers in winter. The lower halves of the antlers of roe deer are rugged, unlike those of other wild deer in Britain; they very rarely exceed 30cm in length. The natural history of the roe deer differs in many ways from that of the other wild deer in Britain. Roe rut in the summer. After mating there is a period of delayed implantation (see p.20). In no other member of the deer family is this known to occur. Roe usually have twins.

The summer coat of adult roe varies from sandy to the more usual bright reddish-brown with paler underparts. The winter coat is thick, dense and varies from greyish brown to almost black merging with a white or fawn-coloured belly. There may also be one or two pale patches on the throat. Newborn fawns have a sandy-brown coat flecked with black and with white spots on the sides and back. The spots soon start to fade away and have disappeared by about five months old, when the fawns have grown their winter coat.

Distribution The roe deer is indigenous to Britain but probably most of those in England are descendants of animals introduced during the nineteenth century. The species was common in England in mediaeval times but by the early eighteenth century had become extinct there, except near the Scottish border. They were reintroduced into Dorset in 1800 and deer from Germany were liberated on the

Suffolk Breckland in about 1884. They are now widespread in southern England, occurring from Surrey and East Sussex to Cornwall and Gloucestershire in the west, and in Cambridgeshire, Essex, Norfolk and Suffolk. They are common also in the Lake District, in Northumberland and parts of Lancashire and North Yorkshire. They are common over much of Scotland but are absent from Northern Ireland and Wales. Roe deer occur over much of Europe and closely related forms are found in China, Korea, northern Asia and Siberia.

Food Roe are predominantly browsing animals choosing, for preference bramble and the twigs of trees, although they do graze in fields to some extent.

Habitat and Breeding Roe deer occur in a wide variety of woodland, in open moorland provided there is deep heather, and in marshy reed beds. Some kind of cover seems obligatory although they can be seen in fields and along woodland edges. Roe are either solitary or live in small groups of male, female and young, but they may congregate to form herds in winter. Males exhibit aggressive and territorial behaviour from April to August even though the rut is only in July and August. The territorial behaviour of female roe is limited to when they are giving birth, from about mid-May to mid-June.

About 75 per cent of adult females carry twins, about five per cent carry triplets and the remainder singletons. Fawns are suckled and can walk within a few hours of birth. After being fed, fawns are usually left hidden and they 'freeze' to avoid detection, if danger looms. As the young males grow up they try to establish territories of their own. If successful, they remain in the area; otherwise they emigrate in the spring, when in their second or third year. Females may also emigrate at this age.

Man has hunted roe deer for food since prehistoric times and hunting them for sport is still very popular in this country and in continental Europe.

The Sika Deer

The sika deer, *Cervus nippon*, is similar in size to the fallow deer and it is easy to confuse the two species. In summer, adult sika are a glossy chestnut red with a dark stripe down the spine and a row of white spots on each side. More spots are present from the base of the neck, over the flanks to the rump. The belly and inside of the legs are fawn coloured. Sika have a white rump patch, bordered with black, which can be flared out when they are alarmed and appears like a large, heart-shaped powder puff. In this respect sika are like roe deer but can be distinguished from them by a long, white tail sometimes with a thin dark line down the middle of the upper side. In winter, sika are much darker and lose most of their spots, if not all. Females are light grey with pale underparts whereas the males are much darker and may be almost black. In September adult males develop a thick mane which lasts until they moult again in the spring. Sika calves are born with a brown coat spotted with white. By about three months of age they have almost lost their baby coats and resemble adults.

The antlers of adult sika deer are similar to those of red deer except that they rarely have more than four points on each antler.

A sika deer stag driving his hinds, all in winter coats. Sika antlers never have more than one forward branch at the base.

Distribution The sika is a native of eastern Asia including China, Japan and Taiwan. It was introduced into Britain just over a hundred years ago.

In England, sika deer have become established most successfully on the heathlands of south-east Dorset. Smaller numbers occur in the New Forest and in the Bolton-by-Bowland area of Lancashire. Escapes from parks have been reported in several other areas, but they have not flourished. Sika have been more successful in Scotland and may be seen in the Mull of Kintyre in Argyllshire, near Loch Ness in Invernesshire and in Caithness, Peebleshire and Ross and Cromarty. They are established in a few places in Northern Ireland.

Sika have been introduced to several other European countries, North America and Australasia.

Food Sika appear to be grazers rather than browsers, at least in south-east Dorset which is the only area in England where their natural history has been thoroughly studied. They seem to feed in fields at night and are rarely seen in daylight.

Breeding Male and female sika live apart for most of the year, coming together only for the rut in September and October. Female sika usually live either with their calf or in small parties during the day, but congregate into loosely-knit herds in the feeding areas at night. They are less secretive than the adult males, which usually live singly or in small parties. Male calves leave their mothers when about seven to nine months old, but female calves remain with their dams until the next year's calves are due, when they are driven off. During the rut, the adult males mark out and defend territories. They appear to spend most of the time in these areas whereas the females continue to move out of the woods to feed in the fields at dusk. The male's rutting call is distinctive, being a three-times or four-times repeated whistle, which rises and falls. After a gestation period of about eight months, a single calf about 3kg in weight is born, usually in May or June.

Pain in Animals

Nigel Hawkes

In the year 1756 the philosopher Burke remarked that 'pain and pleasure are simple ideas incapable of definition'. The English language, so well equipped in other directions, is ill-adapted for describing pain except in a crude and mechanistic way. It is surprising that a sensation so universal and so vivid should have remained almost beyond the range of language. In her essay *On Being Ill*, Virginia Woolf wrote that 'the merest schoolgirl, when she falls in love, has Shakespeare and Keats to speak for her; but let a sufferer try to describe a pain in his head and language at once runs dry'. The purpose of pain is clear enough. It is nature's warning signal, her way of urging the sufferer to escape from a potentially damaging situation. Without this mechanism all kinds of injuries could ensue. For instance, if a leper whose hand is badly affected, and therefore does not feel pain, accidentally touches a hot iron, he will not withdraw his hand unless he has otherwise perceived the danger. By then his hand may be irretrievably damaged. A few human beings, congenital analgesics, are born insensible to pain. They never live long.

If pain is hard to define or to describe, it can at least be anatomized. What happens when we or any other mammal damages itself? The first step is that nerve endings lying in the skin are stimulated to transmit a message of pain through the nerves to the spinal cord. The nerve endings lie in a series of overlapping networks of fibres in the skin, so that any injury triggers more than one network, despatching a series of parallel messages. The rates at which these messages travel depend on the characteristics of the fibres carrying them; the first sharp stab of pain is carried by thick nerve fibres at high transmission speeds, but the aching or burning pain which follows, often after a perceptible delay, is carried by finer fibres at a much slower speed.

Common sense might suggest that pain would be transmitted directly up the spinal cord to the brain, taking priority over more humdrum sensations, in the same way that a general's orders will monopolize an army's telegraph system. But this is not quite what happens. Before the pain signals can begin their ascent to the brain, they have to pass through a region in the spinal cord packed with short interconnected nerve fibres which appear to act as filters or discriminators. These have the ability to modify the message presented to them, or even to abolish it altogether.

Once in the spinal cord, sensations of pain are carried upwards through bundles of nerves in the front and side of the spinal cord. They pass through the lower part of the brain along several distinct routes to reach the higher regions of the brain. Three of these routes can be blocked by anaesthetics, while one is only slightly affected and one not affected at all. Cutting the pathways surgically can reduce or eliminate pain, but the picture is far from simple. In general, attempts to eliminate pain by cutting the nervous pathways have had only modest success; it appears that, in some circumstances, the nervous system can adapt itself and find new pathways fairly easily.

Within the brain itself, it now appears that the pain can be modified chemically. One of the most striking discoveries in brain chemistry over the past ten years has been that the brain possesses its own opiates, morphine-like chemicals which are assumed to act as natural pain-killers. Some people have speculated that the existence of these chemicals in the brain may explain why it is that soldiers injured in battle often feel no pain, or provide a mechanism to explain how anaesthesia can be produced in some subjects by acupuncture needles. Significantly, when human patients anaesthetized by acupuncture are injected with the drug naloxone (which abolishes the effect of opiate-like drugs) then the pain returns. Whether the discovery of the natural pain-killers, known as endorphins ('the morphine within') or enkephalins, will lead to the production of totally safe and effective pain-killers remains to be seen; but that is certainly the object of much of the research.

All these anatomical mechanisms are common to man and to most mammals; indeed, it is through research with animals that most of them have been discovered. Endorphins, for example, have been isolated from the hagfish, the oldest vertebrate known, and from the earthworm. It might then be tempting to assume that since the mechanisms are the same in man and in other animals, all species have the same experience of pain. In fact, no such general conclusion can yet be drawn. The reason is simply that the existence of an apparatus for transmitting pain provides no conclusive evidence as to how that pain is perceived. Even within a single species, the human being, there are some remarkable examples of how the perception of pain differs from individual to individual. In some cultures, for example, childbirth is not regarded as a particularly uncomfortable or difficult experience; yet in Western society it is not only regarded as painful, but actually *is* painful. Cultural conditioning can transform the nature of an experience.

Clearly then, the sensation of pain varies greatly according to circumstances. In the chase, for example, pain may be less acutely perceived – as in the heat of battle. If the distractions are sufficient, the perception of pain may be diminished or even eliminated and this may have consequence in our attitude to those sports which involve inflicting pain or death on animals. Intuitively we may recoil from sports such as bear baiting and bull fighting which are little more than torture chambers with spectators, but many people find more acceptable other sports such as fox hunting, which simulate the behaviour of a predator hunting its prey.

If we cannot even generalize within our own species, it is clearly improper to generalize across the species. We cannot say that animals perceive pain as we do; we cannot, in fact, even say that our next-door neighbour, still less our pet dog, perceives pain exactly as we ourselves would. But we do see that both man and dog react as we would and we know that both are provided with a mechanism for transmitting pain similar to our own. Both man and animals strive to avoid repetition of painful experiences – if that were not so the training of animals by the infliction of punishment would be impossible. We may therefore conclude that there is common ground between the human and the animal experience of pain, and that sympathy for suffering should be extended beyond our neighbour and our dog to include every wild animal.

Poisons, Snares and Traps

W. J. Jordan

There are two main issues involved in man's attitude to animals – their right to share the earth with him and man's moral responsibility to avoid causing animal suffering. Both these issues are raised when man seeks to kill animals which damage or destroy his property. Man's 'right' to exploit or destroy other species rests entirely upon his ability to do so and his methods have usually been chosen for their effectiveness and low cost, rather than for their humanity.

Man's exploitation is frequently equated with that of other species which, in their natural situation, it is suggested, do exactly as he does – the tiger preys on sambar deer, whales consume millions of krill, some species of ant actually farm aphids. But all do these things in a natural way, to which natural selection has adapted them. Moreover, unlike mankind they are prompted by need. Man on the other hand generally kills for economic gain, for sport or for fashion, with little regard for suffering. But why has this unfeeling attitude developed within our society?

There is evidence that early man treated nature with both respect and reverence. Certainly when the white man first made contact with so-called primitive tribes such as the North American Indians, the Australian Aborigines and the South American Bushmen, he found that they looked upon animals as their brothers. This feeling is epitomized in a letter written to the President of the United States in 1855 by Chief Seathl (now Seattle) of the Suwanish tribe, regarding the proposed purchase of the tribal land.

> We know that the white man does not understand our ways. . . . The earth is not his brother but his enemy and when he has conquered it, he moves on. . . . There is no quiet place in the white man's cities. No place to hear the leaves of Spring or the rustle of insect wings. . . .
>
> The white man does not notice the air he breaths. Like a man dying for many days he is numb to the smell.
>
> If I decide to accept I will make one condition. The white man must treat the beasts of this land as his brothers. . . . If all the beasts were gone, man would die from a great loneliness of

> spirit, for whatever happens to the beasts also happens to man. All things are connected.
>
> What befalls earth befalls the sons of the earth.

If the philosophy of the Indian peoples has power, it is because it is based soundly on a humanitarian ideology and is profoundly in opposition to our own materialistic attitude. How could two such different attitudes have developed? For an answer we might look to the words of another American Indian, Chief Luther Standing Bear:

> The man who sat on the ground in his tipi meditating on life and its meaning, accepting the kinship of all creatures and acknowledging unity with the universe of things, was infusing into his being the true essence of civilization. And when native man left off this form of development, his humanization was retarded in growth.

The attitude of modern man is reflected in the way in which he has made use of poisons, traps and snares. Not only are they usually cruel but they also frequently kill animals other than the 'target species' for which they were intended. Fur trappers, for example, constantly find that three-quarters of their catch is 'trash'. This trash consists of normal healthy animals whose fur is of no commercial value and whose suffering is therefore pointless.

Poisons

By the late 1950s the British public had become so concerned about the use of poisons against wild animals that in 1962 the Animals (Cruel Poisons) Act was passed. This Act banned the use of red squill and yellow phosphorous and, in general, the use of strychnine also; but it allowed the use of strychnine against moles to continue. This exception was not of course made because moles suffered less than other animals, but simply because there was no other equally effective means of control – or so it was claimed. The Ministry of Agriculture said that they had tested 15 compounds (including strychnine) on moles but that 'none had met sufficient of the criteria sought, namely: humane method of action, unsuitability of use against other species, operator safety, effective and efficient mole control and safety of other species of wildlife'. Yet strychnine is a highly dangerous poison for man and it is well known to be used (illegally) against other animals besides moles. But let us consider the first of these criteria – humane method of action.

Strychnine is an alkaloid stimulant derived from the plant *Strychnos nuxvomica*. It differs from most other stimulants in that it exerts its action directly upon the spinal cord. Symptoms of poisoning begin with muscular twitching, and these increase until the victim starts having convulsions. All the skeletal muscles contract antagonistically (that is to say they pull against each other) and, because the extensor muscles are more powerful than the contractors, the limbs are extended and the neck is curved upwards and backwards. A mole so poisoned presents a terrible and macabre spectacle for this intense contraction of muscles causes a weird 'rocking horse' motion. In the early stages of poisoning the convulsions are intermittent but the periods of relaxation become progressively shorter and soon the spasms can be induced by any slight external stimulus such as a noise, or even a current of air. Finally the convulsions follow one another more rapidly until death results from asphyxia.

According to the Ministry of Agriculture, moles poisoned by strychnine usually die within ten to twenty minutes of the onset of symptoms. But what does the poisoned mole suffer during that ten to twenty minutes? We know that similar spasms endured during tetanus cause in man cramp and severe pain. Are the moles' sufferings then of no account? Even if we, the human society, decide that our rights over this humble velvet creature are inviolable, are we justified in inflicting such agony upon him? Mole traps are effective but the time involved in setting and checking makes them less efficient, in terms of cost. So, we are back to materialistic values. But what, in real terms, may be the cost of using strychnine?

The Ministry of Agriculture tightly controls the issue of strychnine and licenses the sale of only small quantities for mole control. Every new applicant is carefully checked but he is not again visited to see what use he has made of the strychnine issued to him. Also, in spite of restrictions on re-sale, the import of strychnine into Britain is unrestricted. So, although the Ministry does not think there is widespread abuse of strychnine obtained under permit, its unrestricted import combined with its legal use against moles leaves the door wide open for illegal use against any unwanted animal, wild or domestic.

One use of strychnine against wild animals is called open-cast baiting. In this, a carcass is laced with poison to kill any carnivore which feeds on it – fox, badger or bird of prey. It is even likely that the long-term effect of strychnine poisoning is keeping down the red kite population in Wales. Dogs and cats also fall victims.

All these things follow from permitting the use of strychnine to control moles.

Anti-coagulant poisons With the banning of red squill and yellow phosphorous in 1962, the use of Warfarin, the most important of the anti-coagulant poisons, inevitably increased. Warfarin kills by interference with the clotting of the blood , causing the poisoned animal to bleed internally at various points. If it bleeds into the abdomen or into the lungs, there may be no pain, but bleeding into joint cavities may cause considerable suffering. Warfarin differs from inorganic poisons, such as strychnine, in that it is most effective when administered over a period of several days. On the other hand, the ingestion of very large quantities of Warfarin can cause rapid death without symptoms of internal bleeding. In fact the effect of Warfarin varies but it is a less cruel poison than strychnine.

Warfarin was once hailed as the most effective means of destroying rodents; but it now seems likely that a genetic resistance to it has developed in certain rat colonies and there is no reason to doubt that this could happen with other anti-coagulant rodenticides. Such resistance does not seem to have occurred with inorganic poisons, such as strychnine.

Which animals shall die? The danger of poisoning animals other than those of the 'target species' is as real with the anti-coagulants as with strychnine, and this danger increased when, under the Grey Squirrel (Warfarin) Order 1973, Warfarin was officially enlisted in the war against grey squirrels. A special feeding hopper was developed with the intention of ensuring that only squirrels and small rodents could get at the bait, but a research team from Oxford found that jays, robins, a pheasant, a badger and a fallow deer had also taken it. The Forestry Commission declare that this does not represent the overall situation and that the use of Warfarin has not produced any long-term effect on small animal populations. Perhaps and perhaps not – perhaps there has not been enough research. But we are concerned here not with changes in animal populations, but with animal suffering.

All forms of 'control' inevitably cause suffering, often to animals outside their intention and readers will have noticed that the scientific world has created its own very useful vocabulary for many of its activities. Unfortunately these often mask the true situation. 'Control' means killing. 'Target species' and 'Non-target species' mean intended and unintended victims. Let them be called so. This is an important matter and it is fundamental to man's relationship with other forms of life. It is surely no accident that the American Indian, who spoke of killing his brother when he hunted the bison for food, and often prayed for forgiveness before doing so, managed to exist within his environment without causing it irreparable damage. Whilst we, who poison 'target' and 'non-target' species alike, are endangering our own life upon this planet.

Snares and traps

Although the bones of animals have been found in association with prehistoric man – and there is no doubt that he ate animal flesh and probably used skins as protection from the weather – there is no evidence as to whether he regularly killed animals or was merely a scavenger. In 1969 two anthropologists showed, by putting it to the test themselves that it was possible to survive by scavenging the kills of other animals, dead or dying animals or the defenceless young.

More rhetoric than science has been used to establish man as having inherited the qualities of an aggressive killer, insensitive to the feelings of human beings and animals. Now the sketchy archaeological record is being read again with a different interpretation. A state of continual aggression denies the possibility of altruism and makes no biological sense. It has now been shown by Dr. Brain that the damage to skulls which had previously been interpreted as signs of homicide could equally well have been caused after death and often after they became buried. Hominid teeth have always been more suitable for a vegetarian diet and anyone proposing that man was primarily a carnivore ignores the fact.

There is no doubt that early man hunted – but in a personal way with stones, spears and arrows. Neolithic man of 20,000 years ago could draw with sensitivity and remarkable accuracy. In the detailed murals which he created at least some might reasonably be expected to portray methods of capture and of killings. But most do not, unless the rectangles depicted in the Lascaux caves were tread traps. Was this because their methods were so simple and primitive – for example driving animals over cliffs or into swamps – or because Stone Age man had the same ethical and religious attitude towards nature as the Red Indians? The first known traps were developed for fish during the Neolithic period, towards the end of the Stone Age. One of them, a creel, may be seen in the Copenhagen Museum.

As the Neolithic gave way to the Bronze Age, human settlement and rapidly increasing populations discouraged nomadic hunting and the use of more land for agriculture restricted hunting areas, all, no doubt, leading to more sophisticated means of catching animals to increase the take. Dating from this period is the treadle trap for deer, examples of which have been found in Scotland, Ireland and in several other parts of both western and eastern Europe. It consisted of a heavy rectangular block of wood about 1 metre long with a hole in the centre large enough for a deer's foot. In the hole is a hinged door and above it a stick which can be pulled into a curve and held there by the door. When the animal puts its foot through the hole the stick springs flat and grips the leg making it impossible for the animal to run.

From the tombs of ancient Egypt there is evidence that traps were used for fish, but none of traps for mammals. The Israelites however, according to the Old Testament, used nets, snares, traps and pit falls.

The Romans, of course, trapped animals extensively for their games and circuses, but it would seem that few were trapped for food and none to control pests. Indeed, it was not until the fifteenth century that trapping, as a means of pest control, began to occupy the attention of Europeans. The North American Indians, having no wool-bearing domestic animals, had to use furs and feathers extensively for clothing and had developed great skill in trapping. It was from them that the Europeans learned most about how to make and use snares and traps. They improved them by the use of iron. A record of the first iron trap in Europe appeared in a book by Mascall published in 1590. This had a double flat spring and resembled a modern leg-hold or gin trap (derived from the word engine).

The burgeoning population of Europe and North America and the wealth created by the Industrial Revolution caused the rapid expansion of the fur-trapping industry, particularly in North America, bringing suffering and death to millions of animals to satisfy the demands of fashion. In Britain there were few such suitable fur-bearing animals and it was the demands of 'sport' rather than killing for profit that accounted for the great reduction in predators, especially predatory birds. It is estimated that today some 8,000 gamekeepers snare, trap and shoot up to two million animals a year to protect game birds, such as the partridge and the pheasant (an introduced and artificially reared species).

In 1951, the Scott Henderson Committee, set up to enquire into cruelty to wild mammals, reported to Parliament that the gin trap was a diabolical instrument causing incalculable suffering and should be banned. This recommendation was enacted as law in England in 1954 and in Scotland in 1973. The Committee went on to say that 'it should be made illegal for any spring trap to be used, the design of which has not been approved by the Minister of Agriculture and Fisheries or by the Secretary of State for Scotland, and those Ministers should approve only spring traps which will catch and kill wild animals without causing them unnecessary suffering'. The Committee also thought that knotted snares were less cruel than other snares and that, if an officially approved trap came into general use, it might be possible to ban the use of all snares.

All that was 30 years ago but snares are still being set and gin traps manufactured commercially (only the *use* of gin traps is prohibited by law).

A snare is simply a noose, usually of thin flexible wire, set where an animal is likely to be caught by neck, leg or body. The end of the noose is pegged to the ground or else tied to a heavy object or to a tree, so that the noose tightens when the captive struggles. The knotted or stop snare was invented to reduce suffering for, as its name implies, it will not tighten beyond the knot. This certainly prevents an animal caught around the middle from almost cutting itself in two. One lactating badger, for example, was found dead near the entrance to her sett with a snare round her abdomen. The noose had reduced her bulky girth to a diameter of three inches, cutting through skin and flesh to expose the intestines. Eventually the snare had snapped. She had dragged herself in this terrible condition for over two miles, trying to return to her cubs. The farmer who had set the snare said that he had set it for a fox, because he was rearing pheasants for autumn sport. He was therefore within the law.

Traps are of many sorts, but they work on only a few principles. Pit-fall traps are now used in Britain only to catch insects, although they were originally developed for much larger animals. This trap is simply a pit into which an animal falls and cannot escape. Often water is put into the bottom to drown the captive. In dead-fall traps a stone or other heavy object is propped up above a bait, in such a way that when an animal takes the bait a trigger is released and the heavy object falls upon the animal. Dead-falls were widely used in North America and perhaps by early man. A mouse trap of this kind was made in Europe as long ago as the mid-fifteenth century.

The cage trap relies upon enticing the quarry into a suitably baited cage; whereupon the captive's movement releases a trap-door which it cannot open. Special cage traps have been made for almost every species. In Britain they are used chiefly to catch foxes, badgers, squirrels, coypus, rats, mice and other small mammals. Some are caught for field studies when it is important that the animal should suffer as little distress as possible. The Longworth trap was specially designed for this purpose and it is a measure of its success that even after catching, weighing and marking, many animals will get caught in it again, sometimes in the very same trap.

The spring trap is a product of Western industry. The animal either springs a trigger accidentally or when taking a bait. Then a strong spring snaps steel jaws together upon some part of the animal. Until recently spring traps were of the gin trap variety, designed to hold the captive until it died or was found and killed. But not infrequently the animal would gnaw through its foot and escape. Now more humane spring traps have been designed which, when properly set, kill the animal instantly, in most cases. Only seven of them have been approved by the Ministry of Agriculture, namely; two Fenns, Fuller, Imbra, Juby, Lloyd and Sawyer. The species for which each has been designed are stipulated, as well as the situation in which it may be set. The Scissors and the Duffus mole traps are also in essence spring traps but, as they normally kill the animal immediately, are not investigated for approval by the Ministry.

Conservation Little is known with certainty about the effect of trapping and snaring upon mammal populations. Clearly sporting estates would not continue to pay for predators to be killed if they did not believe it to be worth while. It can also be argued that as predators continue to be trapped and snared, their populations must be able to replenish themselves.

In the Mammal Review of December 1977, Langley and Yalden discuss the decline of the rarer carnivores in Great Britain during the nineteenth century. Polecats, pine martens and wild cats all declined and indeed became extinct in many areas. These reductions did not match the decline in their habitats, woodland, for, as the authors say, the decline in woodland was largely completed before the predator populations began to fall. But they do coincide with the development of sporting estates and gamekeeping, and differences in patterns of decline can be explained in terms of variations in the intensity of persecution. The increase in predator populations during and shortly after the 1914 war confirms this hypothesis.

Recently the RSPCA carried out an investigation into the prevalence of snaring and trapping. Of the 56 replies from RSPCA Inspectors, 51 confirmed that either snares or traps had been used in their areas during 1978. It also seemed clear that both snares and traps were sometimes left unattended for several days, or even forgotten. Incidentally – and showing the indiscriminate nature of these devices – 61 cats and 12 dogs were caught in snares; 5 cats and 1 dog in traps.

Ethics There may be debate about degrees of suffering, but nobody, unless he believes that only man can suffer, will deny that many traps and almost all snares cause suffering. Only cage traps and those which kill immediately can be humane, and then only if used properly. The ethical controversy relates this short-term suffering to long-term gain. But killing animals may not result in any long-term gain at all, nor may it be a worthwhile goal. Moreover much killing is done to curtail population numbers of species which have increased because of man's interference with their environment. Rats and mice have followed man throughout the world and have multiplied because he supplies their food. Squirrels thrive on monoculture plantations and seagulls on rubbish dumps. Rabbits are not only supplied with food, but their natural predators are removed to protect pheasants.

The killing of animals, especially in ways that cause suffering, will eventually affect men. It may cause a feeling of revulsion, or one of indifference or it may have a brutalizing effect. If the reason for the slaughter is trivial – or the slaughter itself unnecessary in that its purpose can be fulfilled in some other way – then there is a strong moral obligation to stop it. Some go further and maintain that if the purpose is sport then, ethically, it should be forbidden.

Further Reading

GENERAL TITLES

P. Bang & P. Dahlstrom *Collins Guide to Animal Tracks and Signs*, Collins, London, 1974

F. H. van der Brink, *A Field Guide to the Mammals of Britain and Europe*, Collins, London, 1967

G. B. Corbet *The Terrestrial Mammals of Western Europe*, Foulis, London, 1966

G. B. Corbet, E. N. Arnold & D. Ovenden *The Wild Animals of Britain and Europe*, Collins, London, 1979

G. B. Corbet & D. Ovenden *The Mammals of Britain and Europe*, Collins, London, 1980

G. B. Corbet & H. N. Southern (Eds.) *The Handbook of British Mammals*. Published for the Mammal Society by Blackwell Scientific Publications, Oxford, 1977

M. Crichton *Provisional Atlas of Amphibians, Reptiles and Mammals in Ireland*, Am Forbas Forbatha, Dublin, 1974

B. Kursten *Pleistocene Mammals of Europe*, Weidenfeld & Nicolson, London, 1968

M. J. Lawrence & R. W. Brown *Mammals of Britain, their Tracks, Trails and Signs*, Blandford, London, 1973

C. Lever *The Naturalized Animals of the British Isles*, Hutchinson, London, 1977

D. Patterson & R. D. Ryder *Animal Rights*, Centaur Press, London, 1979

E. P. Walker (Ed) *Mammals of the World*, John Hogarth Press, Baltimore, 1975

INSECTIVORES

Hedgehog

M. Burton *Hedgehogs*, André Deutsch, London, 1969

K. Herter *Hedgehogs*, Phoenix House, London, 1965

Mole

G. K. Godfrey & P. Crocroft *The Life of the Mole*, Museum Press, London, 1960

K. Mellanby *The Mole*, (New Naturalist Series) Collins, London, 1971

Shrews

W. P. Crowcroft *The Life of the Shrew*, Max Reinhardt, London, 1957

BATS

G. D. Sales & J. D. Pye *Ultrasonic Communication by Animals*, Chapman & Hall, London, 1974

R. E. Stebbings *Artificial Roosts for Bats, Journal of the Devon Trust for Nature Conservation*, 6, 114–19

D. W. Yalden & P. A. Morris *Biology of Bats*, David & Charles, Newton Abbot, 1975

LAGOMORPHS

Rabbit

R. M. Lockley *The Private Life of the Rabbit*, André Deutsch, London, 1964

J. Sheail *Rabbits and their History*, David & Charles, Newton Abbot, 1971

H. V. Thompson & A. Worden *The Rabbit*, Collins, London, 1965

Hares

S. Eabry *A Bibliography of European Hare Lepus europaeus*, N.Y.S. Conservation Department, Delmar, 1969

H. Tegner *Wild Hares*, John Baker, London, 1969

C. S. Webb *A Hare About the House*, Hutchinson, London, 1955

RODENTS

S. A. Barnett *A Study in Behaviour*, Methuen, London, 1963

Squirrels

M. Shorten *Grey Squirrels* (Animals of Britain No. 5), *Sunday Times*, London, 1962

M. Shorten *Red Squirrels* (Animals of Britain No. 6), *Sunday Times*, London, 1962

M. Shorten *Squirrels*, Collins, London, 1954

M. Shorten & F. S. Barkalow *The World of the Gray Squirrel*, Lippincott, Philadelphia, 1973

Voles

S. R. Ryder *Water Voles* (Animals of Britain No. 4), *Sunday Times*, London, 1962

House Mouse

W. P. Crowcroft *Mice All Over*, Foulis, London, 1966

Harvest Mouse

M. Knight *Harvest Mice* (Animals of Britain No. 19), *Sunday Times*, London, 1963

Common Rat

C. Matheson *Brown Rats* (Animals of Britain No. 16), *Sunday Times*, London, 1962

Dormice

E. Hurrell *Dormice* (Animals of Britain No. 10), *Sunday Times*, London, 1962

CARNIVORES

P. A. Gouldsbury (Ed.) *Predatory Mammals in Britain*, Council for Nature, Seel House Press, London, 1973

Red Fox

R. Burrows *Wild Fox*, David & Charles, Newton Abbot, 1968

H. G. Hurrell *Wildlife Tame but Free*, David & Charles, Newton Abbot, 1968

D. W. Macdonald *Rubris and Wildlife*, Oxford University Press, Oxford, 1979

B. Vesey-Fitzgerald *Town Fox, Country Fox*, André Deutsch, London, 1965

Weasel

P. Drabble *A Weasel in my Meat Safe*, Collins, London, 1957

Badger

E. G. Neal *The Badger* (New Naturalist Series), Collins, London, 1948 (4th ed. 1975)

E. G. Neal *Badgers*, Blandford, Poole, 1977

R. J. Paget & A. L. V. Middleton *Badgers of Yorkshire and Humberside*, Ebor Press, York, 1974

RSPCA *Badgers & Bovine Tuberculosis*, RSPCA Special Report, 1980

Otter

C. J. Harris *Otters: a Study of the Recent Lutrinae*, Weidenfeld & Nicolson, 1968

M. N. Stephens *The Natural History of the Otter*, Universities Federation for Animal Welfare, London, 1957

The Joint Otter Group *Reports*, produced by the Society for the promotion of Nature Conservation, 1977 and 1979

PINNIPEDIA

Seals

H. R. Hewer *British Seals* (New Naturalist Library), Collins, London, 1974

G. Hickling *Grey Seals and the Farne Islands*, Routledge & Kegan Paul, London, 1967

R. M. Lockley *Grey Seal, Common Seal*, André Deutsch, London, 1966

ARTIODACTYLS

Deer

D. & N. Chapman *Fallow Deer*, British Deer Society, 1975

O. Danic *Muntjac*, British Deer Society, 1970

R. A. Harris & K. R. Daff *Wild Deer in Britain*, David & Charles, Newton Abbot, 1970

F. Holmes *Following the Roe*, Bartholomew, Edinburgh, 1974

M. T. Horwood & E. H. Masters *Sika Deer*, British Deer Society, 1970

L. MacNally *The Year of the Red Deer*, Dent, London, 1975

G. K. Whitehead *The Deer of Great Britain and Ireland*, Routledge & Kegan Paul, London, 1964

FOR YOUNG READERS

K. Mellanby *Talpa: The Story of a Mole*, Collins, London, 1976

R. Chaplin *Capreolus: The Story of a Roe Deer*, Collins, London, 1978

D. Macdonald *Vulpina: The Story of a Fox*, Collins, London, 1977

J. Taylor *Sciurus: The Story of a Grey Squirrel*, Collins, London, 1978

P. Wayre *Lutra: The Story of an Otter*, Collins, London, 1979

About the authors

Priscilla Barrett, B.A. Animal artist, with five years experience of research at Cambridge University into animal behaviour. Specializes in the illustration of mammals and their behaviour.

C. L. Boyle, O.B.E. retired lieutenant colonel. Secretary – Fauna Preservation Society, 1950–63. A Vice President F.P.S. since 1975. Chairman Survival Service Commission, I.U.C.N., 1958–63. Ridder: Order of the Golden Ark.

Michael R. Brambell, M.A., Ph.D., M.R.C.V.S. Director, North of England Zoological Society, Chester Zoo, formerly Curator of Mammals, the Zoological Society of London.

P. Chanin, M.A., Ph.D. Tutor in the Department of Extra Mural Studies, Exeter University. Has carried out research into the ecology of mink and otters.

D. I. Chapman Amateur mammalogist, especially interested in deer. Has studied muntjac and fallow deer intensively. By profession a chartered chemist.

W. M. Condry, M.A., M.Sc. Teacher-naturalist at the Ynys-hir reserve of the Royal Society for the Protection of Birds, in Wales. Author.

L. K. Corbett, M.Sc., Ph.D. Has recently completed a three-year field study of wild cat ecology and behaviour in Scotland. Previously spent ten years studying dingoes and other fauna in central Australia, and is now studying predators in tropical northern Australia.

A. C. Dubock, Ph.D. Studied grey squirrels for his doctorate and has maintained his interest. Now engaged in research on rodent control.

P. G. H. Evans, B.Sc. Secretary of the Cetacean Group of the Mammal Society. Has worked on a wide range of mammals in various parts of the world. Now at the Edward Grey Institute of Field Ornithology, Oxford.

J. R. Flowerdew, D.Phil. Lecturer in Applied Biology Cambridge University. Hon. Secretary, The Mammal Society.

Gillian Godfrey, M.A., D.Phil. (Mrs Crowcroft). Jersey Wildlife Preservation Trust, Jersey, C.I. Has studied the European mole, shrews and small American and Australian marsupials.

L. M. Gosling, Ph.D. A principal scientific officer in the Ministry of Agriculture, Fisheries and Food, working on coypu biology. Awarded Ph.D. at Nairobi University for work on antelope social behaviour. Honorary lecturer, University of East Anglia.

S. S. Harris, Ph.D. Research Associate Department of Zoology, Bristol University. Now studying the ecology of foxes and badgers in Bristol.

N. Hawkes, B.A. Science Correspondent of *The Observer*. Since graduating in metallurgy has written on a wide range of sciences in many publications and has published two books – on computers and on early scientific instruments.

R. Hewson, M.Sc. Biologist employed by the Department of Agriculture and Fisheries for Scotland. Now doing research on foxes.

Elaine Hurrell. Teacher in field studies. Owes her interest in natural history to her father, H. G. Hurrell, and to her Froebel College Principal, the late Dorothy Venour.

W. J. Jordan, M.V.Sc., B.Sc., M.R.C.V.S., M.I.Biol. Director of the People's Trust for Endangered Species. Formerly Chief Wildlife Officer of the RSPCA. A founder member of the British Veterinary Zoologists Society and its secretary for several years. Held university appointments in Britain and in S. Africa. Was consultant clinician to the Iranian Government for six years and a zoo vet for many years. A frequent broadcaster.

I. J. Linn, B.Sc. Senior lecturer in the Department of Biological Sciences, University of Exeter. Previously at Makerere University, Uganda.

D. W. Macdonald, M.A., D.Phil. Fellow of Balliol College, Oxford. Ernest Cook Research Fellow in Animal Behaviour at the Department of Zoology, Oxford University.

Ian S. MacPhail. Born in the Highlands of Scotland. First full-time executive of the World Wildlife Fund. European Co-ordinator of the International Fund for Animal Welfare.

K. Mellanby, C.B.E., Sc.D., F.I.Biol. Founder-Principal of the University of Ibadan, Nigeria, 1947–54. Head, Entomology Department, Rothamsted Experimental Station, 1955–61. Founder-Director, Monks Wood Experimental Station, 1961–74. Editor, international scientific journal *Environmental Pollution*.

E. G. Neal, M.B.E., M.Sc., Ph.D., F.I.Biol. President of The Mammal Society. For 14 years Chairman of the Somerset Trust for Nature Conservation. Writer and broadcaster.

N. J. Reeve, B.Sc. At Royal Holloway College. Has recently completed a study of hedgehogs in the suburbs of west London.

ABOUT THE AUTHORS

J. C. Reynolds, B.Sc. At the University of East Anglia investigating the interactions between red and grey squirrels for the Nature Conservancy Council.

R. D. Ryder, M.A., D.C.P., A.B.Ps.S. Senior Clinical Psychologist, Warneford Hospital, Oxford. Research Fellow, Columbia University, New York. Chairman RSPCA Council, 1977–79.

R. E. Stebbings, Ph.D., M.I.Biol. A research ecologist working on bats for the Institute of Terrestrial Ecology. Chairman of the Chiroptera Group of the Species Survival Commission, IUCN. He has researched into bat conservation for 30 years.

C. F. Summers, Ph.D. Officer in charge Sea Mammal Research Unit, National Environmental Research Council, 1974–78.

K. D. Taylor, B.Sc. A photographer and rodent control consultant. For 20 years a Government rodent ecologist.

M. J. A. Thompson, M.B., B.S., L.R.C.P., M.R.C.G.P. General medical practitioner. Member of Council, Yorkshire Naturalists' Trust, 1972–78, re-elected 1980. Amphibian and reptile recorder, Yorkshire Naturalists' Union, 1970–78 and past Chairman, Yorkshire Mammal Group.

The Animal Kingdom

This chart shows the place in the Animal Kingdom of those mammals known to be wild in Britain. It omits Sub-classes, Infra-classes, Families and Genera.

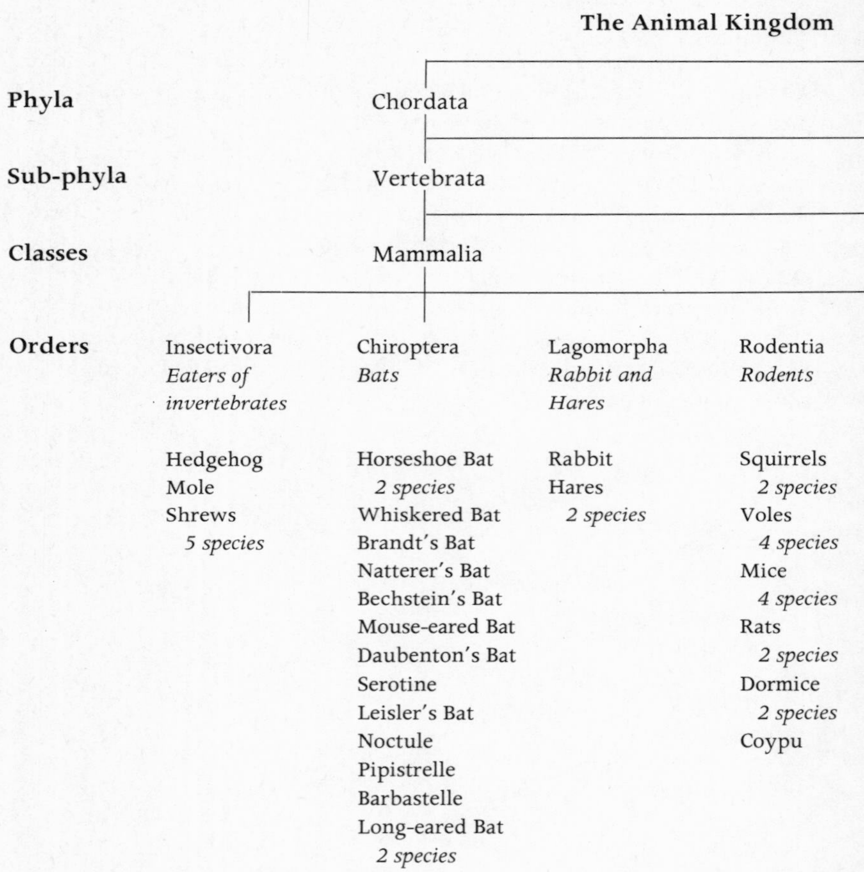

Classification The Animal Kingdom consists of 22 Phyla, one of which is the Chordata. Within the Chordata there are four Sub-Phyla, of which one is the Vertebrata (the Vertebrates). The Vertebrates contain a number of Classes of which one is the Mammalia (the Mammals).

Within Classes there are Orders, Families, Genera, Species and further subdivisions.

This book deals only with the Mammals, and only with such Orders and Species of mammals as are established in the wild in Britain.

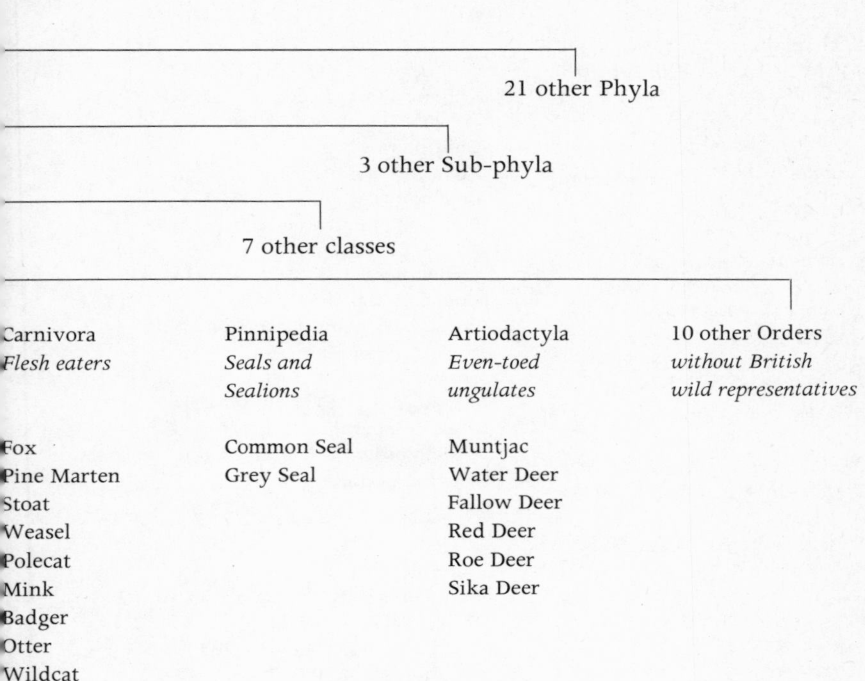

For further classification of British mammals readers are referred to *The Handbook of British Mammals* (1977) published for the Mammal Society by Blackwell Scientific Publications, for all European mammals they should consult *The Mammals of Britain and Europe* by Gordon Corbet & Denys Ovenden (Collins, 1980), and for a total classification of all animals *A Classification of Living Animals* by Lord Rothschild (2nd edition, Longman, 1965).

Index

References to illustrations are shown in **bold** type, for colour illustrations the facing page is listed.